Living Religion

Living Religion

*Embodiment, Theology, and the
Possibility of a Spiritual Sense*

JAMES W. JONES

OXFORD
UNIVERSITY PRESS

OXFORD
UNIVERSITY PRESS

Oxford University Press is a department of the University of Oxford. It furthers
the University's objective of excellence in research, scholarship, and education
by publishing worldwide. Oxford is a registered trade mark of Oxford University
Press in the UK and certain other countries.

Published in the United States of America by Oxford University Press
198 Madison Avenue, New York, NY 10016, United States of America.

CIP data is on file at the Library of Congress
ISBN 978-0-19-092738-7

1 3 5 7 9 8 6 4 2

Printed by Sheridan Books, Inc., United States of America

This book is dedicated with gratitude to the Faculty of Divinity of Cambridge University, its faculty, post-docs, graduate students, and administrators, and to the members of the Faraday Institute for Science and Religion, and to the Master and Fellows of St. Edmunds's College, and to the various Deans of Chapel and local clergy, all of whom made my year in Cambridge a marvelous time of intellectual and spiritual flourishing.

Contents

Prologue

THROUGHOUT HISTORY HUMANS have reported an awareness of transcendental, spiritual realities. What might this claim to sense a transcendental, spiritual reality mean? There are at least two ways to answer such a question. We might give a formal definition on the order of "a square is a shape with four equal sides." Armed with that definition a person could examine a variety of shapes and decide whether or not they were squares. Likewise, we might try to construct a formal definition of such a "spiritual sense."

Or if asked to define a flower, instead of a formal definition from a botany book, we might take a person into a garden and point out plants that were flowers (roses and morning glories, for example) and plants that were not (shrubs and grass, for example). Gradually, after enough examples, a person would learn to recognize flowers and then might list some features they have in common. But that list of features would be something other than a formal definition. A more subtle example: someone says this is a glass of fine wine. If asked what that means, a formal definition would probably not help the uninitiated recognize a fine wine. The person calling it "fine" might describe it as "full bodied," containing "hints of pear and peach," and being "oaky." But obviously such words are not being used in a literal way. Again, the only way to know what they mean is by tasting several bottles of wine, some of which are "fine" and some of which are not. Hopefully over time one learns which to call "fine" and which not to. Here nothing even resembling a formal definition would come into play.

Definitions of terms like "spiritual," "religious," even "experience" or "awareness" are notoriously difficult to arrive at or deploy. Instead let us look at several accounts of experiences that are generally recognized as displaying a sense or awareness of something transcendental or spiritual.

I beheld the plenitude of God, wherein I did comprehend the whole world, both here and beyond the sea, and the abyss and ocean and all things. In all these I beheld naught save the divine power. . . . [T]he soul cried out with a loud voice "the whole world is full of God." (Alston, 1991: 25–26)

A veil seemed to be lifted from my eyes. I found the world wrapt in an inexpressible glory with its waves of joy and beauty bursting and breaking on all sides. (Happold, 1970: 140)

After this my sense of divine things gradually increased and became more and more lively and had more of that inward sweetness. The appearance of everything was altered; there seemed to be, as it were, a calm, sweet cast, or appearance of divine glory, in almost everything. God's excellency, his wisdom, his purity and love seemed to appear in everything; in the sun, moon, stars; on the clouds and blue sky; in the grass, flowers, trees; in water and all nature; which used to greatly fix my mind. I often used to sit and view the moon for continuance; and in the day spent much time in viewing the clouds and sky, to behold the sweet glory of God in these things. (Jonathan Edwards, *Personal Narrative*, in Jones, 1972: 445)

One day when I was at prayer . . . I saw Christ at my side—or, to put it better I was conscious of Him, for I saw nothing with the eyes of the body or the eyes of the soul [the imagination]. He seemed quite close to me and I saw it was He. As I thought, He was speaking to me. . . . All the time Jesus Christ seemed to be at my side, but as this was not an imaginary vision I could not see in what form. (St. Teresa, in Alston, 1991: 13)

Christ himself came down and took possession of me. In my arguments about the insolubility of the problem of God I had never foreseen the possibility of that, of a real contact, person to person, here below, between a human being and God. I had vaguely heard tell of things of this kind, but I had never believed in them . . . in this sudden possession of me by Christ, neither my senses nor my imagination played any part; I only felt in the midst of my suffering the presence of a love, like that which one can read in the smile of a beloved face. (Simone Weil, in Happold, 1970: 141)

I had come through the darkness into a world of light. That eternal truth and beauty which the sights and sounds of London threatened to banish from my sight was here the universal law. I heard its voice sounding in my ears. The very stones of the house seemed to be the living stones of a temple in which this song ascended. It was as though I had been given a new power of vision. Everything seemed to lose its hardness and rigidity and become alive. When I looked at the crucifix on the wall, it seemed to be a living person; I felt that I was in the house of God. When I went outside I found that the world about me no longer oppressed me as it had done. The hard casing of exterior reality seemed to have been broken through, and everything disclosed its inner being. The buses in the street seemed to have lost their solidity and to be glowing with light. I hardly felt the ground as I trod, and I think I must have been in some danger of being run over. I was like a bird which has broken the shell of its egg and finds itself in a new world. (Bede Griffiths, in Vardey, 1995: 88)

Such experiences are extraordinary, unlike our regular sensations and perceptions. They compel our attention. This means that their connection to our more ordinary sense experiences is filled with ambiguity. On the one hand, they are described by using the language of ordinary sensing: something is seen, felt, sensed. On the other hand, in many cases, reliance on our regular senses is qualified or completely denied. So rather than offering a definition, what we have here is the recognition that to speak about a spiritual sense is to speak in a profoundly paradoxical way. It is to use the language of sensation and perception and to negate it at the same time.

I WRITE THIS at the end of my teaching career. I now look back over more than half a century of standing at the intersection of many disciplines. Not raised in any religious tradition, I came to think about religion seriously for the first time as an adult. For me, that was a blessing. I had few childish religious ideas to overcome in order to entertain the religiously lived life as a serious option for me. I had been a student activist in the '60s and was already well versed in philosophy and history before discussions with friends and my own curiosity led me into thinking seriously about religion. That, in turn, led to graduate school. First a master's in theology and then a PhD in philosophy of religion with an emphasis on "epistemology," which led into the philosophy of science and a lifetime of thinking and writing about the similarities and differences between scientific and religious knowledge. That enabled me to spend over forty-five years teaching religious studies (especially psychology of religion and religion and science) in the fiercely secular and totally pluralistic milieu of a large, American, public research university. Then came a second doctorate in clinical psychology, involving training in both psychoanalytic psychotherapy and cognitive psychology (I did my thesis on cognition and emotion in depression) as well as neuropsychology. That was followed by many years of clinical practice that included psychodynamic psychotherapy, family systems work, and later what is now popularly called "mind-body medicine" or psychophysiology, biofeedback, and hypnosis.

Alongside teaching religious studies and doing some clinical training and supervision, there has been the practice of religion as well as the study of it: as an active priest in the Episcopal Church (which required a graduate degree in theology); a long time, if rather intermittent, meditative discipline in both the Christian and Buddhist traditions; conducting retreats with my wife; training in martial arts at a fairly high level; and affiliation with an Anglican Benedictine monastic community. All of this has gone into my teaching graduate courses in contemplative studies and strengthened the conviction on which the argument of this book is premised: that a religious tradition is primarily a set of practices and that the subject of study and debate should be the religiously lived life and not isolated beliefs torn out of context.

In addition to whatever education and experience I brought to this project, this book would simply not have been possible without the year I spent as a Fellow at the Center for Advanced Religious and Theological Studies in Cambridge University. Thanks are due to Fraser Watts who first invited me to come to Cambridge and to join his Psychology of Religion Research Group and who directed the research group on embodied cognition and religion and provided me thoughtful analysis and insight about that and many other subjects throughout the year. And I am happy to give special thanks to Leon Turner, the other member of our "two-man seminar" on embodied cognition, whose reflections and commentary provided a depth of knowledge and reflection that were invaluable to the writing of this book. Leon also shared with me his many papers and his own book manuscript on these topics—texts without which my own book could not have been written.

During my year in Cambridge I also had the privilege of attending Sarah Coakley's lectures on philosophical theology after Kant as well as being welcomed by her into the theology society's seminars, and given the opportunity of reading and commenting on her recently delivered Gifford Lectures. In addition, she was available for tough discussions of the difficult philosophical and theological issues connected with this project. All of this gave me

tools that deepened and focused my current rethinking about religious epistemology for which I am very grateful. Also during that year, Fred Aquino came
to Cambridge and gave a series of presentations on "virtue epistemology" after
which he and I did our best to keep the United Kingdom's Scotch distillers
in business. I am grateful to Fred for his thoughtful and thought-provoking
lectures and conversations, and especially for introducing me to the topic of
virtue epistemology.

Fraser Watts, Leon Turner, Sarah Coakley, Tom Simpson, Ryan Williams,
and Annalena Schriever all read the manuscript (sometimes more than once)
and graciously produced extensive critical commentaries and encouragement,
but not necessarily agreement.

Papers by John Teske and Mark Williams on embodied cognition research
were invaluable to me as I worked through some of this material, as well as papers by Fraser Watts and Leon Turner on its theological implications.

This work was supported in part by a grant from the John Templeton
Foundation; the opinions expressed here are those of the author and do not
necessarily reflect the views of the John Templeton Foundation. Rutgers
University provided a sabbatical leave for the time I spent in Cambridge and
the University Research Council provided an additional grant.

In 2016 I published a book entitled *Can Science Explain Religion? The
Cognitive Science Debate*. That previous book argued that the popular attempt
to use findings from cognitive science to undermine or debunk religious
beliefs is neither logically nor empirically successful. In that sense, that book
was primarily negative in tone. It refuted arguments deployed against religion
but offered little in the way of discussion or evidence supportive of religion.
It cleared away opposing points, but, except for a few suggestions in the final
chapter, it offered little in the way of constructive alternatives. This present
book offers a positive position, giving logical and empirical reasons in support
of the claim that the religiously lived life is a rational and reasonable life.

My moving to the United Kingdom for a year required a sacrifice on
the part of my wife, Kathleen Bishop. That she was so supportive slightly
mitigated the pain of separation and made it possible for me to carry out this
project. As always, she is the source and object of my deepest gratitude.

Living Religion

Introduction

Living Religion

An ambiguous title. Is this a book *about* living religion? How to study it? Understand it? Undermine it? Justify it? Or is it a book on how to *live* life religiously? A book of practical tips for conducting such a life? These days those two possibilities represent two very different (some would say opposed) projects. Most books seeking to study or understand religion by scholars, philosophers, or social scientists often contain little mention of the implications for the lived dimensions of what they discuss. On the other hand, "how to" books by clergy, spiritual directors, and other practical teachers often contain little reflective analysis of what they are suggesting people do.

It was not always so. The first theologians of the Christian faith, the so-called church fathers, were often monks or others deeply rooted in the liturgical or contemplative life. The same is true of the great Buddhist philosophers of Tibet, Japan, or China. All were men (occasionally women) of extensive and disciplined meditative and intellectual training. The current tendency to separate theory and practice, reflection and contemplation, has done inestimable mischief to the life of religion in the modern world. Religion's claims about God or the world or the nature and destiny of the human spirit have been ripped from their context in religious practice and treated as discrete doctrinal abstractions to be justified or refuted in isolation from the living religious life that is their natural home. Many of the intellectual dilemmas faced by those who think seriously about religion today arise from or are intensified by this separation of theory and practice. Here some trends in contemporary psychology might help the theologian, partly by returning theory to practice and thereby opening up new avenues of religious knowing and new ways of justifying the commitment to a religiously lived life. Such, at least, is the claim of this book.

This text is a dialogue between psychology and theology: two disciplines often concerned with the life of lived religion. In different ways, they both deal with understanding the religiously lived life and with the question of whether there is any validity to living that kind of life. Those two topics are the major themes interwoven in this text. The central question that this text seeks to answer is whether it is meaningful and reasonable to speak of a "spiritual sense," whether there are ways we can "sense" or perceive the reality of God. But we do not get to that question until the final chapter; it will take several chapters to lay the groundwork for the answer that is offered here.

The first chapter develops an "embodied-relational" approach to human understanding. To do this, the chapter draws upon two very different psychological paradigms: clinical psychoanalysis and laboratory research into the role embodiment plays in human understanding. On the surface these can appear completely discontinuous and unrelated, if not actually opposed to each other. I will suggest that despite their different foci (clinical treatment and laboratory research) they might also complement and enrich each others' implicit epistemologies. Some forms of psychoanalysis and some laboratory models contain both themes of embodiment and of relationality. Contemporary psychoanalysis provides a richer understanding of the relational nature of human understanding than is found in most laboratory-based models. And laboratory research demonstrates a more complex and central role for embodiment than does much post-Freudian psychoanalysis. This chapter reviews some of the major themes and findings in research on the ways our embodiment influences the processes by which we understand ourselves and the world. Since extensive information on both fields is available in many other places, these models and discoveries are not discussed in any great depth or detail here. Readers wanting more detail or to follow up on any of these studies should consult some of the literature mentioned in the notes at the end of the book.

The second chapter builds on and goes beyond this review of the empirical findings to discuss some of their implications for the traditional and virtually universal theological topic of human nature. All the religions of the world have, in different ways, insisted that there is more to human nature than what can be easily described by contemporary natural science. This chapter defends that claim by arguing that any purely physical account is necessarily incomplete and so is not as compelling as it is often assumed to be in currently popular discussions of neuroscience. This chapter also describes the impact of our embodiment on our theorizing about our bodies and their sensory capabilities. This then lays the basis for the possibility of a spiritual sense and for another approach to the "mind-body" dilemma.

An increasingly popular approach to thinking about religion from a psychological perspective is to treat religions as "meaning systems." A lot of research in the psychology of religion has been conducted within this "meaning systems" paradigm. The research cited in this book suggests that our embodiment directly impacts our understanding of how we arrive at meanings. This, in turn, affects the ways in which we understand religious meaning-making. That is the subject of chapter 3.

The fourth chapter looks at the impact of our embodiment on studying and understanding religion. I argue that taking our embodiment seriously impacts (and perhaps alters) the way religion is defined and theorized in the discipline of cognitive psychology and in other religious studies disciplines, including theology. I also suggest some avenues of research that would follow from adopting an embodied perspective. I also argue that an embodied perspective transforms the way we think about traditional topics concerning religious knowledge that have bedeviled theology for decades. In particular, I analyze the often argued parallel between ordinary perceptual experience and certain religious experiences commonly described as religious perceptions. Along the way I offer an appreciative critique of William Alston's 1991 book *Perceiving God*. His arguments for conceiving of religious experience as a form of perception are strong but the way the argument is framed is seriously flawed psychologically. I offer a reframing of the argument in terms of an embodied-relational model that I think strengthens it and also broadens and strengthens my argument in this book that reason is on the side of those who choose a religiously lived life.

That exploration of the argument from perception leads naturally to the fifth chapter. This directly theological chapter explores a case for a "spiritual sense" grounded in an embodied approach to human understanding. There is a long tradition, going back to at least the earliest days of Christian theology, of conceptualizing religious knowledge as a form of perception—a tradition of the existence of a spiritual sense. This tradition has continued right to the present. What would that traditional claim look like if articulated in ways that foreground our experience of embodiment? Beginning to answer that question is part of the burden of this book.

The reader should be forewarned that some unusual moves and juxtapositions occur in the coming pages. First, most discussions of perception in Western science and philosophy are limited to the Aristotelian "Five

senses." I argue for the epistemological (and not just neurological) importance of additional senses, especially proprioception: the way we are directly
aware of where our bodies are, what they are doing, and what is going on in
them. Such psychophysiosensory input is crucial for medical diagnosis and
psychophysiological treatments (such as biofeedback and hypnosis) of the
kind I rely on in my clinical work. But I also argue that it is epistemologically
important and may provide another way to think about the possibility of a
spiritual sense.

Second, commonly in the literature (e.g., Varela et al., 1993) when embodiment is discussed in connection with religion, Buddhism is the religion in
play. This is usually because some authors see a connection between the tendency of such embodied approaches to reject Cartesian dualism and the rejection of a substantial spiritual self in Buddhism's so-called doctrine of "no
self." Many also claim that Buddhism too sees the self as embodied. While
the popular notion of the Cartesian substantial spiritual self, disconnected
from the body (which is probably not a completely accurate presentation of
Descartes's position), bears some relationship to the Hindu notion of *atman*,
which Buddhism does reject (*anatman*—"no atman"—is the term translated
into English as "no self"), such generalizations about Buddhism and embodiment are something less than convincing to me. First, there is no uni-
tary understanding of how "no self" is to be understood within the many
schools of Buddhism. And second, most schools of Buddhism rely on a transcendental notion of consciousness (often associated with the *dharmakyia*
or *tathagatagarba* or "Buddha nature") that is vigorously denied in most
embodied psychological paradigms. And that teaching, which is central to
much Buddhist philosophical anthropology, is much more complex than
simply the denial of a "self." In addition, any Buddhist notion of embodiment
is going to be radically different from the rather mechanistic and physicalist
model of the body found in most discussions of embodiment in cognitive
science (for a critical discussion of these points, see Federman, 2011). All this
is far beyond the scope of this brief book except to forewarn the reader that
Western theism, not Buddhism, forms the religious foundation of this text,
although references will be made to other traditions to underscore the fact
that the topics discussed here are shared by many of the world's religions.

Third, psychological paradigms that stress embodiment are universally
seen as anti-Cartesian and therefore as inevitably radically anti-dualistic. I do
not dispute the anti-Cartesianism, although I wonder if the Descartes that is
dismissed in these discussions is not a bit of a straw man. But, no doubt surprisingly, I do argue in the coming pages that an emphasis on embodiment

does not necessarily deny dualism and may even support certain types of dualism. Dualism is usually automatically and reflexively dismissed in a sentence or simply assumed to be long gone from off the seminar table. But there are many forms of dualism besides Descartes's supposed dualism of two incompatible substances. And as long as a purely physicalist position remains unconvincing (we'll get to that in a coming chapter) and no coherent conception (let alone explanation) is forthcoming of how consciousness might arise directly from the brain, some form of dualism will still be on the table. I will suggest one model that I call (in an apparently oxymoronic phrase) "embodied dualism."

Fourth, both implicitly and explicitly this book argues that the research on specific ways that embodiment impacts our processes of understanding could profoundly influence and even transform the way we can (should?) think about religious knowledge.

Much, but not all, of the laboratory research drawn on in this book was conducted under the rubric of what is commonly called "embodied cognition." And for a while I thought about this as a book on "embodied cognition" and religion. However, the embodied cognition paradigm is extremely controversial in the field of cognitive science. Inevitably some of that controversy must be discussed in the coming pages. But the points I want to make about how embodiment impacts understanding depend on specific research findings that are widely recognized by those on all sides of the debate about "embodied cognition." I will argue that much on this controversy is not about the actual research results (which form the basis of my argument here) but rather on how those results are located and interpreted within different psychological paradigms. I have argued in many places that this distinction between actual scientific findings and their interpretation is a common theme in the philosophy of science and is one that plays a central role in many controversies between science and religion (Jones, 1981, 2016). My argument here is based on certain empirical findings that are widely accepted, not on their interpretation by those who hold to a position called "embodied cognition." And while the embodied cognition position is well supported in the research literature, research supports alternative interpretations as well. Relying on such research here does not imply that I think the embodied cognition view has been proven correct in all areas of controversy. I am only saying that the research it cites has important things to say to those interested in thinking about religion in new ways. This book is not written to convince the specialist skeptic about the truth of the claims that pass under the title of "embodied cognition." That is not my goal and to do that would require an extensive and detailed review of a wide range of research literature. That would take the text far, far beyond its original intention. Rather, this book is written to introduce the religiously interested non-specialist to some research that could have important and far-ranging implications for theology and religious thought in general.

These points converge on the claim that how we see the role of embodiment transforms not only the way we theorize human understanding, including religious understanding, but also the way we conceive of the body, at least our own body. Such a more nuanced and complex view of the body might legitimately be referred to as a "spiritual body." And if a "spiritual body," then perhaps also a "spiritual sense."

I

Understanding as Living

RELIGIOUS UNDERSTANDING IS the topic of this chapter. What does that mean? Does it mean how to understand life from a religious perspective? Or how to understand a phenomenon called "religion"? Or a little bit of both? Here it probably mainly means the latter. For reasons that will become clearer as the chapter proceeds, I have chosen to use the broadest term I could think of—"understanding"—and to stay away from narrower terms like "thought," and especially the term "cognition." For me "understanding" is more than only "cognition" as defined by contemporary cognitive science. As cognitive scientists Bradford Mahon and Alfonso Caramazza (2008) have written, "conceptual information that is represented at an 'abstract' or 'symbolic' level does not exhaust what we know about the world" (68). While drawing upon psychological research about cognition and philosophical reflection about knowledge and thought, when it comes to religion, my concern here is much broader.

The Real Is the Relational

My first epistemological foray, during the 1960s and '70s, into the domain of religion involved the intersection of the philosophy of religion and the philosophy of science. The philosophy of science I gravitated toward at that time was heavily influenced by the work of Ludwig Wittgenstein. The emphasis was on the constructed nature of scientific models and their pragmatic function. Works by Paul Feyerabend, Thomas Kuhn, N. R. Hanson, and especially Stephen Toulmin, as well as Michael Polanyi, were my primary influences. Out of this came a series of papers and books on religious knowledge in relation to science for both scholars (*The Texture of Knowledge* [1981] and *The Redemption of Matter* [1984]) and a more general audience (*Waking from*

Newton's Sleep [2006]). The deep influence of this Wittgensteinian philosophy of science will be evident in the coming pages.

This was the understanding of science that I took with me when I earned a second doctorate in psychology in the 1980s in a department that was committed to the role of psychological science for clinical practice. This was a time of intense controversy about whether clinical psychology, and especially psychoanalytic psychology, could be considered a science. And if so, in what sense? With my background in the philosophy of science, I was well prepared to participate in those discussions. As a veteran of many epistemological debates, I recognized that psychoanalysis was an epistemological, as well as a clinical, project and that contemporary psychoanalysis contained an implicitly relational epistemology as well as an explicitly relational clinical method (Jones, 1991a). That relational emphasis, in a variety of domains, will be central to the argument in the coming pages.

Freud had cast his discoveries in the materialistic and mechanistic language of Newtonian science. A central pillar of Freud's intellectual edifice was the "reality principle"—metaphysical theory now become a diagnostic category. The "reality" behind the reality principle was the physical world as described by nineteenth-century physics. Armed with this clear and concise definition of what could be true and what had to be false, what could be real and what had to be imaginary, Freud could easily attack religion and philosophy as the products of faulty thinking and imagination (Jones, 1991a).

In a book entitled *Playing and Reality* (1971), the twentieth-century British psychoanalyst D. W. Winnicott (one of the founders of the so-called object relations school of psychoanalysis) sought to move beyond Freud's dichotomous thinking by proposing "a third area of human living, one neither inside the individual nor outside in the world of shared reality" (110). Between inner and outer lies *interaction*. Neither the objective environment nor the isolated individual but, rather, the interaction between them defines this third domain, for it "is a product of the *experiences of the individual* . . . in the environment" (107, emphasis in the original). This intermediate reality is interpersonal from its inception. Beginning in the interactional space between mother and infant, it *remains an interpersonal experience* as it gradually spreads out from the relation to the mother to encompass "the whole cultural field" for "the place where cultural experience is located is in the *potential space* between the individual and the environment (originally the object)" (100).

Winnicott was a pediatrician before he trained as a psychoanalyst and one of the things he noticed was that at a certain developmental period, children become inordinately attached to certain objects—teddy bears, blankets, odd bits of clothing. Key to the infant's move from the infant-parent bond into the outside world is the use of these "transitional objects" which "is not *inside* . . . [n]or is it *outside*" (41); rather, it occupies that intermediate space that is interactional and thus carries for the infant the security of that first interpersonal experience. Children play with transitional objects, and thus play is an essential part of the transitional process. Playing stands at the interface of the physical world and the world of inner psychological process, for

> into this play area the child gathers objects or phenomena from external reality and uses these in the service of some sample derived from inner or personal reality. . . . In playing, the child manipulates external phenomena in the service of the dream and invests chosen external phenomena with dream meaning and feeling. (51)

In play, the child gives physical things an imaginative significance and occupies a psychological space resonating with the earliest experiences of intimacy. Even when the baby plays alone, he or she is still operating interpersonally; the very experience of play (even by oneself) carries echoes of those first interactions: "the playground is a potential space between the mother and the baby or joining mother and baby" (47). Thus, Winnicott's is not primarily a theory about certain kinds of objects—teddy bears and blankets—but is rather a theory about certain kinds of interpersonal experiences.

Encompassing inner and outer reality, the transitional experience overcomes the dichotomy of objectivity and subjectivity for it is "an intermediate area of *experiencing*, to which inner reality and external life both contribute" (2). From the modern perspective, which rigidly dichotomizes objectivity and subjectivity, the transitional process appears paradoxical for it is neither subjective nor objective but contains elements of both. Winnicott expresses this paradox when he writes:

> In health the infant creates what is in fact lying around waiting to be found. . . . Yet the object must be found in order to be created. This has to be accepted as a paradox and not solved by a restatement that by its cleverness seems to eliminate the paradox. (Winnicott, 1965: 181)

The world of the infant's experience (and our own adult world as well) is both created and found, constructed and discovered. We are neither the passive recipients of brute facts imposed on us from outside nor (in health) do we make our own realities out of nothing.

Human understanding is an active, creative process (Jones, 1981) in which reality is simultaneously discovered and constructed. Heuristically, we can separate subject and object but, for Winnicott they are, in actual experience, two sides of the same process. Subject and object are inseparably connected as the human mind creates the object it finds. For Winnicott the external and internal are reciprocally joined and mutually influenced.

So our understanding occurs in and through our relationships with the world of our experience that we both find and create. It arises not from the self alone nor the world alone but from the interaction between them. Human knowing is a transitional process and like all transitional processes, that interactional and relational space that is human knowing echoes with the child's first interpersonal experiences. This makes possible the psychoanalysis of the various forms of human knowledge (science, art, religion, philosophy, even psychoanalysis itself), for the structures of our knowing carry themes laid down in our earliest interpersonal encounters. Thus, psychoanalysis is an inherently epistemological enterprise, laying bare the dynamic forces at work in the various forms of human knowing.

As a transitional process, human understanding transcends the dichotomy between inner and outer. For Winnicott, like play, human understanding is virtually synonymous with creativity and insight. The infusion of meaning from the inner world into actions and objects in the public sphere and/or the expression of inner-generated truths by means of external physical and verbal forms describes not only children playing with teddy bears and empty boxes but also the creation of symphonies, sculptures, novels, and scientific theories.

Since "cultural experience [is] an extension of the idea of transitional phenomena and of play" (Winnicott, 1971: 99), when transitional objects recede into the background, there remains the residue of creativity that will drive the arts and the curiosity that will drive the sciences, that is, the capacity to create culture. In an oft-quoted and moving passage about the fate of transitional objects, Winnicott writes:

> Its fate is to be gradually allowed to be decathected, so that in the course of years it becomes not so much forgotten as relegated to limbo. By this I mean that in health the transitional object does not "go inside" nor does the feeling about it necessarily undergo repression. It is not forgotten and it is not mourned. It loses meaning, and this is because the transitional phenomena have become diffused, have become spread out over the whole, intermediate territory between "inner psychic reality" and "the external world as perceived by two persons in

common" that is to say, over the whole cultural field. At this point my subject widens out into that of play, and of artistic creativity and appreciation, and of religious feeling, and of dreaming. (5)

In discussing transitional objects, Winnicott is not just talking about child's play but is proposing nothing less than a psychoanalytic theory of culture that begins from the interpersonal matrix of infant and parent, moves to the development of creativity through play and the use of transitional objects, and ends with the symphonies of Beethoven, the paintings of Rembrandt, and the theories of Einstein. Culture, science, religion, and art are thus normal extensions of the transitional realm. They develop naturally from the pleasures of this intermediate experience rather than (as Freud felt) being foreign structures heteronomously imposed on the individual from outside in the service of instinctual control. The creative intuition fostered in the transitional space is a crucial human mode of knowing. Playing with reality is not only for psychological relief; it provides the perspectives that nurture creativity in the arts and sciences. In summary, the transitional process involves three components that stand in different ways at the intersection of objectivity and subjectivity: (1) a state of consciousness or "intermediate area of *experience*," fashioned in an interpersonal matrix; (2) external objects used in the service of internal states; and (3) a process encompassing inner and outer worlds (Jones, 1992).

In his drive to go beyond the dualism of objectivity and subjectivity that has dominated not only psychology but much of modern culture (Jones, 1996), Winnicott carried into psychoanalysis a theme central to much late twentieth-century thinking about science (Bernstein, 1983; Jones, 1981) as well as other contemporary movements. Winnicott's search for "the intermediate area between the subjective and that which is objectively perceived" (1971: 3) was clearly part of a larger, late twentieth-century, cultural concern (Jones, 1982).

For example, Richard Bernstein, in a book whose title *Beyond Objectivism and Relativism* (1983) summarizes its intent, chronicled a transformation in our understanding of science since Freud (a discussion of these changes can be found in Jones, 1981). Drawing on the writings of philosophers of science like Feyerabend, Rorty, and especially Kuhn, he describes a

shift from a model of rationality that searches for determinate rules . . . to a model of practical rationality that emphasizes the role of . . . interpretation. . . . The real point is to show what is wrong with a

theory or understanding of the "cognitive" which restricts this honor-
ific term to what can be explicitly formulated in a series of propositions.
(Bernstein, 1983: 57)

Bernstein demonstrates that the supposedly inviolate dichotomies between
objectivity and subjectivity, reason and emotion, depend on an indefensibly
narrow restriction of rationality to rule-governed procedure (e.g., laboratory
science and math). This, in turn, relegates everything else to the intellectual
hinterland of subjectivity.

A careful analysis of the actual conduct of science reveals that "many traditional or standard theories of what constitutes the rationality of science are
inadequate and need to be revised if we are to make sense of how science
functions and in what sense it is a rational activity" (Bernstein, 1983: 59).
Instead of the usual empiricist model of reason as a set of universal rules,
scientific rationality (and by extension reason in general) requires "imagination, interpretation, the weighing of alternatives, and application of criteria
that are essentially open" (56). Bernstein proposes replacing the hard and fast
model of rationality, which undergirded the modern ideal of knowledge, with
a "practical rationality" (230). His more nuanced view of science challenges
the dichotomies often assumed in discussions of rationality.

Similarly, Nelson Goodman, in his *Of Mind and Other Matters* (1984),
insists that all cognitive activities, especially "knowing, acting, and understanding in the arts, sciences, and life in general involve the use—the interpretation, application, invention, revision—of symbol systems" (152). Art
and science share a "common cognitive function" and can both be "embraced
within epistemology conceived as the philosophy of understanding . . . since
science and art consists very largely in the processing of symbols" (146).
Goodman insists that we have no "self-evident truths, absolute axioms, un-
limited warranties to distinguish right from among coherent versions" (37).
Bernstein's response is to rely on pragmatic criteria and accept those claims
that are proven in practice. Goodman proposes a radically pluralistic viewpoint in which there can be many separate "versions . . . true in different
worlds" (31).

Bernstein builds his epistemology from materials provided by the history
and philosophy of science, George Lakoff and Mark Johnson in their 1980
book *Metaphors We Live By*, arrive at similar conclusions from an analysis
of the ways in which claims are linguistically embedded. Claims to knowledge are systems of language. This linguistic inevitability means we have no
unmediated access to reality. All data are, in the words of a virtual cliché in

contemporary philosophy of science, "theory laden." Theory and data cannot finally be separated; we wouldn't even know what counts for data except in the presence of some theory (Jones, 1981). The characteristics we attribute to objects in our world "exist and can only be experienced relative to a conceptual system" (Lakoff & Johnson, 1980: 154).

Empiricist views of knowledge depend on a "correspondence theory of truth." Statements are called "true" when they correspond to some outside reality. The mediated nature of knowledge marks the end of any such theory, for we have no direct access to that external reality against which to compare our claims. There are no claims without contexts; and evaluation is a process conducted within some conceptual network. Lakoff and Johnson call these basic conceptual networks "metaphors." Scientific discourse may depend on a metaphor of causation as a kind of action; business decisions may be made by envisioning labor as a kind of resource; relationships may be conducted under the rubric of love as a journey; and intellectual discussion may be governed by the metaphor of argument as war. Metaphor "pervades our conceptual system and is a primary mechanism for understanding" (Lakoff & Johnson, 1980: 196).

Our actual reality—that is, the world of our lived experience—is shaped by the metaphors through which experience is mediated, and so it is no exaggeration to say that metaphors "create realities" (156). This is because "we define our reality in terms of metaphors and then proceed to act on the basis of the metaphors. We draw inferences, set goals, make commitments and execute plans, all on the basis of how we in part structure our experience, consciously or not, by means of metaphor" (158). The function of metaphor is precisely to "highlight and make coherent certain aspects of our experience . . . [and] be a guide for future action. Such actions will, of course, fit the metaphor. This will, in turn, reinforce the power of the metaphor to make experience coherent" (156).

The empiricist ideal of objectivity was based on the metaphor of truth as correspondence. Given the dichotomous nature of modern thought, undermining the myth of correspondence seems to leave only subjectivity. So to argue for a contextual epistemology is to confront the charge of subjectivity. (For example, see Kuhn's [1972] "Postscript-1969"; and Jones, 1981: chapter 5.) Lakoff and Johnson, like Bernstein and Winnicott, respond by pushing us past this dualism:

The mistaken cultural assumption [is] that the only alternative to objectivism is radical subjectivity—that is, either you believe in absolute truth or you can make the world in your own image. If you're not being objective, you're being subjective, and there is no third choice. We see ourselves as offering a third choice to myths of objectivism and subjectivism. (1980: 185)

They call their third alternative "experientialism." Knowledge arises neither from the external world impressing itself on our passive minds or from the projection of our subjective ideas onto a blank screen, instead "we understand the world through our interactions with it" (194). Like Winnicott's "transitional process," such a viewpoint is neither subjective nor objective, but is rather a third alternative. Lakoff and Johnson write:

> Its emphasis on interaction and interactional properties shows how meaning always is meaning to a person. . . . It gives an account of how understanding uses the primary resources of the imagination via metaphor and how it is possible to give experience new meaning and to create new realities. . . . We see the experientialist myth as capable of satisfying the real and reasonable concerns that have motivated the myths of both subjectivism and objectivism but without either the objectivist obsession with absolute truth or the subjectivist insistence that imagination is totally unrestricted. (228)

Perhaps a better name for their proposal (in keeping with Winnicott's terminology) would be an "interactional or relational epistemology" since "understanding emerges from interaction, from constant negotiation with the environment and other people. . . . From the experientialist perspective, truth depends on understanding, which emerges from functioning in the world" (Lakoff & Johnson, 1980: 230). Or, in Winnicott's more vivid language, truth is both "created and found." Such an account, Lakoff and Johnson say, "meets the objectivist's need for an account of truth . . . [and] satisfies the subjectivist's need for personal meaning and significance" (230). Metaphors stand conceptually between objectivity and subjectivity, involving discursive reason and creative expression. Metaphor is thus a "transitional" phenomenon. Our most rule-governed activities, such as experimental method, depend for their construction, elaboration, and expression on metaphors that "unite reason and imagination" (193). Lakoff and Johnson suggest that this is equally true of the worlds of science, culture, and critical philosophy, for all "human conceptual systems are metaphorical in nature and involve an imaginative understanding" (194).

Another argument for the metaphorical nature of human knowledge can be found in a book authored jointly by a cognitive psychologist and a philosopher of science. Michael Arbib and Mary Hesse, in their 1986 book *The Construction of Reality*, insist that "all language is metaphorical" (Arbib & Hesse, 1986: 150) and apply this maxim to psychology, religion, and the philosophy of science. They write that "the rise of science was accompanied by the conception of an 'ideal language' that would enable us to read off from the 'book of nature' the true science that exactly expresses reality" (149). Empiricism requires "an ideal, universal language exactly matching the world" (158). But a careful analysis of language leads them to reject the empiricist's "view of language as an ideal static system with fixed meanings which are dependent upon . . . rules" (148). Rather, language systems in the sciences and humanities are a "complex web of semantic interactions in which there is no rigid distinction between the literal and the metaphorical" (146). Changes in scientific theory or moving from the sciences to the humanities involve primarily a change in categories. New theories in science or scientific and artistic models achieve a "metaphoric redescription" of experience (156).

Inevitably a view of knowledge as mediated (rather than passively imprinted on our brains) leads them to an interactional, relational model of human knowing. Arbib and Hesse write in this regard: "There is an essential interaction between the knowing subject and the world, both in terms of the linguistic categories brought to the world in describing it, and in the activity of the subject in physical relations with the world" (1986: 159). Here, the philosopher's concern with metaphor dovetails with the psychologist's theory of cognitive schema:

> Schema theory interprets human perception, action, and communication in terms of cognitive schemas . . . [T]hese schemas change with experience. They do not reflect the full meaning of external reality but are always (at least potentially) in a state of flux, subject to change through our dialogue with the world. (181)

Only through cognitive, linguistic categories do we understand the world of our experience. The furthest reaches of scientific theorizing belong to the domain of human creativity, for even "scientific theory provides constructed models of scientific reality" (159).

Winnicott struggled to move beyond the nineteenth-century dichotomy of reason and imagination, objectivity and subjectivity, represented by Freud, through the articulation of a third, or "transitional," realm rooted in interpersonal experience. Late twentieth-century philosophy of science, as summarized by Arbib and Hesse, converges with Winnicott's concern to transcend these dualisms and reinstate imaginative interaction as a source of knowledge:

> Scientific models are a prototype . . . for imaginative creations or schemas. . . . Symbolic worlds all share with scientific models the function of describing and redescribing the world; and for all of them it is inappropriate to ask for literal truth as direct correspondence with the world. . . . We do not suddenly put on a different hat with regard to "truth" when we speak of the good or God from what we wear for natural science. (Arbib & Hesse, 1986: 161)

And they go on to draw an implication of special relevance to contemporary controversies: "There is little difference in principle here between the human and the natural sciences" (177).

So relational psychoanalysis contains an implicit epistemology that, paralleling others writing specifically about natural science, emphasizes a relational, interactional and more open model of human understanding that implies that all knowledge is transitional and interactional in Winnicott's sense. *Discursive reason and imaginative creation interpenetrate. Pragmatic realities constrain imaginative reconstructions while creative reinterpretations reframe empirical experience. No hard and fast line can be drawn between objective and subjective spheres or between the products of reason and of imagination.*

For Winnicott, human life is impoverished if deprived of access to the transitional realm. Reemersion there through moments of rapture and ecstasy are necessary times of psychic refreshment and rejuvenation and are the source of creativity, sanity, and a full human life. Winnicott's "transitional process" means not only a developmental stage or the use of certain soon-to-be-outgrown objects but also entering a certain "transitional" state of consciousness or psychological space. Teddy bears and blankets are hopefully put aside, but the capacity to enter and reenter that transitional consciousness where the subject-object dualism is transcended abides as the source of "creative living" (Winnicott, 1971: 100) and a deeper rationality. Winnicott points to the creative power of that state of consciousness where the usual distinctions of inner and outer, subjective and objective, fade and a creative power is accessed that can be understood in terms of the metaphorical nature of human understanding. In this state of disciplined imagination, or what the theologian Paul Tillich calls "ecstatic reason," new metaphors and paradigms can be encountered. From the transforming interpretation that reframes a patient's experience, to Watson's dream of the DNA spiral, to the imaginative encounter with the holy, transitional experiences become epistemologically creative and psychologically restorative through the generation of new metaphors and therefore new realities.

However, in contrast to Freud whose epistemology was grounded in the human body as conceived by Victorian science, contemporary psychoanalysis has sometimes tended to play down the role of the body, rejecting Freud's nineteenth-century Darwinian model of humanity as a bundle of antisocial, biological instincts in favor of attachment and relationality as basic motivations. This eclipsed Freud's insistence on rooting the process of human understanding in the body. More contemporary, laboratory-based psychological theories of embodiment preserve Freud's insight that human understanding is embodied understanding but in a way that also emphasizes rather than ignores its relational nature.

Embodiment

Embodiment shapes what we see, hear, taste, sense, and experience. People carrying heavy packs were compared to those without them on the task of estimating the incline of a hill they were about to climb. Carrying a heavy backpack caused them to over-estimate the steepness of the hill. The same happened with runners facing a hill at the end of a long race compared to those who had not yet run. The same experiment was repeated with estimating distance, and analogous results obtained. Hills look steeper and distances look longer if you are tired (Proffitt, 2006). Likewise, obese people tend to over-estimate the distances they have to walk (Sugovic & Witt, 2011). Viewing an object evokes the neuronal and motoric processes associated with the object (Tipper, 2004, 2010; Tucker & Ellis, 1998). Likewise, listening to action words evokes the neuronal and motoric processes associated with the actions (Gibbs, 2005: chapter 5; Malock, 2004; Martin et al., 2000; Pulvermuller, 2005; Willems et al., 2005).

Posture affects attention. "Sit up and pay attention" actually means what it says. When people sit up, they are more attentive (Riskind & Gotay, 1982; Strack, 1988). They are also more resilient in the face of stress (Nair, Sagur, Sollers, Consedine, & Broadbent, 2015). Subjects were randomly assigned to sit in a straight back, upright position or a slumped, head lowered position. Baseline psychological and physiological measures were taken. Then the subjects were asked to compose and give a five-minute speech, which would be evaluated by a panel of expert judges, while remaining in these positions. Participants seated upright showed higher self-esteem, better mood, and lower fear than the slumped over participants who used more negative words, expressed more sadness, reported fewer positive emotions, and reported feeling fearful, sluggish, and hostile. In another study (Neidenthal, 2007), two groups received reports of their success on an achievement test. The group that was sitting in a slumped posture felt less esteem and success and were in a worse mood than those who received the same news sitting upright with shoulders back and head held high. Maintaining an erect posture in the face of stress maintains self-esteem and reduces negative mood.

Posture and bodily movement have other effects as well. Tilting left or right, forward or back, affects judgments (Wells & Petty, 1980). Extending your finger can impact interpersonal evaluations (Cacioppo et al., 1993; Chandler & Schwartz, 2009). Looking down or away can improve recall (Glenberg et al., 1998). Nods and smiles increase positive affect (Stepper & Strack, 1993; Strack et al., 1988). Drawing your hands apart may help you distinguish one idea from another (Lakens et al., 2011). Pushing away motions with the hands and arms increases willpower in resisting food or cigarettes (Cacioppo et al., 1993; Hung & Labroo, 2011; Neidenthal, 2007). Images that typically evoke positive or negative emotions were flashed on a screen. Participants were asked to signal the pictures' arrival by either pushing a lever away or pulling it toward themselves. Participants instructed to push the lever away responded more quickly to negative images while those instructed to pull it toward themselves responded more quickly to positive ones. These results suggest a mutual, interactive relationship between concepts and actions so that bodily activity influences the way information is processed.

When people imitate the bodily expressions that go with certain emotions (smiles, frowns, slumped body) they report feeling the associated emotions. Conversely, when motor or bodily activity is inhibited, the experience of emotions and the processing of affective information are also inhibited. Individuals who held a pencil in their mouth that made them unable to smile experienced cartoons as less humorous than those whose mouths were forced into a smiling position. Those who were forced to smile rated the cartoons funnier than those who were inhibited from smiling. Likewise, persons fitted with devices that kept their face in a smiling configuration will rate a short story more positively than those who read the same story with a frown on their face. Or participants in these two positions (smiling or frowning) were asked to evaluate whether a sentence described pleasant or unpleasant events. The smiling subjects recognized the events described as pleasant significantly faster than when they were inhibited from smiling. Conversely, sentences describing unpleasant events were recognized significantly faster when participants were unable to smile. Another study showed that smiling could positively influence cardiovascular and affective responses to stress and increase resilience (Nair et al., 2015). So the comprehension of words and ideas with an emotional salience appears linked to the bodily reenactment of the relevant emotions; when the possibility of that bodily enactment is restrained, comprehension of the words is affected. Adopting the bodily expressions of emotions affects a person's preferences and attitudes so that adopting the bodily features associated with negative emotions causes people to evaluate things more negatively while the opposite is true for the bodily positions connected with positive emotions.

Tactile experiences of warmth or cold, sweetness or bitterness, influence appraisals of those traits in others and of their tendency toward prosocial behavior (Inagaki & Eisenberger, 2013). Holding a warm cup leads subjects to rate others as interpersonally warm; holding a cold cup has the opposite effect. Neural imaging finds that the same neural circuits are involved in experiencing sensations of physical and interpersonal warmth (Sagioglou & Greitemeyer, 2014). Subjects drank either a bitter drink (a specially prepared drink or grapefruit juice) or a sweet or neutral (water) drink. Those who experienced the bitter taste showed significant increases in felt hostility, hypothetical aggressive affect and behavior, and in actual aggressive behavior, both when they were provoked and when they were not provoked. So physical taste sensations can significantly impact our evaluation of and reaction to social situations.

Reactions were also affected by one's bodily position (Kille, Forest, & Wood, 2012). Subjects were seated on either a wobbly chair or a stable one. Participants in the unstable condition judged interpersonal relationships in general to be less stable than did participants seated on stable chairs. They also expressed a greater desire for stability in any future partner than those in the already stably situated group (Forest, Kille, Wood, & Stehouwer, 2015). In a further study, students who reported being in a committed relationship of more than a year were randomly put either into conditions of physical instability (seated at a desk on a wobbly chair, composing a letter standing on one leg, or sitting on an inflatable cushion) or physical stability (solid chair, standing on both feet, firm cushion). On a series of measures, those in the more physically stable condition rated their intimate relationships as more solid and stable than those in the less secure positions. Physical position can influence the evaluations people make of even their most intimate relationships. When remembering experiences of feeling controlled by others, people underestimate their own height; conversely when remembering experiences of being in control, they over-estimate their height (Duguid & Goncalo, 2012). All this suggests that subtle bodily states can impact one's perceptions of others and one's own preferences.

Much of our thinking is associated with enacting the corresponding bodily reactions, that is, thinking about taking a nap involves imagining yourself going into your room and lying down; or thinking about dinner means imagining yourself eating something. Brain scans confirm this. When people think about physical objects, the motor areas associated with picking them up become more active. When we think about food, the parts of our brain associated with digestion (not just associated with thinking) become active and our stomachs rumble. If we think about flowers, the olfactory areas become engaged (studies reviewed in Barsalou, 2008). When we think about animals, the visual cortex "lights up" since we know about animals primarily by seeing them. We simply name an object ("ball") and the circuits associated with catching it become activated. Action words stimulate the motoric system, even if no action is contemplated. Reading a list of verbs evokes motor areas; reading a list of nouns activates visual areas. Even abstract metaphors stimulate any possible associated activity. Thinking and imagining move the body (Ehrsson et al., 2003; Michaelson et al., 2006; Tipper, 2004, 2010; Tucker & Ellis, 2004).

The body enters into thinking in other ways as well. Gesturing is a prime example (Gallagher, 2005: chapter 5; Goldin-Meadow, 2003; Krause, 1998; McGilchrist, 2009; McNeill, 2005; Sweetser, 1998). People with phantom limbs experience the limbs gesturing when they speak even if the limbs don't exist. Blind people gesture when talking to other blind people. Are these just reflexes? Research suggests otherwise. Clearly they are not primarily communicative motions as the examples of phantom limbs and blind people gesturing to each other show. Rather, Shaun Gallagher suggests, gesturing "may at the same time accomplish something within ourselves, capturing or generating meaning that shapes our thought" (Gallagher, 2005: 122). Gestures do not simply express ideas within us; "gesture helps to accomplish thought" (128). Appropriate gesturing helps us remember words. Likewise, I may tap my fingers or look away when I am concentrating. These are not just epiphenomena. These bodily actions also "help to accomplish thought."

Eve Sweetser (1998, 1990) reviews research on the metaphoric use of gesture cross-culturally. Often speakers gesture a straight line ahead of them when making points about honesty or "doing the right thing." This is reflected in languages in which "straight" means honest. Likewise, gesturing upward is associated with good actions (we speak of having "high" morals) and down for immorality ("low" morals). Or in seminars when speakers use metaphors that picture reasoning as a motion through space (e.g., "Are we getting anywhere?" "Where was I?" "Should we really go on?"), her research finds they almost always gesture with their hands in a way that embodies motion (or lack of it). And she provides many other such examples arguing that all languages rely on embodied spatial metaphors to refer to more abstract constructs. So social connection is expressed through shaking hands or hugging; respect is shown through bowing or at least briefly lowering one's head. Even our most abstract concepts are situated spatially and so rely in part on bodily action to convey their meaning. Brain scans too reveal tight links between speech and gesture. All this reveals close connections between language (either in speaking or thinking) and bodily action (Willems & Hagoot, 2007). That moving can affect thinking has important implications for spiritual practices and rituals that involve movement.

As we described earlier, Lakoff and Johnson also insist that abstract thought rests on embodied foundations. Even the most abstract thinking is continually represented in embodied metaphors. The body is a (the?) major source for abstract and metaphoric speech: we speak of the "body politic"; we "embrace" ideas or "spit" them out; we seek to "balance" different positions; we can't "digest" that book; the argument is "shaky"; I could never "grasp" that idea; the news "hit" me hard; she was forced to "eat her words." Human cognition often requires experience informed by a human body, including proprioception. So language and metaphor are tightly tied to bodily experience (Gibbs, 2005: chapter 4). A review concludes, "High level cognitive processes (such as thought and language) use partial reactivations of states in sensory, motor, and affective systems to do their jobs. . . . [A]n admittedly incomplete but cognitively useful reexperience is produced in the originally implicated sensory-motor system, as if the individual were there in the very situation, the very emotional state, or with the very object of thought" (Neidenthal, 2007: 1003). Recognizing another's emotions from the facial expressions and experiencing that emotion oneself utilize the same neurological areas. When making a judgment about whether a word was associated with an emotion, the subjects' faces reflected the relevant emotion if there was one. When exposed to the word "slug," the subjects' facial muscles immediately showed the pattern associated with the feeling of disgust. Storing and processing ideas and associated emotions involves relevant embodied physiological as well as neurological activity.

But we should not disembody this discussion of the ways in which the body is represented in our abstract symbols. This transformation of body into symbol and metaphor is not simply a process of abstraction. There is no clear theory to explain how the cognitive system comes to draw upon bodily functions, that is, how we naturally come to speak of "digesting an idea." But clearly it happens. And clearly it happens because human understanding is carried out in conjunction with the body and not by a disembodied cognitive processor. So this is another indication that thinking often involves our bodies, that thinking is a full-bodied activity. But we must remember that our process of understanding our embodied understanding is itself an embodied process. It occurs and is itself grounded in an embodied social and historical context. This is particularly true, for example, in the ways that political or religious symbols become gendered and acquire masculine or feminine connotations beyond their inherent meaning, speaking (for example) of the "the fatherland," "the body politic," "mother church," or "father God." Speaking of politics or religion in embodied metaphors is, itself, an embodied process, rooted in the body and in culture. And our current understanding of the body itself is embodied, that is, it too is shaped by our embodiment and by our embodied location in history and culture.

Our use of embodied metaphors in our thinking is a very complex process. We do not know how it occurs. That is part of the unresolved question of how consciousness and cognition are related to the brain, and through the brain to the rest of the body. Using bodily metaphors in thinking is not simply a literal transcription. We do not literally "digest" an idea in the way that we digest food. The metaphor works because we have a certain idea or cognitive schema about the nature of ideas—that they come to us from outside and that we have to take them in and make them our own. That is how we think of learning. If we thought of ideas as already innate within us so that leaning was really remembering, the metaphor of digesting an idea would make no sense. The metaphor also depends on how we think about digestion. Speaking of the "body politic" not only involves the metaphor of "body"; it works only because of a certain idea of the "polis" which is represented in our minds as a set of schemas. Without a certain idea of the "polis" as an organic whole with differentiated members, the metaphor of the "body politic" would not work. It also would not work without a certain idea about how our bodies are constituted. But that idea of the nature of the polis that makes the metaphor work is not a natural fact like our digestive system. Our schemas about where ideas come from or how the polis is structured are given us by our culture, like our ideas about the body or about digestion. They are not natural facts nor the direct and literal expression of natural facts. They are cultural products. So the bodily metaphors we use in thinking are not immediate products of our bodies but are rather shaped by the culture in which we live that teaches us to think about ideas, societies, and bodies in certain ways. That these metaphors, including our metaphors for our bodies, are themselves embodied does not mean they are "objective" in some sense or culture free. Quite the reverse.

So our reliance on embodied metaphors in thinking is a more complex process than it sometimes appears in discussions of "embodied cognition." First we do not understand anything about the neuropsychology of how these bodily metaphors show up in our thoughts. Then there are interaction effects not just between body and thought but also involving bodily activity, cognitive processes, and culture, especially since the schemas for understanding the body and cognition are themselves provided by our culture. Later we will raise the question of how theories of embodied understanding would work based on models of the body radically different from those that are currently dominant in contemporary, Western scientific cultures.

Imagining

Imagining does not just occur in an "inner theater"; rather, picturing yourself doing an action evokes the same muscular potentials and the same neurological processes in the brain and body as does actually doing the imagined activity. Imagining moving your arms evokes the requisite electrical activity in the arms even if they stay at your side. Positron emission tomography (PET) scans reveal that imagining running or using a hammer stimulates the same motor areas in the brain as actually doing it. Just naming a tool stimulates the motor areas involved in using it (Ehrsson et al., 2003; Gibbs, 2005: 131; Lotze et al., 1999; Michaelson et al., 2006; Pulvermuller, 2005). If you imagine a person and know, or think you know, what he or she is doing, motoric activation takes place. People who imagined they were lifting a heavy weight were then on average able to lift heavier weights than people in the control group who did no imaginal simulations (Gibbs, 2005: 128). This close connection of mental imagery and bodily responses along with proprioception in which bodily processes are registered in the brain and in awareness shows the intimate relationships that can exist between consciousness, thought, and the body.

That connection between imagination and physical simulation is part of what makes certain psychotherapies (hypnosis, desensitization) and spiritual practices (Ignatian Exercises) that evoke complex imagistic experiences so powerful. Imaginary scenarios that put the person in the imagined or remembered experience by containing the fullness of the experience (the sights, sounds, smells, tactile sensations, actions) rather than being simply memories or images viewed from the outside evoke all the physiological, cognitive, and affective aspects of that experience. Research suggests that if people reprocess the whole of a traumatic experience in their imagination while in a safe environment, the whole psycho-physical complex is modified, as opposed to rumination where only part of the experience replays in a context in which no processing takes place (Ogden et al., 2006; van der Kolk et al., 1996). This clearly illustrates that strong connections can exist between memory or imagery and bodily activity, even if that bodily activity is not expressed in action. And when learning a new skill—shooting a basket or performing a movement in ballet or tai chi—visualizing doing it can improve performance after it has been learned to a certain point. This is another example of the connection between visual and motoric systems and the efficacy of imagined actions.

A similar phenomenon occurs with feelings. Emotional words stimulate the associated emotional centers and motoric actions, even if they aren't expressed, even if the emotions are not conscious, as any well-trained psychotherapist knows: the body's gestures (clenched fists, tightened jaws, incongruent smiles) can betray unexpressed, or even unfelt, emotions. As we have already noted, the process works in reverse. Using smiling muscles or nodding increases positive affect; shaking the head or slumping in your seat produces negative affect (Cacioppo et al., 1993; Stepper & Strack, 1993; Strack et al., 1988; Wells & Petty, 1980). Like thinking, the relationship of affect and body is a two-way street. Emotional scenes and memories impact the body; moving the body evokes emotions (these connections between embodiment and emotion are explored in more depth in a later section of this chapter).

Perceiving

Since the subject of this book is the possibility of perceiving God, research and theorizing about the embodied nature of perception is especially important for the argument to follow. Most researchers writing about perception agree that perception is something we do; it is not simply something done to us. "Visual experience is not something that happens in individuals. It is something they do" (Gibbs, 2005: 65). Things don't just appear to us; we reach out for them in innumerable ways. Unexpected things happen, but our experience of them, our reaction to them, is shaped by our preconscious, bodily experience. A wind-blown object comes flying at me; I instinctively raise my hand to ward it off or I duck—actions that I have rehearsed over and over in other times and places. Perceiving means we turn, we look, we touch, we smell. Visual information is always from the perspective of our body, where it is located in space. If we see an object, even if we know we are not going to touch it, our body still tacitly responds as though it were going to touch the object (Barsalou, 2008). Seeing a cup automatically evokes the neurophysiological processes associated with reaching for it (Tucker & Ellis, 2001; Teske, 2013) "Perceiving something is not simply a visual experience, but involves non-visual sensory experiences such as smells, sounds, and movement of one's entire body, such as the feelings of readiness to take specific action upon the object. On this view perception is tightly linked to subjunctive thought processes" (Gibbs, 2005: 64).

It appears that vision requires extensive bodily connections. In some cases, if the nerves connecting the eyes to the visual cortex are intact but the connections to the motor cortex are broken, the individual is blind. The eyes and brain may work, but if the organism cannot bodily enact visual experience, the person does not "see." Mortimer Mishkin and his colleagues report a series of experiments in which the visual cortex and its connections to the eyes were left intact but the visual cortex was surgically disconnected from the rest of the nervous system. What they call the "highly dramatic and puzzling" result was that the monkeys thus treated were blind even though their visual system was completely functional (Iwai & Mishkin, 1969; Nakamura & Mishkin, 1986). This suggests that non-visual input, including a wide range of bodily inputs, is necessary for vision. Visual processing requires more than a strictly visually oriented physiology.

The same is true of hearing and comprehending language. If people cannot speak the words, they cannot hear them, even if their auditory-processing faculties are fine. Mottonen and Watkins (2009) used magnetic waves to temporarily interrupt the signals between the lips and the part of the brain that receives those signals so that the brain was not aware of lip movements. This blocked subjects' ability to differentiate sounds that required lip movements. It did not block the recognition of sounds whose articulation did not require the lips or tongue. Using a similar method, a group of Dutch experimenters used magnetic waves to temporarily block the connection between the premotor cortex (which serves bodily action) and brain centers involved in processing the meaning of speech. Participants subject to this intervention had difficulty processing words referring to bodily activity. Particular changes in the functioning of the premotor cortex directly impacted the processing of related language, thus demonstrating that understanding verbal descriptions of an action partially depend on the brain's motor areas and that activity in the motor cortex forms part of a verb's semantics (Willens et al., 2011). A similar conclusion comes from a study in which subjects in a functional magnetic resonance imaging (fMRI) scanner were simply asked to read a list of words. Included in this list were words describing bodily actions ("lick," pick," and "kick") (Hauk, Johnsrude, & Pulvermuller, 2004). The relevant motor areas in the cortex (head, arm, and leg, respectively) became active. Again, suggesting the simple word recognition can implicate the motor cortex and that knowledge of categories is closely linked to relevant bodily dimensions. Thus a variety of different studies converge to support the conclusion that motor-action systems and language systems are not independent modules in the brain. Rather, language processing and bodily activity are recipro- cally connected through widely distributed neural networks to the extent that, in many cases, verbal comprehension relies on activity in the motor cortex. *Processing speech is not localized in a particular cortical region. Rather, semantic processing implicates a wide range of brain regions including those subtending bodily behavior.*

From my perspective as a clinical person, the most striking evidence that language comprehension is intimately connected to bodily activity and becomes compromised when that connection is damaged comes from clinical conditions in which lesions in the motor areas impact the comprehension of words related to those motor activities (Pulvermuller, 2005). This involves not just action-oriented words (run, jump) but even objects we relate to through bodily activity. If we lose the capacity to bodily simulate certain categories, we lose the category even if our cortical areas (the ones in which category recog- nition are supposedly localized) are fine (Barsalou, 2008). If our visual area is damaged, we may not have access to categories that arose from visual experi- ence (dog, bird, etc.) (Damasio & Damasio, 1994). If motor areas are injured, we may lose tool categories like hammer since we learned about hammers by using our motor areas (Barsalou, 2008; Damasio & Damasio, 1994). Present problems in the color processing centers may cause us to lose color knowl- edge, and not just color vision, that we formerly knew well (Barsalou, 2008; Damasio & Damasio, 1994). Lesions in the spatial orientation area may im- pact not only our ability to navigate in the world but also to use knowledge about the locations of things we were formally familiar with (further lesion studies supporting these claims are reviewed in Barsalou, 2008: 627; Damasio & Damasio, 1994). *Neural anatomical, magnetic resonance, and lesion studies concur in finding that sensing, experiencing, and comprehending are closely linked to our capacities for implicit and explicit bodily activity.*

So our bodily state impacts our sense experience in ways far beyond whether the sensory apparatus is intact or not (Clemero, 2009). Gibbs writes, "What people perceive depends on what people are able to do, and what they do, in time, alters what they perceive" (Gibbs, 2005: 17). All of this research suggests that a variety of widely distributed neural connections join sensory experience (and therefore the human understanding derived from it) with bodily action. Through these distributed neural networks, perception and comprehension are diffused across many cortical regions and many physiological sites throughout the body. Most every thought, image, and memory is a multi-modal, multi-sensory, virtually whole-body event, spreading across different perceptual and motoric brain regions. There is little evidence here of relatively autonomous brain "modules" (Gibbs, 2005: chapter 3 & 277–281; Teske, 2013). Later in this chapter we exam in detail additional research supporting these conclusions.

Beyond these fundamental neurological and physiological factors, conscious mentation also directly affects sensation and perception. Expectancies are a prime example. We see what we expect to see. People rapidly shown a deck of cards in which the hearts were colored black and the spades red almost universally report the deck looked fine. An experiment involved two people conversing; two workmen carrying a door walked between them and while their view was blocked one of the workmen changed places with one of the conversation partners in a pre-arranged move. Within a few seconds the other conversation partner found himself talking to an entirely different person, dressed differently, and so on. Only 5 percent of the people caught up in this experiment noticed the difference (Gibbs, 2005: 66). In the famous movie of men playing an intense game of basketball, a man in a gorilla suit walks through the middle of the game but most people concentrating on the action don't see the gorilla (Mack & Rock, 1998; Simons & Chabris, 1999). *Experiment after experiment demonstrates that people's expectations govern what they see.*

Our actual sensory experience and our conceptualizations of it are always mediated neurologically, and bodily, and cognitively. We cannot possibly be conscious of all the sights, sounds, smells, thoughts, sensations, or feelings that impinge on us. Normally only those stimuli we can attend to or have cognitive schema for enter our experience. "We experience only the things we specifically attend to, depending on our current needs and goals" (Gibbs, 2005: 67). Our minds can never produce a complete, multi-dimensional cognitive representation of the world. Our maps of our experience are not direct representations but are the product of the dynamic interactions among our actions, our physiology, and our cognitive-processing systems. Such maps or schemas, in turn, then influence what we see and don't see and what thoughts and feelings are engendered.

So perception and sensation are not simple, direct phenomena. They may seem simple when we look at a tree. But research from neurology and cognitive science uncovers processes implicated in our sensory experience that are anything but simple or direct. Rather, perception is a multimodal, and probably non-linear, process. Later in the chapter we will review more research that further supports this more complex picture of our sensory experience. The epistemological implications here are potentially tremendous and we will discuss those at the end when we address the question of a possible spiritual sense.

Proprioception

Embodied understanding partially involves what Shaun Gallagher (2005) refers to as a body schema. He has made a helpful distinction between body image and body schema. Body image is how we see, think, and feel about our bodies. The body schema is a semi-unconscious cognitive schema about our body built on our continual proprioceptive experience of location, movement, what our limbs are doing, how to walk, and so on. Proprioceptors in the muscles, the muscle spindles, are responsible for our sense of position and movement. This body schema controls, governs, and shapes our unconscious bodily activities. The body schema is "a certain collection of sensory-motor functions responsible for maintaining posture and governing movement" (Gallagher, 2005: 45). An example of this body schema is the widely reported (Gallagher, 2005) "phantom limb" phenomenon when an amputee (or even a person born missing a limb) still experiences sensations (pain, muscle tension, movement) in the non-present limb. He or she reports sensations of gesturing with the missing limb while speaking. The body schema has an arm or a leg even if the body doesn't.

We are usually not directly aware of this body schema. Gallagher says it is "a system of sensory-motor functions that operate below the level of self-referential intentionality" (Gallagher, 2005: 26). Thus, he refers to this schema as "prenoetic," that is, it "helps to structure consciousness, but does not explicitly show itself in the contents of consciousness" (32). But we are aware of the results of its operation. A friend enters the room and I decide to stand up and shake his hand. My body schema is implicated in standing up, putting out my hand, and related actions. If I am standing up to get a drink, the form of my hand would be different. I am not aware of all the muscles, neurons, and tendons involved. Coordinating them is the task of the body schema. I do not have to decide which neurons to activate and muscles to use to accomplish those actions.

Proprioceptive information (information about what is happening to and in our bodies) is, according to Gallagher, processed according to the body schema: how we know where our limbs are, how our posture is, how we are moving through space. This is how you find your nose with your eyes closed or know whether your hand is open or closed under the table. Gallagher distinguishes proprioceptive awareness and proprioceptive information along the now familiar distinction between cognitive processes that are conscious and those that are operating below the threshold of consciousness. Proprioceptive awareness is our conscious awareness of our bodies. Proprioceptive information is the information from the rest of the body processed unconsciously according to our body schema in order to keep the body upright and moving fluidly, and so on. So we don't have to be fully conscious of our body in order to move. This frees consciousness for other tasks.

But we do need to be aware of our bodies in order to engage in intentional action. To decide to move, we need to know where and how our limbs are positioned and where we are located spatially. That awareness is not primarily visual; it does not come from looking at our body. It is proprioceptive. Proprioceptive information and awareness are necessary for intentional actions. Both apparently utilize the same proprioceptors and neuronal pathways and sometimes the same central structures (Gallagher, 2005: 75–76).

Virtually from the moment of birth, infants are able to imitate simple movements: tongue protrusions, opening and closing the mouth, turning the head. These are clearly intentional actions, not reflexes, implying that a proto-body-schema is present from birth. They require the integration of visual, proprioceptive, and vestibular information. What is seen visually is translated into a proprioceptive awareness so that one's body's position matches what one sees. What are often called "mirror neurons" clearly play a part when one sees someone doing something and one's physiology responds as if one were also doing it: neurons fire, muscles tense; even if one doesn't actually copy the action, one's body schema does.

More precisely, research with monkeys reveals the same neural activation patterns associated with grasping, touching, or holding objects when watching another monkey do these motions as when the monkey does them himself (Rizzolatti & Craighero, 2004). Research confirms that humans too show similar activation patterns when watching someone do an action or even reading about another doing it (Pulvermuller, 2005; Sinigaglia & Rizzolatti, 2011). Two striking implications of these findings: first, we are in continual interaction with other humans in our environment, even if we are not conscious of it. We aware in our own bodies (if not in our conscious minds) of what others are doing or what they might be able to do, how they might move, reach, or grasp. Certain martial arts practices involve developing this capacity to a high degree: knowing someone will throw a kick or a punch before the person does it. Likewise, people singing in a conductorless choir (in a monastery for example or a small vocal ensemble) develop the ability to know when the group will start chanting without any overt signal. Second, watching another act, the parallel neuronal processes become active in me. I watch another shoot a basket—my somatosensory cortex reacts— but I do not find myself involuntarily setting up for a shot. That neuronal activation by itself does not cause me to assume the same stance. I have to voluntarily choose to do so. This suggests that voluntary action can overrule or rechannel neuronal activation, a point with important implications for human intentionality.

Does proprioceptive awareness mean making one's own body an object of perception? Gallagher says no (2005: 73); he claims directly that "proprioception is not itself a perception of the body as an object" (137). The proprioceptive self is "a sense of self that involves a sense of one's motor possibilities, body postures, and body powers rather than one's visual features" (83). Unlike ordinary sense perception, proprioception seems direct and unmediated. We often don't know how we know what we do know proprioceptively. Clinically some diabetics learn to sense their insulin levels and report them to the physician with a high degree of accuracy before the blood test is taken. But they can't say how they know; they just "sense it." Likewise, in patients being trained in heart-rate variability by biofeedback, many develop a proprioception of their heart-rate variability that is quite accurate; but again, they cannot articulate how they know this. Gallagher describes such proprioception as "a pre-reflective (non-observational) awareness that allows the body to remain experientially transparent. . . . It provides a sense one is moving or doing something" (73). So proprioception is often a "felt sense" or awareness that cannot be fully articulated rather than a perception coming through one of the five major senses. Later we suggest that our proprioceptive awareness might function as an analogy for and play an important role in any hypothetical religious perception.

Neural Holism

The title of this section intentionally reflects the term "quantum holism" which refers to the topic in the philosophy of physics regarding whether or not quantum theory reveals a previously unsuspected interconnection among physical parts or properties. For example, in a series of papers published in the 1970s entitled "Quantum Theory as an Indication of a New Order in Physics," David Bohm (1975) argued that at its deepest level the universe is to be understood as a single, interconnected system. Clearly, at one level the universe is made up of individual particles, atoms, and molecules. At another level, Bohm says, the universe is a single, interconnected system characterized by an "unbroken wholeness" (Bohm's work is reviewed in Jones, 1984). Whether Bohm's claim or something like it is correct and what that might mean is far beyond the scope of this book on cognitive science and theology. Here I simply want to suggest that some neural-imagery findings may be an indication of a new order in neuroscience in which, at some level, the brain is best understood as a single, interconnected system.

Certainly when I was being trained in clinical neuropsychology the reigning paradigm was concerned exclusively with localization. This made good clinical sense since determining where a brain lesion was located was crucial for diagnosis and treatment. The assumption was that symptoms were caused by trauma to a specific part of the brain. But this drive for localization was not simply powered by clinical concerns. It also fit with a widespread, reductionistic model of scientific investigation that was always breaking things apart, looking for simpler, more precise underlying causes. So loss of speech resulted from trauma to Broca's area or vision problems probably indicated issues in the occipital cortex at the back of the head.

Even then this singular focus on localization was being challenged. In a series of studies on the sense of smell starting in the 1970s, using electroencephalogram (EEG) readings of the electrical activity in the brain, Walter Freeman and his group found that information was contained not in the firing of individual neurons but in the amplitude of the wave produced when all the neurons in the olfactory bulb fire together in a particular pattern. Identifying a specific smell is not done by a specific neuron or subset of neurons specialized for that odor but rather is accomplished by every olfactory neuron firing together to produce a wave with a certain configuration. The meaning of a sensation resides in global neuronal activity, not in the firing of individual neurons. These signals are then sent throughout the brain and combined with input from other senses and from memories of past experience. A single perceptual event (in this case a smell) results from the reciprocal interaction of neurons in the olfactory bulb combined with information from other senses and stored information from the past. Together they produce an experience unique to each individual. The smell of bacon and eggs cooking instantly triggers images of bacon strips and fried eggs and evokes happiness in one hungry child and revulsion in another vegan adult.

Freeman's studies of particular sensations suggest that there is no simple, single set of neuronal connections and patterns infallibly associated with specific perceptual experiences. The neuronal pattern associated with the sight or smell of a predator or the taste of a particular substance differs from organism to organism, depending on the organism's lived history that formed its particular pattern of synaptic connections. These neurological markings do not "represent" a predator or a poison or something edible in some direct, literal way since the patterns are constantly shifting and vary from individual to individual. Therefore, Freeman argues that the neurology of sensation seems better represented by non-linear dynamical models than models of linear causation where a particular sight or smell always produces the same neuronal effect. In non-linear (so-called chaotic) dynamical systems there are continually shifting patterns (in this case, of neurons firing) that are constrained within certain limits (not really chaotic in a strong sense, which is why I don't like the term "chaos theory" for this model). From these continually reciprocating processes (new stimulations continually coming into the brain, neighboring neurons firing, etc.) emerge those sensations we experience as smell, sight, taste, and other senses.

These basic physiological structures and the patterns of neuronal firing to which they give rise are shaped and reshaped by an organism's embodied life: by its behavioral history, the experiences it has encountered along the way, its current activity. The underlying neuronal patterns are constantly reformulated as new sensory information arrives and new actions are performed. The same sight, sound, or smell may evoke different neuronal configurations in different individuals who, nevertheless, report the "same" experience. Freeman's research again suggests that even simple perceptual experiences (a sight or a smell) are incredibly complex neurologically. At that level they are anything but simple or direct. It also points away from any narrowly focused modular understanding of how human experience is realized in the brain. (The material in these paragraphs is based on Freeman's [2001] EEG research on olfactory sensation and other research reviewed in Gibbs, 2005: chapter 3.)

It is possible to find brain regions salient for specific functions: occipital areas for vision, and specific locations on the somatosensory and motor regions where neuronal activity is associated with sensations in specific parts of the body or with moving specific parts of the body (in both cases, the largest cortical areas are associated with the hands and the face, much smaller regions with the legs and the feet). But these experiences also involve neurological activity beyond these specific locations. And there is no one-to-one correspondence here. Injury can cause a function to shift to a new location; exercising the body can change the configuration. The body shapes how the living brain gets formed. Research on "neuroplasticity" demonstrates the capacity of the brain's "circuitry" to configure and reconfigure throughout life. Experimenters operated on newborn ferrets to reconnect the neuro-circuits from the eyes to the parts of the ferret's brain associated with hearing. The ferrets were then able to see using what is normally the auditory part of the brain (Noe, 2009: 53–59)

In the late 1970s and early '80s, I remember the way in which the clinical diagnosis of neural pathologies was done through a combination of intense clinical interviews, physical exams, and paper and pencil tests. With the arrival of computed tomography (CT or CAT) scans, much more precise localization of tumors and aneurisms became possible. Basically an X-ray of the brain, CT scans produce a static image. The more precise but static images produced by CT scans reinforced the focus on localization as the only "scientific" way to understand the brain. Later, fMRI technology traced blood flow to the various parts of the brain and thus produced a dynamic picture of neural activity. The dramatic and colorful fMRI slides that soon became de rigueur in neuroscience articles only added to this singular focus on localization as different parts of the brain were said to "light up" (i.e., become more colorful on the computer screen as blood flow and oxygen consumption shifted there) as the subject performed different cognitive tasks (doing mental arithmetic, deciding on a course of action, remembering a happy or sad event).

But as we know, frames-of-reference allow us to see some things and blind us to others. The fact that some parts of the brain received increased blood flow and oxygen during certain tasks did not logically mean that the rest of the brain was necessarily dormant or irrelevant during that task. Looked at through a singular localization lens, the brain scan might look that way. But that conclusion was not necessarily the whole story. At one level there are areas in the brain that are particularly active during certain tasks (for example, speaking, reading, understanding speech, decoding visual signals, or experiencing fear). But that does not logically suggest that they are "special-ized" for that task or that other areas are not equally crucial for or also in-volved in the same task. Some recent research suggests otherwise.

For example, the classic case for the localization of emotion was the amyg-dala as the seat of fear. Individuals with amygdala damage show lowered responses to fearful and aversive situations and are less able to feel fear in nor-mally fearful situations and to perceive fearful expressions in others. Electrical stimulation of the amygdala produces fearful behavior and increased startle reactions in rats. While the amygdala is certainly involved in fear reactions, further research finds it is equally active in processing perception and atten-tion, or in a variety of domains of social cognition, and for memory formation and retrieval (regardless of whether the material is emotionally salient). The amygdala is actively involved in positive reinforcement and positive expecta-tions, and in processing novel experiences. The amygdala also regulates sensory processes, especially the value and salience of a sensory experience (Duncan & Barrett, 2007). So the amygdala plays a crucial role in perception and other sensory information—topics of particular concern to the theme of this book. There is little evidence that the amygdala is specialized for processing fear or any other particular content. Rather, it appears that the amygdala is just one part of a much larger network that is involved not just in fear processing but also in various proprioceptive and orienting tasks, especially parsing ambig-uous stimuli and also in social cognition (Barrett & Satpute, 2013; Beckes & Coan, 2015; Lindquist, Wager, Kober, Bliss-Moreau, & Barrett, 2012; Kober et al., 2008). This larger grouping of neural sites is sometimes referred to as the "salience network" for it helps attend to internal and external factors that are salient for various tasks (Oosterwijk et al., 2012). But no nodes in this net-work (especially the amygdala) exclusively process fear or other emotions and most are also involved in non-fear-related and non-emotion-focused tasks (Beckes & Coan, 2015).

There was much excitement some years ago around the discovery of "mirror neurons" that responded when a subject observed another person per-forming a task or experiencing an emotion. These were proposed as the source of human empathy. But it turns out that social perception and understanding implicates a vast network of neuronal areas that are also involved with au-tobiographical memory, anticipating the future, moral decision making, se-mantic memory for the meaning of words, seeing the context within which objects are perceived as well as with social relations (Beckes & Coan, 2015). This interactive collection of brain centers is often called the "mentalizing" network (Barrett & Satpute, 2013; Oosterwijk et al., 2012). So there is no singular center that produces empathy. Rather, empathy arises from the work of a wide-ranging set of interacting networks (Beckes & Coan, 2015).

Several other such distributed and more general-functional networks have been identified using brain imaging tools (Barrett & Satpute, 2013; Oosterwijk et al., 2012; Peterson & Sporns, 2015). For example, researchers suggest there is a "limbic network" that deals not only with affect (the traditional function of the limbic system) but also autobiographical memory, and it involves areas beyond the traditional limbic system. And there is a "frontoparietal network" that is involved with cued attention, task switching planning, rule-governed processing, and working memory. And there are others as well. Different researchers call them by different names, but for consistency's sake I am going to follow the terminology found in table 1 in Oosterwijk et al., 2012: 2112). These are often called "resting-state" networks because they are investigated using an fMRI and a subject that is in a "resting state"—that is, the subject is not performing any task at that moment. Even under those conditions, these networks show correlated oscillations and so maintain their functional connectivity even at rest. Because the subject is not performing a task, it is assumed these network patterns emerge spontaneously and so represent the uninfluenced and foundational state of the brain.

It is tempting to simply move the modular, localization model to the network level and argue that these "intrinsic networks" are the sites specialized for specific functions. But that seems over-simplified. Several different networks play a role in many common tasks. For example, reflecting on one's own mental state involves parts of the "mentalizng network," the "salience network," and the "executive control network" (Barrett & Satpute, 2013; Oosterwijk et al., 2012). There seems to be no one single set of circuits involved in such a "theory of mind" tasks (Beckes & Coan, 2015). Our "sense of self" and ability to reflect on it results from the highly distributed neurological activity of many different brain centers. Or conscious mental activity involves the "limbic network," the "salience network," the "default network," and the "frontoparietal network" (Oosterwijk et al., 2012). So these networks are not narrowly specialized for particular tasks nor are particular neural tasks limited to a single network (Peterson & Sporns, 2015).

Conversely, as we have seen with the amygdala, a particular neural locale may play a role in more than one such "network." For example portions of the temporal lobe are part of both the "limbic network" and the "default network." Or parts of the parietal area are included within the "salience network," the "frontoparietal network," and the "dorsal attention network." By definition, a network involves more than one area of the brain and each network includes

portions of other networks. The result is a highly distributed and interconnected (rather than a discretely localized) model of the brain (Oosterwijk
et al., 2012; Peterson & Sporns, 2015).

Likewise our mental activities are also widely distributed over several
networks. For example, the "executive network" is heavily involved with
visual perception, motor activity, memory, attention, and cognition, but
it also plays a role in emotions, language, and imagination. The "mirroring
network" is largely taken up with visual and motor activities but is also
implicated in emotion, attention, cognition, memory, and language. The
"salience network" is primarily concerned with affect and emotion but also
processes information about both aversive and positive experiences, active
imagination, cognition, and visual and motor activities. The "mentalizing
network" is about equally involved with emotions, visual information,
memory and cognition, and to a lesser degree with social information, attention, and imagination (these data are derived from Barrett and Satpute,
2013: figure 1). Thus these networks are widely distributed functionally as
well as neurologically. In fact, it appears that virtually all the networks are
involved in virtually all our mental activities to a greater or lesser extent. It
has been theorized that the differences among all our mental activities are
primarily the result of the relative involvement of the different networks
(Duncan & Barrett, 2007; Oosterwijk et al., 2012). Of particular importance for our purposes is the network that Lisa Feldman Barrett and her
colleagues call the "salience network." It is the primary (but not the only)
locus of proprioception, guiding "body-directed attention (and) using
representations from the body to guide behavior and attention" (Oosterwijk
et al, 2012: 2112).

Given that emotional experience and cognitive processes appear to be
widely distributed across many different neurological regions, Barrett argues
against any localization model for the neurology of specific emotions or
cognition. Rather, she proposes that a general emotional system, which she
calls "core affect," underlies all emotional experience (Barrett, 2006). Core
affect is not simply feeling. It is rather similar to proprioception: the awareness of an organism's general psychophysical state organized along the two
dimensions of pleasant-unpleasant and high to low level of arousal (Barrett,
2014; Wilson-Mendenhall, Barrett, & Barsalou, 2013). Core affect refers to
bodily changes that might be felt (for example) as pleasurable, displeasurable,
arousing, or something else. Core affect is the general way a person feels about
himself or herself and the surrounding world at any given moment. Because
it is the psycho-neurological foundation of all our experience, according to

Barrett's proposal our core affect at any given moment impacts all our sensory experience and cognitive processing.

Traditional theories of emotion think of them as "natural kinds," that is, that each emotion (anger, fear, joy, etc.) has its own unique structure. Each has its particular neurological basis, motivates its own inclination to act in certain ways, has its own unique physiological configuration including its own unique and easily recognized facial expression. Barrett rejects this. Rather, she claims that emotions are "constructed" phenomena (Barrett, 2006; Barrett, 2014; Lindquist & Barrett, 2008; Wilson-Mendenhall et al., 2013). On this model, our conscious experience of an emotion arises when our encounter with an external object or some internal event changes our physiological state (our core affect) and so evokes our conscious awareness. This arousal becomes meaningful as an emotion when it is "categorized" as such. That categorization, which transforms a state of arousal into an experience of an "emotion," draws upon stored past experiences. "An emotion is enacted when embodied conceptual knowledge is brought on-line to shape the perception of a physical state" (Barrett, 2014: 293). She calls this a "conceptual act theory" (CAT) (Barrett, 2014; Lindquist & Barrett, 2006). Meaningful affective experience, according to Barrett's model, is the conjunction of three factors: (1) our generalized bodily awareness or proprioception (core affect), (2) which is generated by external, sensory, or internally produced input, (3) along with mental categories that reflect prior experiences (Barrett, 2009). The role of mental categories in creating meaningful experience is what she refers to as "categorization." This makes this a "constructivist" model of experience (Barrett, 2009). "Categorization" constructs meaningful emotional experiences out of the dialectic between the storehouse of past experience and core affect generated by the impact of the present internal or external environment on the organism. Thus experience, including sense perception, is a constructed phenomenon at the neurological level as well as at the information-processing level (Barrett, 2009, 2014; Lindquist & Barrett, 2006; Lindquist et al., 2012; Wilson-Mendenhall, Barrett, Simmons, & Barsalou, 2011). And information gleaned from past experience plays a crucial role in shaping present experiences and the knowledge derived from them. So, for example, the neurological construction of an experience of divine presence like those described at the beginning of this book might occur when some external object (a religious text or statue or the complexity of nature) or an internally felt sense impacts our psychosomatic equilibrium (our core affect) and brings with it connections to previous experiences (including religious teachings). Or a sudden theoretical insight into a difficult scientific problem might arise when our present thinking about the problem combined with our prior education suddenly upsets our psychosomatic equilibrium in such a way that it jars us loose from our conventional thought patterns and so enables us to see the situation from a new perspective.

The neurological dimension of the construction of our experience involves the interaction between these various distributed networks that "combine and constrain one another like ingredients in a recipe" (Lindquist et al., 2012). For example, the "salience network" (including the amygdala) helps orient the organism to external information that may be salient for it (Lindquist et al., 2012). From this constructivist viewpoint, the various networks realize the different permutations of core affect that we, through the process of categorization, consciously experience as anger, ecstasy, beauty, useful information, or a sense of the presence of God. And since core affect is fundamentally a result of embodiment, this model underscores the ways in which embodiment and embodied processes and activities play a foundational role in all our perceptual experiences, our emotional states, and our cognitive processing. As Barrett writes, "All mental states are, in fact, embodied *conceptualizations* on internal bodily sensations and incoming sensory input" (Barrett, 2014: 293; see also Wilson-Mendenhall et al., 2011).

One striking implication of Barrett's model is that there is no fundamental, neurological difference between cognition and emotion (Barrett, 2006; Duncan & Barrett, 2007). Many of the same networks subtend both activities we categorize as "emotional" and those we categorize as "cognitive." And brain scans of individuals undergoing "emotional experiences" show increased activity in networks associated with the simulation of past experience, language, the retrieval of semantic information, and executive attention (i.e., areas associated with "conceptualization")—that is, activities usually labeled "cognitive" (Lindquist et al., 2012). On this model it is not simply that "affect" impacts "cognition." A phraseology that suggests that cognition is primary in human understanding and affect is secondary and simply acts upon cognition. Rather, what we call "cognition" and "affect" are reciprocally bound together in every moment of human understanding including religious and scientific knowing. Every emotional experience has its cognitive component; every cognitive process, no matter how formal or abstract, has its affective dimension.

Such a wholistic approach gains additional support from a recently completed, massive research program called the "Human Connectome Project." This five-year, multi-million dollar project, funded in large part by the National Institutes of Health (NIH) involved thirty-nine investigators at eleven institutions including Harvard, Oxford, Washington University, Indiana University, St. Louis University, and several European universities. All were utilizing an array of the most advanced tools available for studying the brain with the goal of mapping areas of the brain and the connections between them in the finest detail currently possible (a process referred to as the "parcellation" of the brain). The results were published in an expanded edition of *Nature* in July 2016 (Glasser et al., 2016). Using a variety of criteria (cortical architecture, thickness, function, connectivity, etc.) the researchers distinguished 180 areas in each hemisphere of the brain rather than the more traditional 83 such areas. Producing such a detailed neurological map (called a "connectome") of distinctive areas in the brain and the connections among them has been an overriding desire of neurologists for decades, if not centuries (for a history of such investigations and the place of this project in that history, see Sporns, 2013).

There are basically two types of connections within the brain. Structural connectivity refers to the physical connections within the central nervous system (CNS). That is what the human connectome project primarily lays out. As we have noted earlier, the neuronal activity taking place in this interconnected network can produce complex, non-linear patterns and processes. These non-linear processes are not random. Rather, they usually organize themselves into coordinated rhythmic patterns involving temporal relations, coherence, and so on; these include the resting-state networks described earlier. Such "functional connectivity" refers to the correlations among these dynamical patterns operating according to non-linear models. Functional and structural interconnections both reflect neural networks but they occur at different levels. The brain demonstrates network connections at both levels: structural pathways of neurons and reciprocal interactions of functional, electrophysiological processes. As Olaf Sporns, a member of the Human Connectome Project, writes:

> A new picture of the human brain is taking place—a picture that views cognitive processes as the result of collective and cooperative phenomena unfolding within a complex network. (2011: 110)

The functional, dynamic neuronal networks on which Lisa Feldman Barrett and her group focus are carried by the underlying structural networks whose activity produces these widely distributed synchronous patterns (the functional networks) that embrace both local and distant, apparently unrelated brain regions. This is the neuronal foundation of human experience.

But, interestingly enough, the parallel of structural and functional connectivities is not absolute. While most often it is the case, functional connections do not map 100 percent directly onto underlying structural connections. Sporns (2013) reports that studies reveal that "many strong functional connections exist among structurally unconnected node pairs." Thus one cannot necessarily infer the presence of a structural pathway from the presence of a functional connection (58).

The actual relationship between structural and functional connectivity is a complex and controversial issue. The last decade has seen a large increase in the sophistication of the measuring instruments and mathematical tools used to investigate this question. This is a very technical topic in which I have limited expertise, although it has clinical ramifications in the case of some neurological disorders. The general consensus is that there is a very strong association between structural and functional levels and that structural connectivities support and constrain functional events. Usually the strength or weakness of structural connections parallels the strength or weakness of functional connections. While functional dynamics clearly depend on structural connections to some extent, the controversy concerns to what extent and under what conditions—and what is the best way to investigate and measure this relationship. For a review of this issue, see Petersen and Sporns (2015) and Damoiseaux and Greicius (2009).

However, research also finds that "functional relationships exist between regions with no direct structural connection" and that "indirect connections and interregional distance accounts for *some* of variance in functional connectivity that was unexplained by direct structural connectivity," but that is "only partially" the case (Honey et al., 2009: 2035, italics added). A relatively recent review whose title illustrates its result (Chu et al., 2015) concludes that brain wave dynamics "partially reflect" underlying neuronal connections but brain structure "has not been shown to fully predict overlying cortical physiology" (31). Petersen and Sporns (2015) similarly conclude that "functional connectivity is constrained (but not fully determined) by underlying anatomy" (212). And Greicius, Supekar, Menon, and Dougherty (2009) in a carefully nuanced summary of their findings write, "In describing the relationship between functional and structural connectivity in this study, we have been careful to note that functional connectivity 'reflects' structural connectivity. As our results demonstrate, although functional connectivity reflects structural connectivity to a large degree there is not a simple one-to-one mapping. . . . In sum, although our data show that resting-state functional connectivity reflects structural connectivity to a large degree, each can exist without the other" (77).

This result may be partially explained by measurement error, and accurate charting of structural fibers is very difficult with current instruments. And there are other limitations to current technologies as well (Sotiropoulos et al., 2015). Many also posit the presence of indirect connections between brain regions that are not directly joined that would then account for the functional correlations without direct underlying structural connections. But often these indirect connections must be posited or "assumed" (Greicius et al., 2009: 76). And there's general agreement with Honey, Sporns et al. (2009) that only "some of the variance in functional connectivity" can be explained in that way (Damoiseaux & Greicius, 2009: 529).

All I need for my argument is the general finding that these two forms of connectivity do not appear to always map onto each other in a direct, linear one-to-one manner and that some functional connections do not appear to depend directly on structural connections and do appear to behave in non-linear ways. The only theoretical point I want to make is that this suggests some degree of openness and dynamic non-linearity in the operation of the brain and its role in human mental life. My task here is simply to offer some philosophical and theological interpretations of this state of affairs regarding what it might imply for our understanding of human nature.

So, the various resting-state networks traced in contemporary neuroscience are not simply the functional expression of a more basic structural diagram. They are rather dynamically recurring and fluctuating waves, arising from neuronal processes and displaying coordinated aspects of such a phase synchrony or phase locking. Likewise the integrated wholism displayed by the CNS is not simply the result of structural connections. Rather, it too results from coordinated dynamic patterns emerging in a non-linear way from neuronal activities, as Freeman also discovered earlier.

So human cognition, understanding, and feeling are not directly reducible to neuroanatomy and physiology alone but rather, from a neurological standpoint, human conscious experiences emerge in an indirect, non-linear way from "spontaneous" (Sporn's term) neurological activity. Network graphing and various computational systems can model these connections and patterns. But they do not dispel the complexity and openness that appear intrinsic to human neurology—perhaps in a way analogous to the fact that mathematical models of electron behavior do not eliminate quantum mechanical openness (for examples, see Haimovici, Tagliazucchi, Balenzuela, & Chialvo, 2013; or Honey et al., 2009).

The structural connectome of neural fiber bundles is often referred to (especially in popular writings about the brain) as the "wiring diagram" for the brain. This impression is reinforced when the network diagrams (e.g., Sporns, 2013) appear on paper as a series of lines drawn between points that look very similar to the wiring diagrams I had as a kid building simple radio receivers from kits. A general audience not so familiar with the ways of science may mistake the map for the territory. But as Sporns (2013) himself emphasizes, neural networks are not hard circuit boards or tightly soldered copper wires. The connectome is constantly remaking itself. New neuronal connections grow stronger; old neuronal connections grow weaker. Meditation, exercise, some brain games cause parts of the cortex to thicken. For example, gaining a new sensorimotor ability rather quickly alters both the volume of gray matter and the configuration of white matter in the relevant sensorimotor areas (Scholz, Klein, Behrens, & Johansen-Berg, 2009). Age, disease, and trauma causes connections to fray. The popular term for this is "neuroplasticity." I often say that neuroplasticity is another word for learning. When we learn something new—a foreign language, information about a historical event, an athletic skill—we reshape our brains, establishing new neuronal patterns. So we must not take the metaphor of a "wiring diagram of the brain" literally. The connectome is in a continual, if subtle, flux.

Not only do brains reveal a structural plasticity and diversity; brains clearly differ widely in their functional connectivity as well (review in Sporns, 2013). Differences in functional, neuronal connectivity are reflected in the wide range of different human aptitudes and abilities: from accurately hitting a fast-moving tennis ball, to composing a complex orchestral piece, to mastering higher-level mathematics, to quickly picking up a foreign language, to following a multi-faceted logical argument, or developing the capacity for abstract thought.

This means that the connectome may differ in subtle, and more significant, ways from one individual to another (another point Sporns, 2013, insists on). The Human Connectome Project went to great lengths technically and experimentally to duplicate and retest its parcellation over many subjects. And the inter-subject reliability was remarkably good (Glasser et al., 2016). We do not know the extent of this structural variability, but brains clearly differ in the density and strength of their connections and the way the interconnections are distributed throughout the brain. This too means there will be no simple, universal "wiring diagram" of the brain.

From this combination of structural neuroplasticity and functional non-linear dynamics emerges a picture of the CNS as simultaneously balancing a high degree of specialization and an equally high degree of complexity, interconnectivity, and openness. And that is exactly what we see in clinical neuropsychology: enough patterned order and structural specialization to make reliable diagnosis and treatment possible; enough openness for unexpected physiological and psychological changes and recoveries to take place. While most neurological research concentrates on the patterned order in the central nervous system, working on the boundary of clinical neuropsychology and religious studies, I have focused on the other pole. Here I have emphasized the openness of the central nervous system, for the combination of neuroplasticity and non-linear processing makes possible the human capacity for transcendental and transformative practices and experiences.

So rather than a simple, rather reductive localization model of how the brain is organized and experience is neurologically instantiated, current brain research suggests a more complex and non-linear picture. In short, "over two decades of brain imaging data point towards a framework where the human brain is intrinsically organized into domain-general, distributed functional networks" (Barrett & Satpute, 2013: 361). No simple, single set of neuronal connections or configurations necessarily underlies particular perceptual experiences. The underlying neuronal patterns constantly form and reform with the advent of new sensory information and new physical activities. Similar sights, sounds, smells, memories, or thoughts may evoke different neural activity in different subjects who, nevertheless, claim to have the "same" experience. The same cognitive process may employ or reemploy different cerebral areas. Different cognitive activities may not represent different circuits but rather represent different interactional patterns among common areas. A single physiological region may be involved in multiple cognitive activities and may underlie several different cognitive processes (Anderson, 2008, 2010). All this calls into question any neat, hard-and-fast models of the brain as organized as a series of rather autonomous modules. Studies of the couplings between environmental stimuli and correlated neurological activity show them to be highly distributed and interrelated in a complex, non-linear fashion (Holden, Van Orden, & Turvey, 2009; Teske, 2013; Van Orden et al., 2003).

All this also suggests there is little or no inherent or necessary connection between certain neurological centers and their ability to subtend particular sensory experiences. That connection is at least partially established through experience. This also suggests that neuro-physiological development does not follow some hardwired, genetically predetermined path. Rather it is the result of the organism's capacity for self-organization working on the interaction with the environment. All of this complexifies and nuances any simple claim of localization and the idea that particular cognitive activities can always be neatly mapped onto particular cerebral locals (Anderson et al., 2012; Teske, 2013).

There is no denying that there is a degree of modularity in the brain. Normally certain areas are particularly associated with certain cognitive and sensory processes. But higher-order thought, complex reasoning, self-reflection, creative activity, and mentalization all emerge out of the reciprocal interactions of many neural networks in complex, non-linear ways.

It is possible that a deeper investigation could find individual neurons or columns of neurons that are uniquely specialized for processing particular sensory data, and so revert to a singularly localization model. But that seems unlikely. Freeman's EEG research suggests that it's the wave pattern, not the output of individual neurons, that carries information. And Barrett's fMRI studies show distributed activity throughout the brain. The fact that both methods give rise to systemic, interactive models may be significant since they measure rather different domains. EEG's are good for issues of time and less good for issues of localization; fMRI's are better for localization but provide less temporal resolution (since the fMRI only scans the brain at approximately two-second intervals). And even simple experiences (the smell of a rose or the color yellow) are phenomenologically so complex that it is hard to imagine them mapping onto a single neuron or even a single column of neurons. So the relevant evidence taken together appears to point to a more wholistic, interactive vision of brain functioning, perhaps even a new order in neuroscience that parallels Bohm's claim of a new order in physics.

My goal is not to defend any particular interpretation of the research reviewed here; for example, Barrett's construct of core affect. Rather I simply want to point out that given the incredibly complex neurological activity behind all sensory events as shown by current brain-scan and EEG studies, sensory experiences and their associated neurological activity leave "bare" sensory input far behind. And we can begin to see some of the ways in which research on embodiment's impact on human experience and information processing potentially has very significant and far-reaching implications for understanding human knowledge, including our religious knowledge. This research calls into question any epistemology that relies on modeling sense experience as a direct, linear, literal representation of external reality. Perception and all sense experiences are much more neurologically and phenomenologically complex than such models allow for and they are heavily influenced by our embodied state (e.g., Barrett's core affect) at any given moment. Given the complexity of even "simple" sensations, there is no evidence here for a simple direct representational view of sense experience at the neurological level. Rather, the evidence appears to point to an intrinsic, non-linear openness in the functional operation of the CNS, again in some ways analogous to the complexity and openness often theorized to characterize the physics of the created universe. And any neat separation of cognition, affect, perception, memory, and bodily activity is seriously undermined, except for the purpose of writing undergraduate textbooks.

In the forthcoming chapters, we explore some of the implications of these more complex models of sense experience for religious knowledge and the possibility of a *sensus spiritalis*.

In What Sense Is Our Understanding Embodied?

Some have used the research on the importance of the body for human understanding to argue that cognition is embodied in a way that it is also "extended." The meaning is that the term "cognition" should not be limited to what happens in the brain but may also include the bodily use of external objects in the service of cognitive tasks. If I use a pencil and paper and the back of an envelope or an electronic calculator to add up a series of numbers (a task I might also do in my head without any external support) these objects are performing the same function as my central nervous system when faced with this task. David Chalmers calls this the "parity principle." If an external object performs the same function as the human cognitive system, there is no reason not to say that it too is a cognitive system since it is performing a function that we would naturally call "cognitive" if it went on in the brain. Most of the controversy around interpreting the research on embodiment involves this notion of "extended cognition," which is often seen as an aspect of "embodied cognition" but which is separable from empirical data on the impact of embodiment on understanding.

The core issue in this controversy seems to be the question of what is meant by "cognitive" and what are its boundaries. Fred Adams and Kenneth Aizawa argue that theories of "embodied cognition" are wrong to extend "cognition" in this way. Various tools (calculators, pencils, etc.) can be used in the service of cognition but that does not make them "cognitive" in the strict sense. For them, cognitive processing is something that only goes on in the brain. They want to insist that "there is something distinctive about the brain" (Adams & Aizawa, 2009: 80) because of its "distinct type of information processing capacities." They also want to advocate what they call a "classical, rules and representations" model of cognition. For Adams and Aizawa, the extended cognition argument falls prey to what they call the "coupling-constitution" fallacy. It confuses a "coupling relationship" (a cognitive mind coupled with a calculator) with a "constitutive relationship" (the cognitive mind that is partly constituted by the calculator). In the service of cognitive processing, the internal cognitive system may link up with external objects so that the brain plus calculator functions as a coupled system, one part of which (the brain) is a cognitive processor. But the fact that one part of this coupled system is rightly called "cognitive" does not make the whole system cognitive. We may speak of a sound system (this is their analogy) but not every component produces sound. Speakers do, but lasers and control knobs do not. The brain plus calculator may produce cognitive outputs but that does not make every component cognitive.

The crucial point here is becoming clear on what the term "cognitive" refers to. Adams and Aizawa insist that what they call "the mark of the cognitive" must involve two dimensions: (1) what they call "intrinsic, non-derived content," which seems to mean contents that are immediately and directly available and that "do not derive their meanings from conventions or social practices" (Adams & Aizawa, 2001: 48). Thus they want to decisively reject any epistemologies that rely heavily on "interpretation" or "flirt with content instrumentalism." Such epistemologies are not a "live option for a would-be science, such as cognitive science" (49). (2) The second condition is that cognitive processes exemplify particular laws or causal processes. Thus they reject the analogy between brains and computers since computers clearly exemplify very different laws than neurons do. Thus information processing is not "a mark of the cognitive," since on their terms, "not all information processing is cognitive processing" (Adams & Aizawa, 2009: 87). These two dimensions are essential for something to be called "cognitive."

In response, Andy Clark (a proponent of embodied and extended cognition) offers a much more general definition: "What makes a process cognitive, it seems to me, is that it supports genuinely intelligent behavior." Thus he speaks of cognition in terms of "hybrid wholes." His model is that the brain and the calculator are "the resultant system as a cognitive whole." He describes his theory as an "extended functionalism" (2010).

This response might make it appear that the dispute is purely terminological. But that is not quite right. Part of the issue is to define the boundaries of the discipline of cognitive science: does it include all "genuinely intelligent behavior" or the more particular processes by which *homo sapiens* reason about matters of concern to their species? Clark advocates a "systems-level cognitive (rather than neuro-) science" whereas Adams and Aizaway insist "there is something distinctive about the brain" because it possesses unique processing procedures. Defining the boundaries of a discipline is always a crucial activity for the participants in that discipline.

On the issue of most concern to me here—the relationship between embodiment and human understanding—the position of Adams and Aizawa does not seem materially different from the one I am taking here, although we clearly arrive at it from radically different starting points. We all appear to agree that cognitive processing, and human understanding in general, are "causally connected to bodily and environmental processes" (Aizawa, 2007: 6). But again, they want to insist on making that claim in a way that avoids any "constitution fallacy." Having accepted the clear evidence that bodily and environmental factors drive our thinking processes, Aizawa goes on to reject "the problematic shift from the observation of causal dependencies to the conclusion of constitutive dependencies" (8). Widely accepted demonstrations of causal connections between embodiment and cognition must not be used to argue that embodiment constitutes cognition in some way, or that cognition is, in any way, constituted by embodiment.

This becomes especially salient in the discussion of an aspect of embodiment that is central to my discussion here—perception. Aizawa rejects the argument that perception is simply a bodily based activity, what Noe calls "not a process in the brain but a kind of skillful activity on the part of the animal as a whole" (2004: 2). Clearly people have to learn to see and hear: to recognize a tree as a tree or to tell a Bach fugue from a song by the Rolling Stones. In that sense, perception is a learned skill. Aizawa agrees that perception is not simply the stimulation of the sense organs or other sensations. Perception clearly involves not only sensory but also "motoric or higher level cognitive inputs" (2007: 10). But again, the argument is that these embodied practices that shape our perceptions are not "constitutive" of perception. He writes, "It is not that the exercise of sensorimotor skills are essential to perception because they are constitutive, in part, of perception; it is that these sensory motor skills are essential for normal perception because they have an essential causal role in shaping perceptions" (16). Again, embodied activity is necessary for perception but that does not entail that perception is constituted by this activity. However, this point—that activity shapes perception—is the one that will be crucial to my argument in the coming chapters.

Bradford Mahon and Alfonso Caramazza (2008) also critique theories of embodied cognition that argue or imply that cognition is constituted by somatic or sensory activity. But they draw heavily on brain imaging studies showing that parts of the brain related to sensory and bodily activity are closely associated with conceptual thought. Activation of the somatic areas often accompanies conceptual processing. But, they argue, this does not entail that conceptual processing is the same as somatic activation or that somatic activation constitutes conceptual processing. It is not clear, for example, that somatic activity constitutes the *meaning* of the words that it accompanies. But Mahon and Caramazza (2008) also insist that the fact that somatic activity does not constitute cognitive processing does not imply that it is irrelevant to it. Rather, they affirm that research undeniably demonstrates, at a minimum, that the motor system is automatically activated when a subject observes manipulable objects, hears words involving actions, or sees others performing an action (60). Experiments like these refute claims that concepts exist separate from bodily information or bodily activity. The motor cortex and embodied processes are not irrelevant to cognitive processes, even if they do not constitute it. It is clear, Mahon says, that "the state of the sensory motor system affects cognition" (2015: 172). But rather than constituting cognition itself, Mahon and Caramazza (2008) argue that there is "spreading neuronal activation" between the higher cognitive areas and the somatosensory cortex.

Willems et al. (2011) critique Mahon and Caramazza's theory on the grounds that the conjunction of the motor and language areas occurs too quickly to be the result of "spreading activation" from the cognition system to the motor system. Willems wants to argue for a tighter connection between motor processes and linguistic meaning than Mahon's theory that cognitive processing occurs first and then cues motor responses through a spreading activation. Along this line Anna Borghi and Felice Cimatti (2010) also provide studies showing that

> the fast activation, the automaticity and the somatotopic organization of the motor system renders the hypothesis very unlikely, that information is first transduced in an abstract format and then influences the motor system. The hypothesis that the motor system is activated in a direct and straightforward way is much more plausible and economical. (766)

Willems wants to claim that motor activity itself is part of an action word's semantic structure. This disagreement parallels Adams and Aizawa's insistence on a distinction between "coupling" and "constituting."

This disagreement between Willems and Adams and Aizawa will presumably be settled when brain measurement becomes even more finely grained.

This disagreement makes little difference to my argument. Mahon and Caramazza conclude that "sensory and motor information . . . contributes to the 'full' representation of a concept" (2008: 68). This is because "conceptual information that is represented at an 'abstract' and 'symbolic' level does not . . . exhaust what we know about the world" (68). "Full" human understanding goes on at other levels besides the processing of abstract representations. They call their position "grounding by interaction"—that is, concepts are grounded by the interaction between "higher" cortical areas and the sensory-motor cortex. This is all that I require. Mahon summarizes their position when he writes, "*connecting* concepts to input/output (i.e., sensorimotor) representations serves to *ground* those concepts—but it does not make those concepts *embodied*" (2015: 175; italics in original). Embodiment may not constitute cognition but human understanding is closely linked to the body through the reciprocal spreading neuronal activation between frontal areas associated with cognition and somatosensory areas. In some ways theirs is an intermediate position between a strict "rules and representations" view of amodal cognitive processing and an extreme version of embodied cognition in which extended, embodied activities are equated with cognition.

In many ways it seems that this discussion hinges on the distinction between laboratory data and the interpretation of that data. Mahon and Caramazza (2008) agree when they write,

> The goal of developing a theory of concepts will not be served by collecting more of the same data. One more fMRI experiment demonstrating that the motor cortex is activated during action observation or sentence processing does not make the embodied cognition hypothesis more likely to be correct. One more patient showing that an impairment to motor processes does not affect action or object recognition will not make the disembodied cognition hypothesis more likely to be correct. In our view the way the hypotheses space is currently cast does not productively serve the development of a theory of concepts that resonates with all the available evidence (67).

Currently there seem to be three interpretations of this collection of experimental evidence that virtually everyone agrees is authentic, scientific data: that embodiment constitutes cognition; that embodiment is irrelevant to amodal cognition (brain in a vat); and that embodied processes are intimately joined to cognition while not being identical with it. This is not a fight in which I care to enter a dog. I have no stake in the question of how cognitive scientists should define their subject matter. And I am not claiming that embodiment is constitutive of cognition. I am claiming that human understanding, which is a broader than "cognition," is influenced by the fact of our embodiment. The ways in which we experience the world and make our way through it, including the ways religious devotees experience and make their way through it, are connected to our embodiment. This research simply specifies many of the particular senses in which that very general claim is true.

Summary

My main point is that contemporary research demonstrates that embodied processes shape what we see, hear, taste, sense, and experience. Four implications for theological and psychological understanding and for practicing religion that flow from looking at this research from an embodied-relational perspective are elaborated in the coming chapters.

First, even at the psycho-physiological level, human understanding is an incredibly complex phenomenon. Thinking, sensing, and feeling reciprocally influence each other and can even be theorized as aspects of a common process (as with L. F. Barrett). Bodily activity impacts all three. Neuroplasticity and the often non-linear connectivity within the various neural networks and between the functional networks and the brain's anatomy give human nature a certain degree of openness. Experimentation, diagnosis, and treatment development all require simplifying and constraining this openness. But in dealing with the kinds of issues touched on this book, we must never lose sight of the intrinsic complexity and openness built into human nature, even at the neurological level. In the coming pages I will be invoking this openness and complexity whenever I sense the presence of the kind of over-simplifications that do mischief in our understanding of the topics developed here.

I have alluded in passing to possible parallels between contemporary neurology and contemporary physics in terms of the possible openness within the physical world. Traditionally it has been said that the probabilistic and indeterminate processes at the quantum level "wash out" or "cancel each other out" at the ordinary physical level that we inhabit. This has, more recently, been called into question in new disciplines like "quantum biology" where it appears that indeterminate quantum processes do affect ordinary physical processes like gene expression (Ellis, 2012, 2013). And physicists recently demonstrated quantum effects in a macroscopic structure: an event that *Science* magazine called the most important scientific discovery of 2010 (reported on ScienceDaily.com, December 17, 2010). All of this suggests a previously unsuspected openness in ordinary physical matter. If true, that could have profound implications for the role of mind and consciousness in the material world. And it would potentially bring the nature of minds and the nature of brains closer together—a possibility we discuss in the next chapter.

Second, perception is really construction. The mind is not passive but active in perception—and not just the mind but our whole body. We shape our perceptions through our bodily activity. Perception and sensation do not simply passively produce an inner picture of the world of experience. For example, often perception doesn't start with a stimulus hitting the eye; it starts with our turning our heads and focusing our eyes; it starts with bodily activity. And, of course, before that were the bodily actions that brought us within range of the stimulus. Embodied activity generates the world of our lived experience; this is a major theme in the argument to follow. Our lived-in world, the world we actually inhabit, arises from our behavior and from our somatosensory capacities. What we see, hear, smell, intuit, and feel depends on the places we choose to look, the things we pay attention to and the things we ignore, the schemas we have developed in our minds through practice, experience, and thought.

One of the very radical possible interpretations of the embodied-relational paradigm is that through our embodied interactions with the world, we create the world we live in; or as Gibbs says, "we bring forth a world" (2005, 17; see also Varela et al., 1993). This, he says, is a realistic alternative to a false objectivism that claims that true knowledge is simply a mirroring of a pre-given, external world and a radical constructivism or idealism that says the world we know is only a projection of our mental or cultural constructs—a point similar to Lakoff and Johnson's "experientialism" and Winnicott's model of knowledge as "transitional" (Jones, 1992b). We are neither entirely autonomous, independent, self-contained subjects over-against an objective world nor totally conditioned passive expressions of physical or cultural forces impinging on us. Rather, the world we actually live in, our lived-world, our known-world, is brought forth by our mutual, inter-penetrating interactions with the objects of our experience. This is not a new idea; many relational, interactional epistemologists have said similar things (Jones, 1997, 1992b). But Gibbs goes on to say "when a person enacts or brings forth a world, the person and the world are coupled" (2005: 17). Through my body and its motor and sensory systems, I am really "one" with the world of my experience (my known world) that I create through my interactions. I am not simply its product and it is not simply my projection. My embodied "oneness" with the world is not a unity in which I am simply absorbed into the world nor is it just a passing emotion on the part of a self that is radically free and independent. I act upon the world and the world acts upon me. My individuality is not lost, but also it is not cut loose from all connections and dependencies; it is a relational individuality. I and my lived-world are our mutual co-creation. A very complex, even paradoxical, vision of the self emerges here: a self that is a unique, existing agent that is also "coupled" (Gibbs's term) with its world. The epistemological and spiritual implications of this vision are explored in the coming chapters.

Third, proprioception may be a bit of an exception to the foregoing. It appears to be more direct and less mediated. I seem to directly experience that my hand is resting in my lap or that my foot has fallen asleep. But that is true only up to a point. The supposedly "direct" experience of pain can be modified by conscious cognition. The hypnotic treatment of chronic pain relies on precisely that phenomenon. Pain sensations can be diminished, shifted to other parts of the body, or pushed into the background of consciousness. Usually when religious experience is discussed in terms of perception, the analogy is almost always to the "five senses," usually to visual perception (for example, Alston's "theory of appearing"). But sometimes religious experiences come in the form of many diffuse somatic sensations: the rising Kundalini along the spine or tingling sensations during the laying-on-of-hands. Might more direct proprioception also serve as an analogue for religious experience? Later we will develop this suggestion in more depth.

Fourth, knowing can be shifted and transformed by bodily activity. Standing, walking, gesturing, carrying a heavy pack can cause us to think differently and change our perception of ourselves and the world. This has been widely and deeply known for centuries within the religions of the world. The whirling Dervishes, the yogic masters, the universal reliance of breathing techniques testify to this. In the West since the Enlightenment the tendency has been to separate theory and practice. Nowhere has that done more mischief than in the area of religion. The result has been an almost singular focus on belief as the defining characteristic of religion. This has been especially true of the cognitive science of religion, some of whose advocates have gone so far as to claim that by explaining the cognitive grounds for a few isolated beliefs they have "explained religion" (Jones, 2016). An embodied-relational model of human knowledge returns beliefs to practices and thereby underscores that understanding requires doing and new understanding requires new doings. Reading, thinking, and arguing alone will rarely give rise to new or transformed religious convictions and moral actions. If knowing is an embodied activity, then new or transformed religious understandings will arise primarily from new or transformed embodied practices.

The coming chapters elaborate some of the implications of these four claims for theology and the psychology of religion as well as for the practices of religious knowing, especially those that might be associated with developing and deepening a spiritual sense.

2

The Embodied Mind and the Mind-Suffused Body

HUMAN NATURE AND THE QUESTION OF PHYSICALISM

THE QUESTION OF human nature—what does it mean to be a human being?—is a universal topic in the religions of the world. It is also a question directly at the interface between psychology and theology. While their answers differ in varying degrees, all the world religions make claims about human nature and all agree that there is a "spiritual" dimension to human nature, that there is more to being human than can be described simply and only in the categories of contemporary physical science. But this fundamental and universal religious claim immediately creates conflict with the current common insistence that natural science requires the contrary claim that all that is really real must be physical in the sense that all of reality can be, at least potentially, described in the categories of the physical sciences. Such a position I will call "physicalism" in the coming pages.

For example, so far in this text, in keeping with the common convention, I have mainly drawn on research that is usually referred to as about "embodied *cognition*" and is often described as research dealing with an embodied *mind*, thus interchanging "mind" and "cognition." Such an equation of terms, so widespread in the literature, conceals tremendous assumptions, particularly that the "mind" is basically about "cognition" and that since cognition is clearly carried on in and by the body, the *mind* is also primarily, or entirely, a function of the body. The assumption (and that is what it is) that the mind in its entirety is a function of the body (i.e., the brain) is, of course, now common (virtually taken for granted) in both popular and professional discourse in the cognitive and neurosciences. Nevertheless, both of these assumptions—that the mind is primarily devoted to formal information processing and that the mind in its entirety is only a function of the brain—are assumptions that I reject. So while I am basing my argument primarily on contemporary cognitive science research, this is where I depart from contemporary, laboratory-based cognitive and neuroscience.

These two assumptions are closely connected, especially in contemporary cognitive science. If the mind is primarily involved with cognition, and cognition is defined primarily as the processing of information, and the processing of information can be understood as something that takes place in a totally physical milieu such as in brains and computers (that is, that it is "multiply realizable"), then it follows that the mind is something that can be totally understood in physicalist terms. In that sense, mainstream "embodied cognition" paradigms, despite their rejection of many of cognitivism's assumptions and claims, would be another version of a reductive physicalist model of mind and of human nature. However, *mind* in its entirety is more than just the processing of information; for purposes of this book *mind* will also be understood as encompassing intentionality or choice and awareness or consciousness. These realities (and I think they are realities) are fundamental to any theological or spiritual view of human nature and they are also much harder, I would say impossible, to completely account for on purely physicalist terms (Jones, 2005, 2016). Therein lies the tension between the way in which *mind* will be understood in the coming chapters (in keeping with most theological and religious traditions) and the way *mind* is most often understood in current discussions of scientific models of human nature. This tension must be confronted directly before we can discuss how the research on embodied understanding might contribute to a theological account of human nature, for theologies generally require affirming the reality of consciousness, freedom, and intentionality—the very things a reductive physicalist account has trouble accounting for.

Can Physicalism Account for Consciousness and Intentionality?

Despite physicalists' breathtakingly extravagant and breezy claims that science has demonstrated that mind/consciousness is but the product of brain activity, nothing could be further from the truth. Assertions of this claim are not reports of experimental findings but are simply a report of physicalist ideology. We cannot even specify what a physical account of consciousness might look like. Virtually all writers agree that no such account is currently available (Jones, 2005, 2016; Kihlstrom, 2002; Nagel, 2012; Velmans, 2000; Wallace, 2007). All attempts to do that based in contemporary science have serious problems. And, more to the point, advocates of relying on, for example, quantum theories or non-linear dynamics agree that such natural processes by themselves probably could not give rise to a strong version of conscious causation, as would be required by claims about free choice or intentionality.

I do not want to push this point too hard. It is, after all, something of an argument from silence. The future may well produce compelling scientific models of how neuronal processes give rise to conscious experience. But all this should, at least, suggest a more humble and nuanced position than a simple assertion that the mind is simply the product of neurological activity. Theologically crucial constructs such as freedom, intentionality, and conscious awareness continue to escape compelling physicalist explanations (Jones, 2005, 2016, for more references; for an interesting parallel discussion, see Crane, 1995). Most physicalists tacitly acknowledge this and end up arguing that consciousness, freedom, and intentionality—phenomena essential to the religious and moral life—are illusions or epiphenomena.

However, there are of course those who claim to be physicalists (and therefore see the mind-brain as a single, *physical* system) but deny such epiphenomenalism and try to stake out a mediating, so-called non-reductive physicalist's position. This position claims to be fundamentally physicalist while also affirming the reality of consciousness, freedom, and intentionality. Many current thinkers, including some theologians as well as neuroscientists (for references, see Jones, 2005), claim to be physicalists and still affirm the reality of the mind and even give the mind the "top-down" causal powers that religion and morality seem to require. Such an affirmation of top-down causation must go beyond simply describing the functioning of neural systems or finding correlations between conscious events and neuronal activity. Those physicalists favoring top-down causation must assert that the higher-order, mind-processes exert direct causal power over the lower, neurophysiological processes. If the mind-brain is a single, physical system in which the mind-aspect is a product of the brain-aspect and yet these higher-level, mind-properties can exert a kind of causality over the system's constituent physical parts, this implies that the top-down part of the system (the mind) has causal properties not controlled by the causal properties of the lower parts of the system (i.e., the brain). In this case, the mind has causal powers not determined by the causal properties of the neurons.

However, if these top-down powers of causality are not determined by the causal processes in the brain, where do they arise from? From where does the mind acquire the property of downward causation? Current physical science appears to assume that the macro features of a system are determined by the causal properties of its parts. The causal processes going on among its macromolecules govern what a cell can and cannot do. The meaning of the words governs what a sentence can and cannot mean. In most, if not all, cases, any causation at the macro level of a system is derived from causation at the micro level. Nowhere in the physicalist's world can macro processes overrule or alter micro level causal activity. But in the case of consciousness, the non-reductive physicalist says that a new principle of causation, "top-down causation," suddenly appears and influences, if not overrules, some of the micro level, neurological processes.

The non-reductive physicalist appears to be in a no win situation. He can maintain the common scientific position that all causality arises from fundamental micro level processes. But then he would be practically indistinguishable from the reductive physicalist. And then mental causality becomes simply the conjunction of neuronal and mental events. Or he can affirm a strong causal power of consciousness to overrule, or at least redirect, those micro level, physical properties but at the cost of leaving inexplicable the origin of this top-down causality.

In addition, if brain processes can be overruled by a higher-order mental causation, then it would appear that the central nervous system is not really a closed, physical system. But the principle of the physical world as a closed system, not amenable to intrusions from beyond, is a major assumption of scientific physicalism. Of course, the non-reductive physicalist can assert that the mind too is physical, operating within the constraints of the physical world. But that brings up a more serious problem. This position that the mind-brain comprises a single *physical* system depends on the assumption that minds and brains are similar enough to be parts of the same physical system, that is, a system constrained by the laws and categories of current physical science. Calling this position a form of physicalism underscores this assumption. If all that is real about human nature is physical, and consciousness is real, consciousness too must be in some sense physical. That is, it must in some sense be, not just correlated with, but also similar to, physiological activity in the brain.

Such a claim has serious difficulties. In what sense can thoughts and neurons be said to be similar enough to be parts of the same physically defined system? In terms of current scientific theorizing, the answer is practically none. Consider:

(1) Neurons and other components of the central nervous system, like all physical entities, are always described in the categories of space and time. Thoughts and images are never described, except perhaps under poetic license, in terms of their mass, energy coefficient, or width.

(2) I may make a claim about the neurons in my brain—their number, density, organization, or development—and be mistaken about it. But I cannot be mistaken about the ideas or sensations I have in my mind. If I say I feel a pain in my foot, I cannot be mistaken about feeling such a sensation, even if I do not have a foot.

All of this is so obvious that it is a little silly to repeat it except that it seems to be a fatal blow to any purely physicalist model of consciousness, no matter how "non-reductive." If thoughts and neurons are neither described in the same categories nor governed by the same logic of explanation, in what sense are they similar? And if thoughts and neurons are not at least basically similar, in what sense can thoughts be part of a system of neurons? Certainly not in the same sense that a word can be understood as a system of letters or a cell as a system of chemicals. (An oft-cited critique of this theory on which the system's model appears to depend can be found in Nagel, 1965; see also Watkins, 1982.) Later in this chapter I will return to the question of possible similarities between minds and physical objects (e.g., brains) but from a very different perspective. Now I am arguing against reductive physicalism so I am relying on a reductive physicalist understanding of what "physical" means. Later I will reconsider this question of possible relationships between thoughts and physical objects from several rather different models of what the "physical" might be.

Put most starkly, a thought is not a thing. The sensation of seeing red is not reducible to or translatable into statements about wavelengths, rods and cones, or neuronal processing (Chalmers, 1995; Robinson, 1976; Velmans, 2000). No description of physics or neurology can lead from there to a description of the experience of redness. They are simply two separate and distinct linguistic systems. One of the claimed advantages of the physicalist model in contrast to dualism is that it removes the dilemma of specifying how mind and brain, spirit and matter, are connected. However, renaming consciousness as a property of a physical system may not account for the origin of consciousness without some way of specifying how two such different things as thoughts and brains can be aspects of a single system. Of course the non-reductive physicalist wants to claim that both thoughts and brains are, in some sense, physical. But my point is that specifying in exactly what sense images, thoughts, and intentions are themselves physical (as distinct from simply possessing physical correlates) is far from clear.

Physicalism is supposed to be simpler than its competitors, but it is not clear in what sense this simplicity is a virtue if it provides no explanation of the process that most needs explaining: the rise of conscious states from neuronal activity. As fervently as the proponents of this model might wish it to be otherwise, it is not clear that just calling consciousness a systems property removes the need (which dualism also has) to provide a theoretical bridge between brains and thoughts. If you simply say that everything that is real is physical, and that consciousness is real, then consciousness becomes physical by definition. A tautology is all that has been produced here: that mental entities are real entails that mental entities are physical, because real is equivalent to physical. The problem has been solved by definition.

But a new problem has been created: what exactly is meant by physical? What are the limits of the physical in the non-reductive physicalist account? Since it includes entities like thoughts and feelings, the domain of the physical would appear to lack clear boundaries. The reductive physicalist says simply that the physical is what is described by the physical sciences. Period. Here the reductive physicalist has the virtue of simplicity. Non-reductive physicalists, on the other hand, need to assert that mental properties cannot be completely described in terms of physics and chemistry. Otherwise they would be reductive physicalists. Yet they also want to say that mental properties are physical? In what sense?

Once again, the non-reductive physicalist appears to be in a no-win situation. She can insist that mental processes are really physical and that she is a genuine physicalist. But that claim borders on identifying the mental with the physical: a position that is problematic for reasons we've just given and that also undercuts any real difference between reductive and non-reductive physicalism. Or she can reject this identification and stress the differences between mental and physical domains, and so maintain her non-reductive stance. But then it becomes less clear in what sense her position is really one of physicalism as understood in the categories of current physical science. I'm not sure the non-reductive physicalist can have it both ways: trying to maintain both the reductive physicalist's tie to current natural science and the traditional theological affirmations of consciousness and active mental causality without either vicious reductionism or scientific incompatibility.

One currently popular attempt to get around these problems is by use of the term "supervenience." Supervenience defines a dependent but non-reductive relationship between properties: Property G in said to supervene on Property F, if an x instantiates G in virtue of x also always instantiating F under circumstances c. So property G depends on Property F but it cannot be simply reduced to Property F. The property of being a US penny supervenes on being a copper disk with Lincoln's head under the circumstances of being minted by a legitimate US mint (the example is from Nancey Murphy, 1999: 150).

So supervenience describes relationships between properties in a way in which there is dependency but not over-determination since the lower level, physical processes may underdetermine the macro properties (not every copper disk with Lincoln's head is a penny—the one I stamped out in my basement clearly isn't). Thus the subvenient property (being a copper disk) can cause the supervenient property (being a penny) without determining it. The property of being a penny is codetermined by the circular, copper disk, the presence of Lincoln's head, and the US currency laws. Neither the physical properties nor the legal context by themselves make something a penny.

Being a copper disk can cause this object to be a penny but by itself it does not determine it to be a penny. Since supervenience requires dependence and non-reducibility, it suggests a way of describing a real genuine dependence of human understanding and intentionality on the brain without reducing these mental activities to neurology. The mind supervenes on the brain but is not reducible to the brain alone. But such underdetermination is not the same as top-down causation—a fact that Murphy herself acknowledges when she says directly, "I reject all moves to make supervenience or realization a causal relationship!" (Murphy, 1999a: 154). Focused primarily on relationships between properties, the category of supervenience alone cannot speak to mental causation (Jones, 1992a, 2005, 2016).

A fine discussion of supervenience in relation to neuroscience and theology can be found in the 2006 book edited by Philip Clayton and Paul Davies (2006), *The Re-Emergence of Emergence*. This extensive text makes it clear that this is far from a settled issue. Nancey Murphy and Michael Silberstein are strong advocates for supervenience. Jaejwon Kim is a fierce critic of those ideas. David Chalmers is, at best, an ambivalent supporter. In addition, both Silberstein and Chalmers critique traditional physicalism, and their arguments, along with Kim's, illustrate my main point in this chapter, that consciousness and mental causation cast serious doubts about any form of physicalism. In addition, for a fine, critical review of these debates see Tim Crane's papers, the 1995 "The Mental Causation Debate" and the 2003 "Mental Substances." In these papers, Crane supports mental causation and is critical of the concept of supervenience. For another discussion supporting my main point here, see Tim Crane and D. H. Mellor's 1990 paper, "There is No Question of Physicalism." That is because physicalism is an indefensible philosophical position. Thus, one should be wary of relying on it in interpreting neural science, especially in the context of discussions with theology. And just invoking the category of supervenience does not, by itself, settle the issue.

So no physicalist interpretations of current neuroscience findings are complete or compelling enough to eliminate or undermine theological models of human nature.

Physicalism and Its Trials

Besides the problems associated with accounting for our experience of consciousness, freedom, and intentionality, there are additional problems with a purely physicalist understanding of the world and of human nature. Basically, they are listed here only to make the point that physicalism is not as automatically convincing as many who insist on a purely physicalist account of human nature would wish. Many questions can be raised about each of these points. And each would require a book or more to develop in depth. But together they sum up to a serious questioning of a purely physicalist viewpoint.

(1) Of course the most basic problem with a physicalist position is that the claim that the only reality is physical reality as demonstrated by the physical sciences is a claim that is itself not demonstrable by the physical sciences. No conceivable experiment could demonstrate that. Nor is it a regulative principle of some kind that science itself requires since clearly throughout history there have been brilliant scientists doing excellent work who do not accept it. Accepting such a proposition is not required for the conduct of science nor is it demonstrable scientifically. So the "prestige" of science cannot be called on as proof for physicalist metaphysics. So what is such a claim? It is a matter of belief; of commitment; of judgment, with exactly the same logical status as the contrary claim that the physical world as investigated by science is not the entirety of all that is real and that empirical science is not the only source of knowledge.

(2) In addition to this logical problem, the *claim* that only physical things exist is clearly not a physical thing, at least in our ordinary sense. It is an idea. Now

some physicalists want to claim that mental realities are really physical realities. But as we have just seen, that claim is hardly straightforward or uncontested. Finally, the only defense for it is that since thoughts clearly are real and since only physical things are real, thoughts must be in some sense be entirely physical. But, of course, such an argument is virtually a tautology and tautologies can tell us nothing about reality since they simply reprise their premises in different words and can be true under any and all conditions. The claim that all unmarried men are bachelors, on the premise that bachelor means unmarried man, is true by definition and would be true whether unmarried men existed or not. Likewise the claim that thoughts are both real and entirely physical, on the premise that real means entirely physical, is true whether or not such things as entirely physical thoughts exist or not. This is not a demonstration of the truth of the claim but once again a confusion of premise and conclusion.

(3) This general problem of specifying the reality of "mental" contents is even sharper in the domain of science than in ordinary life. Modern science depends on mathematical objects and logical truths. But mathematical and logical objects are clearly primarily mental; they are clearly not physical objects perceived by our five senses. Thus their status has been the subject of debate for centuries. There is no need to review that discussion here. But the position that only physical things—things available to the five senses and describable in physical terms—exist raises serious questions about the reality of the mathematical forms on which science depends. Thus one wonders if a purely physicalist position can sustain an understanding of the scientific method that is necessary for the conduct of science.

(4) In addition, it is hard to say what "physical" means in light contemporary physics. Electrons are probability waves only appearing as "particles" when measured in a specific way. Fixed meanings for matter, time, and space are almost impossible to specify. Mathematical formalisms suggest that "matter" is vibrations of "waves"—but waves that lack any physical medium (think of ocean waves with no ocean), and according to some (like Stephan Hawking) that "imaginary time" is the real time and what we experience as time is a function of the limitations of human consciousness that only perceives four (time and three dimensions of Euclidean space) of the many actual dimensions. The same is true with "space," which is so bound up with matter and time that their lack of specifiablity carries over to it. Thus a physicalism that insists that "matter" in the sense of that which exists in Euclidean space and ruthlessly obeys Newton's laws is the foundational reality to which everything must be referred and in terms of which everything must be understood has very little claim today to the title of science.

A corollary of this is that what we do know of the physical world through physics is only a segment of that reality as it appears under very artificially isolated and constrained experimental conditions. The physical world we know is only the physical world as it appears to human consciousness within a restricted framework. There is absolutely no reason to claim that this is the entire picture.

(5) Accounting for morality and values remains problematic. Evolutionary psychology may provide an account of the evolutionary functions of our moral sensitivities and conscience. But no one has found any logical way to derive the actual content of our values from empirical investigations of the physical world. They tell us what is the case in the physical world. However, empirical descriptions of what "is" tell us very little about what "ought to be."

(6) There remains the irony that research suggests that human flourishing requires a sense of meaning and purpose: people who experience life as meaningful, who have values by which they live, who possess a grounded hopefulness appear to do better on almost every epidemiological measure and to be more resilient and better able to cope (some of this research is described in chapter 3 on meaning-making). If meaning, purpose, value, hope, and other such metaphysical variables are really, objectively meaningless (as they are on purely physicalist terms; e.g., physicist Steven Weinberg's famous claim that the more we understand the universe, the more meaningless it appears), then we have evolved into a major psychological and spiritual "double-bind" and psychologists know that double-binds make human beings crazy. Some physicalists do embrace this double-bind and argue that evolution has produced an objectively determined, meaningless species (us) endowed with the illusion that it possesses freedom and intentionality and purpose because such illusions have survival value. I once heard an evolutionary psychologist say, "We are robots designed not to believe that we are robots." How would we possibly know whether such a perplexing assertion was true or false? How could such a confused proposition claim that it should compel our rational assent?

(7) Science itself assumes a rational structure to the world. On purely physicalist terms, there is no reason to think that such a rational, intelligible structure actually exists. Physicalism seeks to understand the world in the most rational way possible but is unable to give any rational account for the rationality it requires. As Nietzsche pointed out, truth itself functions as a value. But if the truth is that all values are meaningless, then truth too is meaningless. Even if it possesses the strictest possible methodology (which evolutionary psychology, cognitive psychological studies of cultural phenomena, and physicalist philosophy certainly do not), it is hard to call a paradigm scientific that

undercuts grounds for believing in the reality of reason and truth. In addition, as Hume pointed out, on physicalist terms which limit "reality" to objects known through the physical senses, inductive reasoning and claims about causation cannot be substantiated since simple sensory experience of events occurring in conjunction is not a sufficient basis for inferring an occult force known as causality. A position that undermines the bases of scientific work—such as causality, rationality, and truth—in the name of science seems a bit self-contradictory.

(8) The age-old question of a final explanation of the universe is not answered but is rather ruled out of court. Why anything exists rather than utter nothingness, and why what exists contains the potential to form into a universe (or universes) that contain the further potential to give rise to and to sustain sentient life—physicalism insists that such final explanations are necessarily impossible. But that does not automatically make them irrational; there is no evidence that it is psychopathological to wonder about such things. Such questions are only impossible in a purely physicalist context. Religious worldviews can provide additional resources and perspectives with which to reflect on such questions

These concerns (and more could be listed) suggest that the assumption that physicalism (and the interpretations of neural science derived from it) is the viewpoint that is most comprehensive, most rationally compelling, and most congruent with science may not be correct. All these problems do not coercively prove physicalism wrong, nor do they demonstrate that alternative viewpoints are necessarily correct. Instead my only point is that popular science writers and polemical atheists are wrong to simply assume or assert, without giving any reasons, that science requires belief in physicalism (i.e., that the physical world as described by natural science is the only objective reality) or that physicalism is obviously the most compelling, comprehensive, and rational viewpoint. If that background viewpoint is not so obviously or intuitively plausible, then neither are those anti-religious interpretations of human nature that are based upon it.

In addition to these arguments against physicalism which I have developed in more depth in other places (Jones, 2005, 2016), various thinkers from a variety of perspectives, many with no religious commitments, have launched a series of additional, telling arguments against physicalism (for example, see the works in the bibliography by Crane, Nagel, and Plantinga). So varied and extensive are the arguments calling physicalism into question that while it appears to be the default position for pundits writing about science in the popular press, in reality purely physicalist claims seem pretty torn and tattered.

The Selectivity, Incompleteness, and Virtue of Humility

In addition to these problems inherent in a purely physicalist viewpoint, when we think about the relationship of current scientific accounts of human nature to the accounts proffered by the religions of the world, we should remember that all accounts, scientific and religious, and the reasons for them have domain limits and so are selective. All accounts of a phenomenon select some aspects of that phenomenon to focus on and others to ignore. Some years ago, there was an unfortunate rash of suicides at a nearby university. Over a three-week period, several students jumped from a dormitory balcony. An intense and unhappy discussion about why this happened ensued. The head of the counseling service, whom I happened to know, was called upon to participate in this process. Interviews with friends and families led her to conclude that at least two of the students were severely depressed. Studies show a close connection between suicide and depression and that became her explanation for this tragedy. A sociology professor who studied adolescent group behavior wrote a column in the university newspaper describing a phenomenon he called "copy-cat activity" based on what he called "the epidemiology of group behavior," that is, adolescents tend to follow each other's behavior whether this involves taste in music or dress or even "acting out" or fatal activities. And it turned out that all these students knew each other and had been talking together about suicide for some time before that horrible three-week period. The head of the university police department weighed in with the results of his investigation, which showed that several of the students had been drinking in their rooms before they jumped. This was confirmed by toxicology reports of high blood levels of alcohol. In all honesty, they did not ask the head of the physics department for his analysis. But if asked, he could surely claim that as a physicist he was positive that each body fell from the balcony at a rate consistent with Newton's inverse square law of gravity.

Out of this whole complex tragic episode, each expert attended to one aspect of the event in his or her explanation: the psychological state of the students, the effect of group dynamics, illegal substance abuse, and the rate of descent of falling bodies. The point here is not who was correct (they all have some supporting evidence) or which explanation was more important (all these factors clearly played a role). My point is that each explanation required selecting one facet of the tragedy to focus on. And that is characteristic of any process of explanation; it is always selective.

In this case, and in most cases, that selectivity is driven by the frame of reference that a person brings to the subject under investigation. Like cognitive schemas, shared disciplinary frames of reference highlight some aspects of a phenomenon and conceal others. The psychologist focuses on psychopathology; the sociologist on group behavior; the policeman on illegal activity; the physicist on natural law. The sociologist may miss the presence of psychopathology; the psychologist may miss the power of group dynamics; the policeman may overlook both. And probably none of them will have the calculation of the rate of descent of falling bodies on their minds. Each frame of reference enabled each observer to offer one account while potentially blinding them to others.

Let me give you a scientific example from my own experience. I am trained in behavioral medicine and psychophysiology; this has been part of my clinical practice for some years and I have taught this material as well. When I first started studying psychology in the 1960s, if someone had applied for a grant to study the impact on health of psychological factors like feelings or beliefs, they would have been ridiculed (and maybe even relieved of their tenure). While there were a lot of anecdotal accounts of personality factors being correlated with medical conditions circulating in the clinical world at the time, we were all taught (for example) that the central nervous system (the CNS—basically the brain and spine) and the immune system were totally separate and that the autonomic nervous system (which controls breathing and heart rate, for example) was "autonomic," working on its own, uninfluenced by other factors or systems, especially the CNS. That was the frame of reference that kept any scientifically inclined clinician from considering the role of psychological factors in health and disease. One might as well have proposed research on the connection between astrological sign and disease. This was not irrational blindness. There simply was no way, then, of scientifically seeing any possible connections among these physiological systems. Decades of research have now clearly established all sorts of interconnections here through neurological, hormonal, and chemical pathways. And that has made so-called mind-body medicine or psychoneuroimmunology a busy field of research and clinical practice. The point is not that researchers and clinicians in the 1960s were irrationally close-minded. They were not. The point is that we are all often encapsulated in disciplinary frames of reference and governed by schemas that shed a clear light on some things and inevitably blind us to others. So, to reflect critically and constructively on scientific and religious accounts of human nature, we must become as conscious as we can about what is clearly illuminated and what is inevitably hidden by these differing viewpoints.

Put another way, the physicalist's viewpoint, the theologian's, and everyone else's are inherently selective and therefore incomplete. None attend to all the facets of a phenomenon. All allow us to see some elements clearly and keep us from noticing others at all. This selectivity driven incompleteness should engender in us a certain epistemic humility about the limitations of any and all claims we make. (I argue more extensively for the inevitability of incompleteness and the necessity of epistemic humility in Jones, 1981, and discuss additional implications in Jones, 2016).

Embodied Dualism

So far, I have argued for the inadequacy of accounts of human nature that are completely constrained by the limits of current physical science (which is what I mean by physicalism). Now I want to argue that the embodied viewpoint provides intellectual resources for an account of human nature that is richer by far and more theologically fruitful than the purely physicalist account, while still being grounded in good scientific research. In other words, the embodied-relational paradigm allows us to expand the framework in which a scientifically informed and theologically fruitful discussion of human nature might take place beyond that which physicalism alone assumes. Such an expanded framework can generate more complex understandings of the mind and the body and therefore new avenues for thinking about the mind-body dilemma and the doctrine of human nature.

If we make three moves that are implicit in what I've said so far and (1) reject the reduction of mind to formal information processing alone and keep in mind (literally) realities like consciousness and intentionality that do not map well onto a purely physicalist account but seem essential to any theological perspective on human nature; and (2) recognize the incompleteness of a purely physicalist viewpoint so as to ensure that any theory that ties human understanding to the body does not also reduce the mind in its entirety to a purely physical reality; and (3) realize that "dualism" is not necessarily synonymous with the popular notion of Cartesian substance dualism, then we can understand that the embodied-relational perspective does not necessarily contradict or preclude dualism. As paradoxical as it may seem, understood in a certain way, an embodied-relational paradigm may actually support some forms of dualism.

Contemporary thinkers insist there are other forms of dualism besides the popular version of Cartesian "substance dualism" containing two self-contained and incompatible substances. There are also property dualists, emergent dualists, and various shades of dualism in between (see Baker & Goetz, 2011, especially Zimmerman's chapter 7; Inwagen & Zimmerman, 2007). By dualism I mean the claim that the human person consists of at least two (there may be more as in Tibetan Buddhism's exceedingly complex philosophical anthropology) distinct and potentially separable realities that nevertheless are known only in and through the physical body (at least in this life). The crucial question is how distinct? Popular Cartesianism and certain forms of Platonism and Hinduism appear to insist on *completely distinct* in the strongest possible sense. And we have seen how a rigid and reductive physicalism also entails a strong separation of the physical and the mental and the virtual elimination of the mental (at least as an active cause in the world). Such positions generate the serious (many say fatal) problem for dualism of how such completely distinct (really opposed) mental and physical realities can interact.

But mind and body can be distinct without being as radically separate and ontologically incompatible as those positions claim (a point insisted on by many authors in Baker & Goetz, 2011, for example). Minds, if they are carriers of cognition, awareness, and intentionality, clearly to some extent inhabit space and time and in that very general sense can be regarded as semi-physical (at least in the sense of existing within the world of time and space) even though their mode of existence is not well understood. Given that in contemporary physics the boundaries of the "physical" are not so clearly defined, minds may possess other "physical" properties without being physical or material in our ordinary, primarily Newtonian sense, the sense that reductive physicalism seems so enamored of. And bodies may be more complex realities than Descartes's physical machines or the purely material entities described in current medical texts. So being separate does not necessarily mean that minds and bodies have nothing in common.

The Mind-Suffused Body

If ordinary physicalism is not a complete account of the physical world in toto, then obviously it is not a complete account of the physical body. Thus, we may well require a more complex understanding of the body. Embodied models of human understanding bring the process of mentation (but not necessarily the mind in it is entirety) into close connection with the body. One might think that this is a powerful argument for the reduction of mind to body—especially since contemporary discussions of the body's role in understanding and perception often sound like the body being referred to and theorized is the Cartesian mechanistic body, the body of Newtonian science and mainstream Western medicine. So often when people bring up the so-called mind-body problem they assume they already understand what the "body" is—the body is what can be described by the biological sciences and ultimately by physics. For them the "mind-body problem" is primarily a problem of understanding the "mind." But reflections based on an embodied-relational paradigm might suggest that the "mind-body problem" may lie equally, or even more so, with understanding the "body." For our bodies are not simply lumps of dead matter. Before we worry about understanding the "mind," perhaps we should be clearer about how we understand the "body."

In his little book *Mind and Matter* (1969), the physicist Erwin Schroedinger points out that the categories (like matter, time, space) through which we describe the world and our bodies are creations of the human mind. For good reasons, in the name of objectivity we remove ourselves from our scientific picture of the world and impose impersonal categories on it. So we should not be surprised when the world (and everything in it) looks impersonal when seen through our scientific lenses. So powerful and compelling (and often elegant and beautiful) is this impersonal picture of the world that we forget that it is a creation of the human mind. And so, Schroedinger argues, the mind becomes a stranger in the world-picture it has itself created. But, he goes on to argue, the mind that creates these categories can thus be said to transcend that impersonal world-picture it has created and in which it remains an alien. The Cartesian mechanistic view of the body is part of that impersonal world-picture the mind has both created and been banished from. Part of rethinking the body in a way that might make the idea of a spiritual sense possible is moving some of our reflections on the body (and not just the mind) past Cartesianism with its mechanical body. And that will involve, among other things, different tools to think with. Here too an embodied-relational approach can play a role.

The embodied-relational paradigm reframes the discussion about the body as well as the mind. Human understanding in its broadest sense does not just take place in the skull; understanding is not only a correlate of the brain. Understanding takes place in a context; it is impacted by the body and the body's relational interaction with its environment. So the boundaries of

the activity of human understanding are the boundaries of the person's relationship with her environment; the limits of our mentation are the limits of
our interactions with our environment. What are those boundaries? What are
those limits? Where should we set them and why? The physical world? The
cultural world? Or is there more beyond the physical and cultural worlds?
Where should we set the boundaries? If we limit the "mind" to the "body"
and we limit the "body" to the Cartesian physical machine, then we create a
"mind-body" problem. If, as part of our reflective understanding, we expand
the boundaries of what constitutes both the "mind" and the "body," that may
diminish the "mind-body" problem.

There is a potentially cosmological dimension to an embodied-relational
approach to the "body-mind dilemma." The body connects us to the rest of
the universe, not just because we are made of the same physical particles but
more deeply because we breathe the air, walk on the earth, ingest physically
constituted plants and animals. Through our bodies we live in constant reciprocal interaction with the universe. And our minds "follow" our bodies there
when we cognitively and imaginatively engage with the universe through our
scientific, artistic, philosophical, and theological explorations of it and our
projections of our ideas and images into it. How far does the relational mind
with its cosmically interconnected body extend?

Please note that my discussion does not concern the debate referred to
earlier about "extended cognition" and whether tools used in the service of
thought deserve to be designated as "cognitive." Rather, I am raising a question from within an embodied-relational approach to human understanding
(which I take to be a broader concern than "cognition" as the term is used in
cognitive science) about what we can consider the boundaries of the most
encompassing environment to which the human mind stands in relation. If we
take account of an expanded notion of the mind and the body, both the mind
and the body can be seen to have a cosmological or transcendental dimension.
But another way, if we allow our imaginations to follow our minds' embodied
connections and interconnections with the cosmos, we may glimpse something of the mind's transcendental nature that Schroedinger presupposes in
his essay.

In pointing to this potentially transcendental, cosmological dimension of
human awareness, we have extended both the relational mind and its body.
What are the boundaries of such a body-mind so tightly connected to its
(potentially transcendental) environment? This question points to one place
where this paradigm is supportive of a semi-dualistic position in a way that
builds upon an argument for dualism offered by Dean Zimmerman (2011).

The view of the body generated here is one of vague (to use Zimmerman's term), even disappearing, boundaries. Zimmerman argues that our experience of the physical world is always somewhat vague. "Where does Mount Everest end, and its foothills begin?" Zimmerman asks (189). Likewise with our brain, is it the cerebellum? Or does it include the brainstem, and the peripheral nervous system, the neuro-chemicals produced throughout the body? There are no sharp boundaries in nature, so we must simply "*stipulate*" (189, his italics) where physical objects begin and end. Yet our conscious experience, he argues, is quite bounded and distinct. We can experience our embodied selves as rather unbounded in the ways just described. But our conscious experience at any given moment, such as talking to a friend or reading a book, is quite bounded in time and space. This suggests a serious disjunction between conscious experience and the physical reality of our extended body-brain. Where in the extended and cosmically interconnected body-brain is the source and subject of our discrete conscious experiences?

So now, after the rise of an embodied model of human understanding, there is a double disjunction of consciousness-mind and brain-body. This disjunction was part of an argument suggestive of dualism that I made earlier in this chapter and in a paper in 2005. There I argued that brains were discrete and thoughts vaguer from a physical standpoint. Here, from the standpoint of embodied understanding, while brains have obvious discrete physical properties that thoughts lack (mass, color, etc.), the reflecting brain-body is theorized as being rather vague and unbounded (following Zimmerman) and the subjects of conscious experience as being rather discrete and bounded. The basic point is that either way you look at it, there is a serious disjunction between our experience of the contents of consciousness and our description, especially in the context of a physicalist model, of our physical nature (as Zimmerman emphasizes; see also Jones, 2005). They simply do not, perhaps cannot, map onto each other very well. This is clear in terms of our immediate experience which is hard to deny and almost impossible not to rely on. But not only in terms of immediate experience, logically, as well, conscious experience and physical reality as ordinarily conceived do not fit together very well (Baker & Goetz, 2011; Jones, 2005).

An embodied model of human understanding brings mind (at least in the sense of mentation and perception) and body close together. But this affects not only how we think about cognition and the mind but also how we think about the body. The body of an embodied model of understanding is a "mind-suffused body" (in the wonderful phrase of my colleague Leon Turner), or at least a mentation and perception suffused body. This deepens the meaning and function of proprioception. Proprioception is not only an awareness of where my body is in space or when it is tense, relaxed, or in pain. The body as experienced, the known-body, is not primarily the Cartesian mechanistic and physicalist body. It is *my* body; the body with which I get around, the body with which I bond intimately and joyfully with my wife, the body with which I train in karate and which enabled me to see the world from the summit of mountains, the body that dreamed of running a marathon but never did, the body with which I stand to pray and sit on a cushion to meditate, the body that daily reminds me that I am growing older and that to dust I shall return. My body both enables me to join the world around me and pulls me back into myself when in pain. And, I shall argue in the last chapter, my body may enable me to perceive God in new ways. This is the body I know directly and immediately, not as a psychophysical machine but as myself embodied, myself situated and often moving in time and space.

As with the Cartesian physical body, the known-body is a situated, contextualized body; the known-body is partly a set of social constructions, apart from which it does not exist (as a known-body). The known-body is different in a gross anatomy lab and in Tibet or in India or in Plato's or Plotinus's philosophies. The inert body the surgeon sees is different from the active body being treated by biofeedback or psychoneuroimmunology. Traditional embodied cognition has a particular view of the body, often a rather mechanistic, Cartesian mechanical body (despite its insistence that it is rejecting Descartes). What would embodied cognition look like if it started from the Tantric body known in India and Tibet or the body being trained tai chi or karate in Japan? There is no one correct way to know the body; the body is known differently in different contexts. The body that is known depends on the functional contexts in which we seek to know it. What do you want to do with your knowledge of the body: excise a tumor, treat irritable bowel syndrome (IBS) with biofeedback, deepen your spiritual practice? The known-body is not simply an inert object that passively receives cultural inscriptions nor is it just a machine made of meat that deterministically causes thoughts and behaviors to occur in the human organism. Here embodied models can make a real contribution by insisting on starting our reflections on human nature from the mind-suffused body, the known-body, that exists only in sets of physical and cultural contexts.

The continual manipulation of the body also belies the notion of the body as a natural or objective fact. Such a notion is undermined by the ways in which the body has become a malleable and plastique thing that can be made and remade by sex reassignment surgeries, plastic surgeries, implanted technological devices, and other manipulations. No theory of embodiment can presuppose there is a natural objective reality called the body. The human body is a cultural artifact as much, if not more, than a biological one.

Does all this discussion of the embodying of understanding and perception entail that I am my body? That there is nothing that I am beyond my body (broadly conceived)? In one sense that is clearly true. I am my body. It's not just my body that is sick; I am sick. It's not just my mind that is worried or angry' the worry or anger runs through my whole body. But if that's true, what body am I? The body I was at twenty? The body I was when I turned forty? The body I am now after I turned seventy? Am I the entirely physical body that my surgeon sees as I slip under the anesthesia? Am I the complex spiritual body that I might experience through tai chi or if I were more deeply committed to Tibetan Buddhist Tantric practice? Contemporary Western theories of embodiment that identify the self with the body take place in a cultural context that is obsessed with the self as body in which technologies of transforming the self become technologies of transforming the body through diet, exercise, surgery, and other practices. Does an embodied-relational paradigm reinforce this obsession with the body? Such cultural questions are far beyond the scope of this book but they arise naturally out of any paradigm that emphasizes embodiment.

The "mind-body problem" is not only a problem with the mind; it is also a problem with the body. If we theorize the body as the Cartesian mechanistic machine made of meat, we inevitably create a "mind-body problem." If we envision the body in more complex ways, in ways nearer to our lived experience of our bodies, then the mind-body problem may look different. Put another way, many thinkers who insist on the reality of mind call for a first-person perspective on the mind. But what about a first-person perspective on the body?

Phenomenologists like Husserl and Merleau-Ponty remind me continually that my body is not an external object that I perceive from outside but is rather the place from which my thinking inevitably begins. Likewise, an embodied-relational model also calls for a first-person perspective on the body. The vastly extended mind and the proprioceptively known and "mind-suffused" body are more complex realities than Cartesian mental substance or cognitivism's information processing calculator or physicalism's meaty machine.

Of course, for centuries the world's religions have experienced and thought about the body in ways far more complex than Descartes's material machine. In different ways and at different times, all of the world's religions have spoken of human beings as possessing several "bodies." For example, Tantric Buddhism, following earlier Indian sources, speaks of three bodies: coarse, subtle, and very subtle. The coarse body is what we think of as the physical body; the subtle body roughly parallels our concept of consciousness; the very subtle body is the center of consciousness and survives the death of the coarse body (Williams, 1997: 222). Strikingly even the most subtle, spiritual aspect of the living organism is referred to as a "body"; it is embodied but not physically. Likewise, Chinese and Japanese Buddhism speaks of an embodied but non-material energy called "ki" or "chi" that circulates through the material body (Yuaso, 1993). Neoplatonism too speaks of a variety of bodies with names like "celestial, astral, etheric, spiritual, and physical," and some of this terminology entered Neoplatonic Christianity. And in the New Testament, Paul speaks of a "spiritual body," which is probably an oxymoron in purely Platonic terms. (More examples of such non-physical "bodies" from the world's religions can be found in Coakley, 1997, and Cattoi & McDaniel, 2011.)

The idea of a bodily but non-material reality, of course, sounds outrageously foreign to modern ears. We are conditioned to think of our body in purely and simply reductive physicalist terms, which then virtually drives the religious person into dualism if he or she wants to affirm the reality of a spiritual aspect to humanity. The cultural power of this purely physicalist conception may make it impossible to recover a more traditional and complex view of our body (or "bodies") and therefore of the person. But an embodied-relational viewpoint with its conceptions of the consciously extended mind, the embodied mind, and the mind-suffused body might point the way to such a recovery.

More complex and multi-dimensional models of the embodied mind and the mind-suffused body generate a greater range of possible interrelationships between mind and body than substance dualism or various forms of reductive physicalism. The mind-suffused, proprioceptively known body is more complex, more subtle, more nuanced than the physiological machine of medical school textbooks. And the embodied-relational mind is more bodily (in some sense) than an entirely spaceless, timeless spiritual substance while still generating thoughts and possessing awareness and intentionality, capacities that cannot be accounted for on purely physical terms. This suggests the possibility of a continuum, not a sharp break, between a mind-suffused body and an embodied mind in which the mind retains its transcendental capacities at the far end of the continuum. Such a continuum does not solve the problem of theorizing mind-body interaction. But bringing closer together an embodied mind (in a very broad sense of the term "body") and a mind-suffused body may lessen the problem.

This model of a continuum is a purely heuristic device. I am not claiming that it represents a developmental trajectory or a physical or metaphysical process. The physicalist would affirm such a continuum but argue that it is all simply permutations of narrowly physical realities. The idealist would claim the reverse: that it is all permutations of the mental. The continuum modeled here grows out of reflections based on work in psychophysiology (which relies heavily on proprioception) and research on embodiment in human understanding, which gives rise to images of the mind-suffused body and the embodied mind. The implicit ontology of this continuum of body-to-mind and mind-to-body is neither purely physical nor purely mental (in the popular Cartesian sense of a substance having no physical properties). Rather this is the ontology of the human person, a more complex, third reality for which we have no term in our ordinary (Western) language.

Most current discussions of human nature, the body, or the mind-body dilemma usually follow Descartes and start from a general understanding of physical reality (often derived from Newtonian physics) that is later generalized to apply to the body as a subset of physical reality. Such a heuristic trajectory makes good scientific sense and has obviously been extraordinarily fruitful in terms of medical science. But it is subject to the same incompleteness that characterizes all finite human frameworks. It gives us an amazing understanding of some things like the functioning of neurons or the precision of the immune system. But if relied on exclusively it may blind us to other realities like our deeply embodied connection with the world around us.

There is no logical reason that trajectory cannot also run in the reverse direction as well and start with the mind-suffused body and then expand to an understanding of physical reality so that we not only seek to understand the body on analogy with physical matter but that we also seek to understand the wider physical world on analogy with the known, mind-suffused body. Exploring the wider implications of this suggestion would require another book and take us too far from the concern of embodied understanding and theology. But this suggestion implies that a more complex and multi-dimensional model of the physical world might be possible: a material nature that contains more variables and processes than described by reductive physicalism; an ordinary world that (like the functionally interconnected, complex, and non-linear human connectome) contains more degrees of freedom and openness than described by Newtonian mechanics (we have already alluded to suggestions that quantum processes may, in fact, show up in the everyday world); a material nature that has previously undisclosed depths and richness.

I began this chapter with a sharp critique of a reductive physicalism but I conclude by gesturing toward a richer and more complex physicalism. A complex physicalism that is not the antagonist of mind and spirit but rather, like the physical body, is a mind-suffused physicalism, a mind-suffused natural world in which a mind-suffused body might find a home. And just as religion requires that the human person possess a spiritual dimension, so this model would suggest that the natural world possesses a spiritual dimension. It is not only a mind-suffused world but perhaps a spirit-suffused world as well. Such a spirit-suffused naturalism accords well with the New Testament vision of the cosmos as the body of Christ, filled with the presence of him who fills "all in all." It also accords well with the Mahayana Buddhist teaching about the Dharmakyia, the universal Buddha nature that infuses the universe (Jones, 2003: chapter 3).

The common position that sounds closest to this would probably be some form of "dual aspect monism" that asserts there is only one reality that possess two aspects—a conscious aspect and a physical aspect. But when such a dual-aspect monism is proposed it often sounds to me like the "one" reality is primarily a physical reality on which a conscious dimension depends or supervenes. That, to me, is really a form of physicalism, which I reject. If the monistic reality is really equally composed of two aspects, consciousness must be theorized as being as fundamental as the physical. That is rarely done in my experience. Also, the mental is seen as inseparable from the physical. I might agree if the boundaries of what is considered physical are left quite vague (and not limited to Newtonian-Euclidian space) so that "physical" is now just a general term. But if the "physical" is primarily the Newtonian universe and the body is defined entirely in those terms, I do not think such a dual-aspect monism (really a dual-aspect physicalism) will really work. I also want make room for the possibility of consciousness, thought, and intentionality going on being after the demise of the material body (as we now know it)—something all religions affirm. While perhaps being physical or bodily in some more general sense, consciousness, thought, and intentionality should also be understood as potentially separable from the material body (as we now know it). Few dual-aspect models allow that.

These embodied-relational reflections do not "solve" the mind-body dilemma. They do not explain if or how consciousness, awareness, and intentionality might arise from the brain nor how these abilities might go on being after the death of the physical body (as all religions affirm), perhaps surviving in an embodied but non-physical form. The New Testament, after all, speaks of the afterlife in terms of a "spiritual body," not simply as pure spirits (whatever they may be). But these suggestions do demonstrate that an embodied understanding is not inimical to dualism and may actually support some types of dualism. My goal, then, is a more complex (multi-dimensional, non-reductive) model of mind, body, and materiality that does not subtly prioritize a narrow, Newtonian definition of the physical. In other words, if we expand and make more complex our understanding of human nature—that dynamic interaction of embodied mind and mind-suffused body—then the relation of mind and body may be less mysterious. But really all I have done is diffuse the mysteriousness over the whole physical world. To the reductive physicalist that is a decided loss but for the person interested in developing a spiritual and religious viewpoint, it might be a decided gain. In any case, all this simply hints at much bigger issues that go far beyond the relationship between embodiment and theology.

So embodied-relational understanding is not only about mentation; it is also about the body. It calls upon us to rethink the body as well as to rethink human understanding. It calls on us to reflect more deeply about the body or rather to experience the body more profoundly. It implies that the known-body, the mind-suffused body, is more than, different from, the Cartesian mechanistic body that has dominated scientific, philosophical (with the exception of the Phenomenologists), and even to some extent theological discourses. The known-body, the body as experienced, the body known directly through a more penetrating and conscious proprioception, is a body beyond physicalism. It may well be a spiritual body. And if a spiritual body, then perhaps the seat of a spiritual sense.

3

Meaning-Making

AN EMBODIED-RELATIONAL APPROACH

THE CONSTRUCT OF "meaning" has sat for a long time directly at the intersection of theology and psychology. Both disciplines have, in various ways, addressed the perceived need for meaning. In a book entitled *Meanings in Life*, the psychologist Roy Baumeister defines meaning as a "mental representation of possible relationships among things, events, and relationships. Thus meaning *connects* things" (1991: 15, italics in original). A definition that refers to a mental representation obviously points the concern with meaning to the domain of cognitive psychology. How that works out in the context of an embodied-relational paradigm that broadens the discussion of human understanding beyond the role of mental representations (as they are usually thought of in cognitive psychology) is the theme of this chapter. But first we need to locate this discussion in its broader psychological and theological contexts.

Meaning-Making and Modern Theology

Baumeister's definition talks about meaning as a relationship, something that "connects" things (see also Heine, Proulix, & Vohs, 2006). This, of course, might gesture in the direction of religion since the root of the word "religion" is the Latin *religare*, which is the prefix "re" plus "ligare" which means to bind (from which we get our English word ligament). So at its root, religion means to "bind up" or "tie together." So it is not coincidence that psychological research finds a close connection between "meaning" and religion; that is, religion is a potent, perhaps the most potent, source of meaning (Park, Edmondson, & Hale-Smith, 2013). So it is not accidental that many twentieth-century theologians, perhaps starting earlier with Soren Kierkegaard, frequently deployed that category. The mention of Kierkegaard underscores that the theologians most focused on the issue of meaning and meaninglessness were those influenced by existentialism. Paul Tillich spoke for that post–World War I/World War II generation of theologians when he wrote, "We were extremely happy when we encountered Kierkegaard" (1967: 163). He and his theological cohort found in existentialism a language that, after the rise of critical philosophy and crises of the two world wars, struck them as a more powerful apologetic language than the traditional theological vocabulary. Tillich refers to this when he writes, "The common point in all existentialist attacks is that man's [*sic*] existential situation is a state of estrangement from his essential nature. . . . The existence of the individual is filled with anxiety and threatened by meaninglessness. With this description of man's predicament, all existentialists agree" (1957: 24).

To this predicament the theologian has a variety of responses. The most obvious is the assertion that belief itself provides meaning. Committing oneself to belief in the existence of a loving and providential God should, by its very nature, provide meaning. This claim was probably the staple of many twentieth-century sermons and popular religious writings in North America. Theologians more steeped in existentialism had a more nuanced response. The Jewish thinker Martin Buber, in a fashion true to Kierkegaard, does not think that purely conceptual belief removes what Tillich called the crisis of meaninglessness. Rather, only a deeper and totally non-cognitive experience of the presence of God can do that. Buber writes,

> Man [*sic*] receives, and what he receives is not a "content" but a presence, a presence as strength. . . . And this is the inexpressible confirmation of meaning. It is guaranteed. Nothing, nothing can henceforth be meaningless. The question of the meaning of life has vanished. But if it were still there, it would not require an answer. You do not know how to point to or define the meaning, you lack any formula or image for it, and yet it is more certain for you than the sensations of your senses. (1970, 158–159)

Meaning is found not in the affirmation of a set of propositions ("content") but in an intensely personal and completely incommunicable experience of divine presence.

Tillich is also clear that simply believing something is not a real response to the problem of existential meaninglessness. Nor can meaninglessness simply be transcended or erased. Instead Tillich says, it must just be embraced,

> The answer must accept, as its precondition, the state of meaningless-ness. It is not an answer if it demands the removal of this state, for that is just what cannot be done. . . . There is only one possible answer, if one does not try to escape the question, namely that the acceptance of despair is in itself faith. . . . Even in the despair about meaning, being affirms itself through us. The act of accepting meaninglessness is in it-self a meaningful act. It is an act of faith. . . . The faith which creates the courage to take [meaninglessness] into itself has no special content. It is simply faith, undirected and absolute. It is undefinable since every-thing defined is dissolved by doubt and meaninglessness. (1952: 155)

This courageous embrace of meaningless is possible, again in good Kierkegaardian fashion, because of a paradoxical experience that is "absolute" but has no "special content" and so remains "undefinable." Such an experience does, however, "point beyond itself" (Tillich's phrase) to the reality that our individual lives are grounded in and sustained by an eternal power outside of ourselves which Tillich calls the "power-of-being" or "being itself," that which "affirms itself through us"—which, for Tillich, is the true referent of the word "God" (1951).

The influence of existentialism on North American theology (the European situation is different) waned as the crises of two world wars and a depression gradually faded. The students of Tillich and his existentialist colleagues often sharply criticized existentialism and turned their focus to other, often social-political, concerns. And the existential theologians' core affirmation of a deeply personal, totally subjective, and completely inexpress-ible but meaning-supplying experience was soon dismissed as pure irration-alism as theology and philosophy moved in more concrete and empirical directions. But its existentialist lineage embedded the issues of meaning and meaninglessness in the discourse of Western religion.

Existential Psychology

Just about the time that American theologians were abandoning the focus on meaning and meaninglessness, some of their colleagues in the psychology department were discovering it. "Meaning" entered the field of contemporary psychology through two routes: existential psychology with its roots in existentialism in which (as we just saw) meaning and meaningless are central themes and, more recently, research on coping and trauma where people's meaning systems are a core ingredient.

As a field, existential psychology tended to gravitate toward the more atheistic versions of existentialism rather than the religious existentialism of Tillich and Buber. One of existential psychology's chief spokespersons has been the clinician Irving Yalom. While rejecting Tillich's theology, Yalom takes over from Tillich's existential philosophy the idea that an individual's life is constructed around a set of "ultimate concerns." Yalom (1998) describes four: *Death* which underscores the absurdity of our existence. *Freedom* which is the capacity to take responsibility for our actions and so live "authentically" (in the terms of J. P. Sartre). Existential psychology is relentless in its opposition to any form of determinism that might be seen to rob humanity of its freedom and responsibility. *Isolation*, which underscores the radical individualism and subjectivity of this set of ideas derived from Soren Kierkegaard. As Sartre writes in one of his plays, "hell is other people." And *meaninglessness* that "stems from the dilemma of a meaning-seeking creature that is thrown into a universe that has no meaning" (9). Here meaning denotes an absence: the world is meaningless; life is lonely; existence is absurd. Unlike the theological existentialism of Tillich and Buber, for Yalom meaning cannot be found in or confirmed by any experience of presence or of transcendentally grounded courage. But in both its religious and atheistic forms, the task of finding ways to live a meaningful life in a meaningless world dominates the discourse of existential psychology.

Of course, the existentialist approach assumes there is a crisis of existential meaning and that meaninglessness is rampant in modern Western society. This is at least a quasi-empirical question, and several questionnaires and scales have been developed to study it. For example, a recent review of some of the relevant research (Heintzelman & King, 2014) describes the findings of many studies using either the *Purpose in Life Test* or the *Meaning in Life Questionnaire*. These reviewers examined studies not only done in North America but also in Sweden, Australia, Japan, and other places. They also reviewed studies involving large clinical and non-clinical populations from different age groups including patients facing serious illness or recovering from significant trauma. Surprisingly, the findings were strikingly consistent across this wide and diverse sample-set: virtually every study found the majority of the people reported a level of meaning in their lives significantly above the mean of the scales. In other words, most people appear to find their lives quite meaningful. The authors discuss some possible objections (limits of self-report scales, response biases, etc.). But they argue that the consistency of the findings suggests that, in fact, most people feel they are living relatively meaningful lives. This is important, they claim, because research also suggests that meaningfulness may be a necessity for human life. To that research we now turn.

The Need for Meaning

A very different emphasis from that of the existentialists can be found in the more recent psychological writings about research on coping and trauma. Here the presence of meaning, or its restoration, are central psychological concerns. These discourses begin from extensive research that finds that human flourishing requires meaning. As one researcher in the field, Crystal Park, writes, "That human beings possess a strong and inherent need for meaning is a widely accepted notion in psychology" (Park et al., 2013: 157; see also Heine et al., 2006). Ironically, whereas Yalom sees this need for meaning as the problem with human existence, researchers in fields like coping and trauma see it as the solution to many of life's problems. Park writes, "People require a strong and functional meaning system that successfully meets [life's] basic challenges" (Park et al., 2013: 158). These researchers, who study trauma and coping, find that "the need for a meaning system is thought to be continuously and pervasively present in everyday life and to be particularly acute in times of severe stress" (157; see also Heine et al., 2006). Both aspects— the pervasive human need for meaning and the acute need for it in times of stress—have recently been the subject of extensive psychological research.

Often in this research, the rather vague claim about a pervasive "need for meaning" is reframed as the study of the psychological presence and function of a "meaning-making system" (Heine et al., 2006; Koltko-Rivera, 2004; Park, 2010; Park et al., 2013). A meaning-making system is usually defined in rather cognitive terms as the quote from Baumeister about a "mental representation" suggests. This cognitive system is variously referred to as a "meaning-system," an "assumptive world," or a "worldview." It is an integrated system of beliefs, assumptions, and values that filters our perceptions, organizes our cognitive processes, and shapes our goals. Thus, a meaning-system is a global cognitive construct encompassing fundamental beliefs about the world, the self, and the relationship between them as well as the basic values that shape one's life and govern one's overriding life goals. Its main function is to respond to the "deepest" or "most encompassing" (depending on which metaphor you prefer) existential questions that human beings encounter. Thus, a meaning-system or worldview is the broadest and most primary framework through which people interpret and make sense of their experience (Heine et al., 2006; Koltko-Rivera, 2004). This central cognitive function of meaning-systems underscores their crucial epistemological role. Because meaning-systems contain people's fundamental assumptions about themselves and the world, they define how correct beliefs are to be arrived at and what a person will consider as a true statement.

Given its all-encompassing nature, the term "ultimate" is often applied to one's primary meaning-system in this literature (for example, Park et al., 2013), even when no religious connotations are (consciously) intended. In this context, to have a meaningful experience, or even a meaningful life, requires being able to connect one's life to a global, and more encompassing, frame of reference (Heine et al., 2006; Koltko-Rivera, 2004; Park, 2010). Making meaning, or having one's life make sense, means experiencing it as a part of something greater than just one's individual ego. Again, such a construct as a global meaning-system inevitably gestures in a religious direction, since that definition of a meaning-system (an encompassing frame of reference that gives meaning to life and functions as a source of values) could also easily serve as a functional, psychological definition of religion. So again, it is not coincidence that research consistently finds a very significant connection between religious belief and practice and being able to experience life as meaningful (reviews in Paloutzian & Park, 2005; Pargament, 2007; Park et al., 2013).

Implicit in this discussion is the claim that every well-functioning human being possesses a meaning-system or worldview. As we have seen, extensive research seems to support this claim (Heine et al., 2006; Koltko-Rivera, 2004; Park, 2010). Also implicit is the claim that there are many possible meaning-systems or worldviews, and much of the research being done seeks to discover the psychological and epidemiological effects of these different possible meaning-systems or worldviews. Clearly such research is a function of, and only makes sense in, the context of the radically pluralistic societies in which contemporary Western theologians and psychologists work.

A great deal of research finds that throughout life, possessing a strong sense of meaning is associated with a greater sense of well-being, less anxiety and depression, better physical health, and even lower all-cause mortality (Heine et al., 2006; Park, 2010; Park et al., 2013). The epidemiologist Anton Antonovsky approaches the relationship between meaning and health from a similar direction. In his 1987 book, *Unraveling the Mystery of Health*, he finds from his research on factors that significantly predict health or illness that what he calls a "sense of coherence" is a major epidemiological variable. Coherence, for Antonovsky, is a schema about life that has three facets: (1) Comprehensibility, which, in his definition, means, "one's internal and external environments in the course of living are structured, predictable, and explicable." That is, my life makes sense (most of the time). (2) Manageability, which means that "resources are available to meet the demands posed" by life. That is, I do not feel overwhelmed by life (most of the time). And (3) Meaningfulness, which requires that there are projects "worthy of investment and engagement." That is, I have things in my life I can be committed to that bring me a sense of meaning and purpose (most of the time). Antonovsky does not over-idealize this sense of coherence; he insists that "only someone who is totally out of touch with reality could claim to have an absolute sense of coherence." No one feels this way all the time and good health does not require that (19). From his epidemiological studies, Antonovsky concludes that a sense of coherence—that life is comprehensible, manageable, and meaningful—is a major predictor of mental and physical health, happiness, and satisfaction with life. So these metaphysical constructs like meaning and purpose turn out to be critical for mental and physical health and for psychological resilience and coping. Again, given that religion is a major source of meaning, it is no surprise that research on religion and physical and mental health parallels the findings on meaning and health: that religion and spirituality are generally (in Western cultures) associated with a greater sense of well-being, less anxiety and depression, better physical health, and even lower all-cause mortality (reviews in Jones, 2004; Koenig, 2012; Pargament, 2007; and vol. 13, 2002, of *Psychological Inquiry*, which is devoted to this topic). And it appears that meaning is a major mediator of that relationship (Jones, 2004)

Meaning, Trauma, and Coping

In addition to research on the continuing need for meaning in order to flourish, there is also research on the role of meaning-making in coping and recovery from trauma. In this literature, trauma is virtually defined as an event that challenges a person's meaning-system; it is an event so dissonant with the person's meaning-system that to make it meaningful is hard (if not impossible); an event that, in the words of a classic text in the field, "shatters" assumptions about oneself and the world (Janoff-Bulman, 1992; see also Park & Folkman, 1997). The extent of the dissonance between the meaning of the event and a person's global meaning-system may be a significant factor in how "traumatic" the experience is to the individual. Therefore, a major ingredient in recovery from trauma is the process of meaning-making (or perhaps meaning re-making) in which victims attempt to reduce the dissonance between the impact of the event and their global meaning system by (1) reframing the event in a less traumatic direction, for example, as a challenge or opportunity for learning; or (2) altering their global meaning-system to incorporate the event, thus revising basic beliefs or life goals; or (3) eliminating from their worldview those beliefs most threatened by the traumatic event (Park, 2010). Any of these moves, or a combination of them, allows victims to retain a (perhaps transformed) global meaning-system and so move from a stance that "my life is now meaningless" to one in which life is again experienced as meaningful (Janoff-Bulman & Frantz, 1997). In some cases this involves finding meaning in a traumatic event; in others it means coming to a place of acceptance. In any case, meaning, its loss and possible restoration, is central to this understanding of trauma, and research consistently finds that the majority of traumatized people at least attempt to find some meaning in their crisis or trauma. And while the coping research is complex and sometimes inconsistent, there is general agreement that "numerous studies have reported that, compared with not having searched [for meaning], meaning-making attempts resulting in meaning made are indeed related to better adjustment" (Park, 2010: 287).

Again, since religion has been found to be a major source of meaning, it is no surprise that religion has also been found to play a major role in facilitating coping with and recovering from trauma (the classic, if somewhat outdated [since so much additional research has been done] source is K. Pargament, *The Psychology of Religion and Coping*). In fact, "research suggests that religion-based meaning systems may be more able to absorb stressful occurrences without shattering than can other types of meaning-systems" (Park et al., 2013: 163).

Beyond religion's role in recovery from trauma by facilitating a move "from meaningless world to meaningful life" (Janoff-Bulman et al., 1997) is the recent research on what is referred to as "post-traumatic growth." This is a process in which negative life experiences can result in new life-possibilities that might not have been available otherwise (Michael & Cooper, 2013; Shaw, Joseph, & Lindley, 2005). Here too the recovery of meaning is found to be a central factor, with religion usually playing an important role. Virtually all studies find that religion or spirituality is a significant (perhaps *the* significant) component in post-traumatic growth both as a facilitator and a result of post-traumatic growth (Bray, 2013; Michael & Cooper, 2013; Park,

Edmondson, & Blank, 2009; Powel, Gibson, & Collin, 2012; Shaw et al., 2005). So in sum, meaning-making—the drive to find one's experience comprehensible and that one's life has a purpose—is a powerful, perhaps the most powerful, resource for coping and maintaining resilience in the face of crises and, maybe even, growing through them.

Embodied Knowing and Meaning-Making

So far, we have reviewed three rather different approaches in the modern psychological and theological literature to the issues of meaning and meaning-making: (1) religious existentialists like Tillich and Buber, who claim that a sense of meaning can be found in a deeply personal, totally subjective, and completely inexpressible but fully experiential encounter with a transcendental and ultimate reality that is the source of meaning; (2) existential psychologists like Yalom, following the path laid out by atheistic existentialists like Nietzsche and Sartre, who affirm both the importance of meaning and its inevitable absence as the paradox of the human condition (Heine et al., 2006); and (3) clinical researchers studying coping and trauma, who conceive of meaning in more cognitive and more functional terms as a cognitive system that connects the individual to a larger, more encompassing frame of reference. In contrast to the experiential emphasis of the theologians, in the psychological literature, cognitive and intellectualistic metaphors predominate: meaning is a "mental representation" (Baumeister, 1991) or "an effort to understand . . . why it happened . . . to answer the question, What is the significance of the event? . . . [W]hat caused the event to happen?" (Taylor, 1983: 1161). And we have seen that such literature defines meaning in terms of "meaning-systems," which are clearly highly cognitive in nature. Meaning-systems are worldviews that are basically systems of beliefs about the self, the world, and their relationship and also about values, which are also really beliefs (Koltko-Rivera, 2004: 5). Or Janoff-Bulman's basic construct of an "assumptive world," which is a "stable, unified, conceptual system . . . a network of diverse theories and representations . . . a strongly held set of assumptions about the world and the self" (1992: 5).

For empirical and heuristic reasons, we have argued for a theory of human understanding that is broader than a singular focus on cognitive processing, particularly approaches to cognition built around models involving mental representations produced by computational processes. Such approaches radically decontextualize and disembody our life in the world and ignore our pragmatic concerns. Rather, much of the research reviewed in this book, by focusing on the role of the body, theorizes understanding, perception, and sensory experience as expressions of our intimate immersion in the world around us. In this paradigm, sensory experience and the understanding arising from it are "world-involving" and so "entangle" us with the world (Gallagher & Zahavi, 2008: 94). Thus our understanding is something we must often enact. It arises as we move our bodies in particular directions, turn our eyes or ears to the right or the left, focus our attention on the sound of a bird singing or the eyepiece of a microscope or the slide from a functional magnetic resonance (fMRI) scan or the words spoken by our beloved partner. Our bodies are continually reaching out to the world. We see a tennis racket and our neurons and the muscles in our hands imperceptibly form themselves into our "grip." The world around us is not simply a container for our activity; it also evokes and shapes our actions.

And we, in turn, shape it. As Gibbs says, through our embodied interactions with the world, "we bring forth a world" (2005: 17). The world we actually know and live in is brought forth by our mutual, interpenetrating interactions with the objects of our experience. Our lived, experienced, known world is enacted, generated for us in part by our embodied movements. But Gibbs goes on to say, "When a person enacts or brings forth a world, the person and the world are coupled" (17). Through my embodied body interactions—where and how I look and listen—I am really united with the world of experience that I thereby engender. I do not simply receive the world of experience passively nor is it simply my mind's projection onto a blank screen. Rather, I live in continual, reciprocal interaction with what is around me. I make sense of world, then, not simply by cogitating about it but also by acting and interacting with it. Understanding and meaning then are not simply the result of a computation process going on in my head; rather, meaning also arises out of the processes and patterns of my embodied interactions. The understandings we embrace and the meanings we make are formed by the way we make our way through the world.

On this view, meaning is not (in the first instance) an attribution in which I reference the cosmos ("the world is meaningless"), ourselves ("my life is meaningless"), or a striking event (a sudden joy or catastrophe). Meaning is not fundamentally an inward, mental representation. It is rather the form, the experiential result, of my embodied and interactive relationship with what surrounds me. Meaning is a relational reality. For example, the claim "the world is meaningless" expresses (in the first instance) a way of relating to the world. The physicist Steven Weinberg's famous statement, "the more we understand about the world, the more meaningless it appears," obviously derives from understanding the world in and through the context of physics. In the name of objectivity, this means understanding the world through a set of practices that (ideally) involve looking at the world from the outside (so to speak), removing anything personal from the process of understanding, and expressing that understanding in our most impersonal language of mathematics. When we study the universe through methods rigorously designed to remove from them any trace of anything personal, we should not be surprised that they result in a picture of the world that is impersonal, mechanical, and meaningless, as another physicist (Werner Heisenberg) once pointed out. So the statement, "the world is meaningless," is first of all a way of relating to the world as meaningless and impersonal. Likewise, any meaning (or lack therefore) we attribute to the world, ourselves, or other people is, first of all, an expression of our relationship to the world, ourselves, or other people. On this view, global meaning-systems and worldviews develop from, and change as a result of, our reciprocal engagements with the world.

We have suggested that an embodied, relational approach draws upon many of the themes seen in contemporary clinical psychoanalytic theorizing. In this case, meaning would be a "transitional phenomenon," made in Winnicott's "third area of human living"; something existing neither simply inside the individual nor only outside in the world of shared reality. This "transitional world," which is really our actual world, the world of our lived experience, "is a product of the *experiences of the individual* . . . in the environment" (Winnicott, 1971: 107, emphasis in the original). The world of meaning is a "paradoxical world"—neither subjective nor objective but containing elements of both. Winnicott insists, "This has to be accepted as a paradox and not solved by a restatement that by its cleverness seems to eliminate the paradox" (1965: 181). Our world of meaning is "both created and found," constructed and discovered. Meaning-making is an active, creative, transitional process in which meaning is simultaneously discovered and constructed and which reciprocally joins our external and internal worlds. Like all transitional processes, human knowing and meaning-making reflect our first interpersonal experiences. Therefore, a psychoanalysis of the various forms of human meaning-making (science, art, religion, philosophy, even psychoanalysis itself) is possible, and even required, for our meaning-systems carry themes laid down in our earliest interpersonal life.

This parallels Lakoff and Johnson's "experientialism" by which "we understand the world through our interactions with it" (1980: 194). Like our emphasis on embodiment, experientialism with "its emphasis on interaction and interactional properties shows how meaning always is meaning to a person" (228). Like Winnicott's "transitional process," such a viewpoint is neither subjective nor objective but is rather a third alternative. We have also examined brain research that weakens the dichotomy between reason and emotion, a conclusion that also parallels Lakoff and Johnson's metaphor of metaphors. For them, metaphors transcend the dichotomy of objectivity and subjectivity, drawing on both discursive reason and imaginative expression (1980: 193). Theirs is also a general model of human understanding including both religion and science, for all "human conceptual systems are metaphorical in nature and involve an imaginative understanding" (194). These ways of understanding human meaning-making combine the relational, interactional emphasis of contemporary psychoanalysis and also bring back to psychoanalytically informed theorizing, in a transformed way, Freud's focus on the body.

Embodiment and Meaning-Making

While rejecting a strict cognitivist, singular emphasis on amodal, disembodied computational processing, nothing said here repudiates the claim that people have "meaning-systems" or "worldviews" that are heavily (but not exclusively) cognitive. Clearly they do. Nor does it weaken the findings that people use global meaning-systems to make sense of their lives or that such systems can be deeply involved in coping with the vicissitudes of life and recovering from trauma. Rather, it supports such claims but reframes the nature and source of such meaning-systems. Meaning-systems and worldviews are not, in the first instance, simply the result of disembodied computational processes working on amodal propositions. Rather, like all of human attempts at understanding, they are the result of embodied and intentional beings reciprocally interacting with the worlds of their experience. As part of this process, human beings generate global meaning-systems and worldviews and use them in the ways this research finds that they do in order to arrive at goals and values, make experience understandable and comprehensible, and cope with life's events.

But there is no evidence that this process of meaning-making (whether in science or religion) is exclusively cognitive in a narrow, information-processing sense. Human beings certainly possess and deploy worldviews and global meaning-systems, but these are much more complex in origin and function than the usual, cognitively oriented psychology of meaning-systems suggests. There are several senses in which that is true.

First, as we have stressed throughout, human understanding is almost always embodied, involving not only the cerebral cortex but also somatosensory and peripheral activity and often the movement of the whole organism. And that is certainly true of the formation and deployment of global meaning-systems.

Second, studies of particular sensations or experiences find that neuronal patterns differ from organism to organism, depending on their lived history that formed their particular pattern of synaptic connections. Often a perceptual experience implicates an organism's whole embodied history up until that moment. The complex, non-linear sensory and neurological activities associated with human meaning-making are much more physiologically, neurologically, and phenomenologically complex than can be described by any cognitive processing model alone.

Third, the human mind contains at least two systems for processing information. One system's contents and operations are often outside our awareness. This semi-unconscious dimension is often expressed by calling this system "tacit" or "intuitive." It contains the material we take for granted or consider "obvious" or "self-evident." Its results are quick and automatic, yielding "snap judgments" and "first impressions." Little or no concentration or energy is required here. The second system is conscious, slower, and deliberate. It involves mental effort and usually produces reasoned arguments and thoughtful analysis.

The immediate products of the tacit, intuitive system are usually the main source of the basic assumptions on which the reflective system works, whether that reflective activity is scientific or theological. In that sense the intuitive system is often the foundation for what goes on at the conscious, reasoned level. So most often the intuitive system governs our rational thinking unless the more reflective system puts forth a great deal of effort to analyze and override the activity of the intuitive system. But, of course, that analysis and reflection, like so much of our meaning-making activity, is also guided by intuitive assumptions about how the world works.

Finally, current researchers agree that emotion and cognition reciprocally influence each other; Barrett says they are two sides of the same coin. Many experiments in cognitive science laboratories report that result. And we reviewed some of the work by Antonio Damasio, Lisa Feldman Barrett, and others that demonstrate the many ways that our emotions are a crucial part of our information processing. When we are sad or depressed, we remember negative events more than positive ones and our minds seem to work more slowly. When we are afraid, we are more apt to see the world in more black-and-white terms.

So much of what governs our meaning-making is unconscious, out of our awareness and control. We may not be aware of how much the worldviews we hold (whether they are theistic or atheistic) and the conscious reasoning we use to support them are governed by assumptions and sensibilities that are usually outside our conscious awareness. The way we see the world just seems obvious and self-evident to us. We do not experience the functioning of the schemas that organize our experience. Nor are we usually aware of the impact of emotional processes on our cognition; we just find, for example, that we think more negatively when we are sad.

For these reasons, and many others, meaning-making (and all human attempts at understanding) is neurologically and psychologically much richer and more complex than abstractly processing information or making isolated attributions.

So the embodied-relational model advocated here does not undermine the contemporary research on the role of meaning-making in human flourishing and coping with trauma. It does claim that meaning-making is more complex cognitively, neurologically, and phenomenologically than a purely cognitivist model suggests. Meaning is not primarily a mental representation or an attribution but is rather an embodied, affective-cognitive process of acting and relating that brings forth a world and entangles us with it. And that process may be shaped by unconscious dynamics in both the cognitivist sense of implicit cognitive activity and the psychoanalytic sense of personal motivations rooted in childhood experiences.

So the meanings we make are a function of our interactions with the world of our experience. But our experience is also partly a function of what we intentionally do or do not do. The research reviewed here suggests that bodily activity can change how we experience ourselves and the world. Bodily practices intentionally undertaken can shift our experience of self and world and the way we process and make meaningful those experiences. If we want to make, or at least explore, religious meaning we may have to undertake religious practices. Otherwise our religious meanings may feel like ungrounded religious abstractions.

The research reviewed here suggests that meaning-making cannot be a purely cognitive activity simply because there are no purely cognitive activities. Neural wholism holds that affect itself is a form of information processing and that more rule-governed forms of information processing (including natural science and theology) are intimately tied up with our affective systems and intuitive systems and our bodily states. Research reviewed here suggests that there are no ungrounded cognitive processes. Our religious meaning-systems may feel or sound like ungrounded abstractions, especially to those who are not engaged in the practices associated with them, but they are still inevitably linked to affective and bodily processes. Religious meaning-systems may appear ungrounded but that may be because we are unaware of, or unconscious of, the role that body and affect are actually playing in the meanings we affirm and the claims we make. Likewise, scientific and philosophical claims also instantiate the outputs of our unconscious, intuitive, and affective systems.

For example, there is laboratory research suggesting that religious claims are more emotionally salient for religious devotees than for militant atheists. I recently attended a panel discussion between two cognitive scientists, one of whom was devoutly religious and the other was militantly atheistic. Afterward I was talking to the atheist and he remarked in passing that his devout colleague was more emotionally connected to his religion whereas he (the atheist) treated it purely intellectually. I suggested that maybe that was why his colleague was religiously inclined. Yes, he replied, religious is just all emotion. No, that's not what I said, I replied. It's just that atheistic ideas have more emotional salience for you than religious ones do. But both positions are equally grounded in part by affect. He was not happy about that reply but he appeared struck by what seemed to him a new thought (I was struck that it seemed to him like a new thought) that the same theories and analyses that he applied to others' positions also applied to his own. Whatever our worldview or global meaning system, affect and embodiment are deeply involved in constituting it.

This emphasis on embodiment and embodied activity pushes the epistemology of religion and religious meaning in a pragmatic direction—not in a superficial sense that whatever "works" must be "true" (in some sense) but rather that there are truths (maybe all truths) that we will never understand unless we understand their function in the world of lived lives and practice them in whatever way is appropriate. So embodied practice is as central to meaning-making as information processing is.

Such a model suggests that meanings (whether religious or non-religious) arise out of our embodied, reciprocal interaction with our environment. Our sensory experience and our cognitive processing are impacted by our bodily activity, including various bodily practices and disciplines, and by our personal psychological histories. Since meaning is a property of the ways in which we interact with the world, and the ways we interact can be transformed by commitment and bodily practice, then the meanings we make arise out of and can be transformed and refined by the practices we choose to undertake. Choosing or refusing to undertake an embodied spiritual practice may influence what we do, and do not, know about religion and spirituality. So again, making meaning is not simply thinking; it is also engaging in embodied, meaning-making practices. Research supporting this claim in the domain of religion and spirituality and its implications for the religiously lived life will be the subject of the coming chapters.

4

Knowing Religion

RESEARCH REVIEWED SO far has implications for how religion is practiced. We will get to that in the final chapter. Does it also have any implications for how religion is understood? Well, it has implications for how understanding is understood. So that must have implications for how religion is understood. This chapter title, like the title of the book, can be read in two ways: knowing about religion, that is the study *of* religion; and religious knowing, how we might come to have religious knowledge. The first is primarily psychological (at least for purposes of this discussion), the second more theological. Both psychology and theology will be the subject of this chapter

Embodiment and the Study of Religion

Most of the discussion in the contemporary cognitive science of religion (CSR) seems primarily focused on beliefs—and not just cognitive science. Since the Reformation and the Age of Reason, religions in the West have often presented themselves as primarily sets of beliefs. And in ordinary language we often refer to religious devotees as "believers," as though non-religious people don't have any beliefs. Most current cognitive science theories of religion describe how beliefs are arrived at and constrained by the action of natural cognitive mechanisms (my own, rather critical introduction to and review of this material can be found in Jones, 2016). For the CSR, the belief in supernatural agents is seen as the defining characteristic of a religion. Such a belief is a combination of two of CSR's favorite postulated cognitive modules: the hyperactive agency detection system and the theory of mind. This "theory of mind" (not a theory about the mind but a theory that other beings have minds) is a representational system that represents the world as filled with agents with minds. It begins to function as soon as the child comes to understand that human beings have minds, that is, have thoughts, feelings, intentions. A great deal of research suggests that between ages three and five (some research claims even earlier) children start to think of others as being "minded"—holding beliefs (that can be true or false), forming intentions, having feelings. The research also suggests (what every parent knows) that children appear to over-generalize (from the parents' perspective) their "theory of mind" to the pet dog and the stuffed teddy bear.

Based on this model, cognitive scientists who apply evolutionary theory to culture claim that a single evolved cognitive process underlies all religious belief and practice—the recognition of supernatural agency. They argue that humans have evolved a tendency to look for and focus on beings who appear to be intentional agents with minds analogous to human minds. It makes a certain amount of intuitive sense that we would evolve a tendency to attend to, and perhaps over-attend to, other humans and other human-like beings (that is, agents with minds) in the service of survival and reproduction. Hence, for survival it would be better to "over-detect" agents, even when their existence was possible but not certain, than to ignore their presence. Better to assume the rock ahead is a bear or the sound in the grass is a lion than to assume it is only a rock or the wind and become a predator's supper. Thus we evolved a tendency to over-detect the presence of human-like agency around us and to attribute human-like agency to natural forces and events. Religion, then, is the natural (perhaps inevitable) result of this normal cognitive process, which developed through evolution for the sake of survival.

Laboratory research in cognitive science supports the claim that people often attribute agency to ambiguous or clearly non-agentic stimuli. Experiments suggest that as early as the first five months of life, infants perceive agency in the self-propelled and purposeful-looking movement of colored disks. And not just infants. This apparently natural attribution by adults has also been demonstrated in the laboratory. All that seems required to evoke this attribution of agency is that the movements have no obvious external cause and appear goal directed. The figures do not have to look like humans or animals or fictional agents. Justin Barrett called this cognitive system the Hypersensitive Agency Detection Device, universally abbreviated HADD in the literature. Like many of the cognitive processes, unless we consciously work to over-ride it, the HADD unconsciously and automatically delivers to us an experience of agency in the face of ambiguous stimuli. We hear a noise in the night and immediately think of an intruder. When we go and investigate, we find it is only a branch blown against the window by an unusually strong wind. Cognitive scientists who seek to explain the origin of religion rely heavily on the idea of a HADD as a major cause for belief in supernatural agents, and therefore for religion, in both children and adults. Such beliefs do seem to be a species of or a cousin to representations. Experiences and objects are claimed to be represented in the mind as examples of agent activity, the presence of mind, or the result of a cause.

We have argued that human understanding is not simply about formulating amodal, abstract representations about the world. Cognition is not only about representing the world or holding certain propositions. The post-Enlightenment and cognitivist picture is of a mind set apart from and over against the world (a little like God) which has to then represent that world internally. But human understanding can also be theorized as first of all about making one's way in the world as an embodied creature immersed in the world of its experience. "Mental representations" may play a part in that but are not at all the whole story. And from a neuropsychological standpoint, human understanding is much more complex than most CSR models allow for. For example, from its roots in evolutionary psychology, CSR stresses a massively modular view of the mind. However, we have seen reasons to suspect that the brain is not actually organized that way, at least not in the strong sense of modularity that evolutionary psychology seems to demand of the mind (Atran, 2002; Boyer, 2001). (An additional critical analysis of the modularity thesis can be found in Jones, 2016.) Thus the CSR model of religious understanding as consisting only of beliefs is rather over-simplified. And the CSR understanding of beliefs themselves is also over-simplified neuropsychologically.

Scientifically, would the cognitive science of religion project change if it adopted a more embodied approach? Such a move would shift it away from simply attending to propositional beliefs (in chapter 5 we discuss how theology might change if it shifted away from a primary focus on abstract beliefs). After such a move, scientific research might address questions such as, How does religion help or hinder our making our way through the world as embodied creatures? What beliefs and practices aid and hinder that? For example, research on stress and religious coping (which are profoundly embodied phenomena) might be reformulated as the study of the contribution of lived religion to human flourishing and include, for example, the physiological dimensions of stress and coping and the specific impact of embodied religious practices on those physiological markers of stress. Shortly we will turn to the epistemic aspects of this point.

Theologically, how might a consideration of embodiment impact our religious claims? An embodied theology is not a theology of the body but rather a set of reflections on the ways in which embodied metaphors get deployed theologically. What bodily metaphors are drawn on when we reflect on the Trinity, or the meaning of *shunyata*, or the relationship of Brahma and Atman? What implications do such embodied metaphors import into our believing and theologizing? What implicit meanings come into our theology when we speak of the church or the Eucharistic bread or the cosmos as the "body of Christ?" Or when people are called on to "digest the Word of God" or assert they are "standing on the promises of God"? The insistence that virtually all metaphors are grounded bodily might provide additional insight into the functioning of religious language.

For example, in the early 1960s when I first seriously encountered religion and began thinking about it (remember that I was not raised in any religious tradition), there was a major controversy about literalism and religious language. Much of this was driven by the German biblical scholar Rudolph Bultmann and his countryman the theologian Paul Tillich. Bultmann advocated a process he called "de-mythologizing," which meant translating a literalistic interpretation of the language of the Bible into more contemporary philosophical (and therefore more abstract-sounding) language. Bultmann's particular target was what he assumed was the biblical writers' "three-story" view of the world—heaven "above," hell "below," the earth in between. Thus the biblical texts and Christian creeds speak of Jesus "coming down from heaven," "descending to hell," "ascending back to heaven." How literally and physically the early Christians meant these phrases is something we don't know. Bultmann and many of his contemporaries assumed these phrases were originally meant very literally, although many early Christians were very allegorical in their treatment of their sacred texts. For example, in the New Testament, Paul writes about Moses striking a rock in the desert and water coming forth, and comments allegorically "the rock is Christ." And Gregory of Nyssa, among the most orthodox of the orthodox church fathers, writes a commentary on the books of Moses in the Hebrew Bible called *The Life of Moses* that is flamboyantly allegorical. In fact, literalism is a modern, post–scientific revolution phenomenon and so it is not wise to assume that the early Christians were literalistic in the modern sense in their interpretation of sacred texts. But there are certainly people today who claim to take them literally but again it is not clear what that really means. But any literalizing interpretations are clearly the target of Bultmann's argument.

We have looked at research that suggests we inevitably see the world from the perspective of our bodies and our sense of our location in space. Our perceptual apparatus means that we naturally see ourselves as located in three-dimensional Euclidian space with ourselves in the middle and directions or vectors of perception radiating out from our center in all possible directions. And for reasons that are not entirely clear but that are profoundly embodied, these directions naturally acquire cognitive and affective meanings. Up is good: we say things are "looking up" and research suggests that looking upward improves mood. Conversely down is bad: we say "the boss is really feeling down today, watch out" and research suggests that looking down or slumping down makes one feel depressed, vulnerable, and ineffective. These spatial metaphors are not simply the result of an archaic worldview; they are the natural and inevitable result of our embodied cognitions and perceptions.

A program to excise them from our theological, devotional, and homiletical discourse is bound to fail. Better to continue to use the language that resonates with our embodied cognition and use one's theological energy to make the point (if necessary) that such language is not literal and descriptive but metaphoric or symbolic (like most embodied language). And to offer alternative (non-literal) ways of understanding how theological metaphors work and what they mean. Hopefully this embodied perspective might free theologians from needless anxiety about the spatial metaphors that are so common in religious discourse. Given our embodied condition, such metaphors are inevitable.

Embodiment and Religious Research

In the process of social-psychological research into religion, an awareness of the impact of our embodiment might also drive a specific kind of self-reflexivity. We might consider the role of the body in conducting any research project and in interpreting the results. Again, what bodily metaphors do we draw on in formulating research questions, drawing up questionnaires, and formulating interpretations of our results? Again what implications do such embodied metaphors import into our researching and interpreting?

A focus on lived religion underscores the role of embodied activities, not disembodied reflections, in human life. While the cognitive science of religion seems to define religion primarily as a set of beliefs, the position taken here would suggest instead that religion is primarily a set of embodied practices. To really understand religion means understanding those practices. We use our bodies to experience what is held sacred: kneel in prayer, sit in meditation, dance with Jesus or Krishna, whirl with Allah, kiss the Torah. Some sense the healing power of God as electricity-like sensations in their bodies.

There are St. Theresa's orgasmic revelations. People see the Virgin Mary or the Goddess Tara or their deceased guru in perceptions experientially indistinguishable from more ordinary perceptions and so presumably involving many of the same neural pathways; likewise with hearing the "voice" of God. Thus bodily perception is crucial in much of the religious life.

This suggests several ways in which psychologists might incorporate the body in their research into religion. Again we might research the role of the body in religious practice. Does imagining doing a ritual have the same effect as performing it physically? Does walking meditation function differently from sitting meditation? Already psychologists are researching these areas. There are already decades of studies of the effects of meditation (which we return to in chapter 5). And there are scores of neuro-imaging studies that seek to uncover what is happening in the brain when people meditate and pray. And I know of several ongoing research projects on the effects of posture on prayer experiences and on the psychophysiology associated with prayer. For example, a recent study found that posture can influence religious attitudes (Fuller & Montgomery, 2015). Subjects (most of whom identified as religiously committed) were significantly more inclined to endorse more conventional religious ideas after sitting in a slouched position or down on the ground than similar subjects who sat in a chair in a relaxed upright position or stood upright with their hands on a table. This study stands in the line of studies that find upright postures to increase attitudes of power and autonomy while slouched and low postures reduce feelings of power. Another found that when Catholic nuns changed their postures and motions during their prayers, their sense of the meaning of the prayers also changed (Corwin, 2012; see also Ladd et al., 2007). From such studies we learn that posture and other physical activities change the experience of prayer and the meanings derived from it as well as the associated psychophysical sensations. Finding significant effects for posture and movement supports the claim that embodiment is important to religious experience and understanding its role is important for understanding religion.

There is much to study here. One can envision qualitative, narrative research that deeply explores different experiences involved in eating the Eucharistic bread and wine. Or how approaching a shrine kneeling differs from walking toward it. Or the effects of bowing when entering the Zendo or Dojo. How does touching one's head to the ground when praying in Islam or davening in Orthodox Judaism, or Sufi whirling, or doing the hundred thousand prostrations in Tibetan Buddhism change one's cognitive processes? How does listening to crystalline chanting and singing in a medieval cathedral or chapel where all the senses are evoked at once shift one's state of consciousness? All such studies directly address some of the possible connections between embodiment and spiritual practice. They demonstrate various ways that spirituality is something done with the body as well as the mind and the spirit.

These are just hints of some of the ways that incorporating an embodied perspective might impact the cognitive science of religion, theology, and social scientific research generally: moving cognitive science away from an over-reliance on simplistic models of representation, expanding the theologian's understanding of metaphor, deepening the social scientist's awareness of the implications of the terms they use, and increasing the focus on the effect of bodily practices.

Another Way of Knowing

We have reviewed research here that supports the claim that human understanding is a whole body process, not a disembodied one. If we are to know God (or the *Brahman* or *Dharmakyia*), it is with our bodies, not just with our minds or brains. This suggests at least two things:

(1)   When we are thinking about God, knowing God, experiencing God (or some other religious object), we are using our bodies (even if we are perfectly still in sitting meditation or contemplation). The process of shifting our awareness, focusing our attention, thinking about concepts, all evoke psychophysiological activities in our brains and in our bodies. Our attention may be stilled, our bodies calm, but psychophysiological activity goes on: brain waves shift, heartbeat and respiration change, oxygen consumption drops. These are not just effects passively caused by adopting a meditative stance; they are part and parcel of the meditative stance itself and its associated experiences.

(2)   Embodied practices can help us know God, or maybe they are even necessary to know God. Embodied practices do not simply add to what we know, but they also change *how* we know. Living religious experience is not simply about knowing new things (gods or angels or bodhisattvas) in the same old way that we know tables and chairs. Rather, religious experience is also about knowing old things (like ourselves, nature, sacred texts and practices) in a new way. The shift that takes place through spiritual practice is not simply that we have added some new objects to our list of things that we know in our usual way. The shift that takes place is that we are developing other ways of knowing (Jones, 1972). That is part of what the spiritual senses tradition means when it talks about a

new spiritual sense. Even if turns out that that phrase refers to a transformation in our ordinary senses and not literally the creation or uncovering of a new sensory faculty, it still points to the reality that spiritual practice can produce other ways of knowing. That is part of what it means to say that religious knowing is transformational knowing. Embodied practices transform our way of knowing; they generate other ways of knowing. This point we return to and illustrate more extensively in chapter 5.

But why do we need another way of knowing? Why a new (or re-newed) religious epistemology now? Let us put that question in its historical context. In the last century, positivism or verificationism and cognitivism made reference and representation the central epistemological concerns not just for cognitive science but also, indirectly, for philosophy of religion and theology as well. These issues of representation and reference have bedeviled theology, at least since Kant, and actually they go back to the earliest religious thinkers. They are not new issues or simply post-Kantian, modern issues. But they made particular trouble for theology in the modern world. If understanding is representing, especially representing in a detached, amodal way (as required for understanding on a strict cognitivist model), then how in the world can we claim to know God who, by definition, cannot be represented?

One solution to the problem of theological knowledge that is beyond representation has been to invoke symbolism or analogy. We represent God using symbols, not literal representations. This is somewhat on an analogy with physics, which also invokes "entities" that are not really entities in an ordinary sense—"particles" without mass, "particles" that travel backward in time, fields of force, curved space. These, of course, can be represented symbolically, that is, using mathematical symbols. The power of these mathematical, symbolic representations is that they fit together in elegant and coherent ways. And they can be tied back indirectly to experience (for example, the tracking lines on a bubble-chamber photograph). In systematic theologies and religious philosophies (Aquinas's *Summa*, Tsong Kappa's *Lam Rim*), religious symbols too can fit together in elegant and coherent ways. And they can be tied back indirectly to experience (the order found in nature, mystical moments, insights generated by meditative and contemplative practices).

But even when understood as symbols, these religious forms are still often taken to be referential representations in some sense: to represent God even if symbolically, to refer to God even if indirectly. And so the question of how they could possibly represent God or refer to what is beyond the finite world continues to plague theology. Both those believers who vigorously defend religious belief as referential in some sense and those atheists who vigorously oppose them agree with the cognitivist model that understanding means working with representations. That agreement is the basis on which they can oppose one another. On the other hand, we have suggested that an embodied-relational psychological paradigm, and much of neuroscience in general, can move us away from an abstract view of representation and the model of direct reference toward an understanding of understanding that is both more complex and more pragmatic. Such a movement weakens and constrains the positivism that powers much of the popular atheism in the modern world. And it also opens up the possible reconsideration of religious knowing and the justification of religious claims (for a discussion of the relationship between contemporary atheism and positivism, see Jones, 2016). The weakening of positivism and verificationism opens a space in which to look for other ways of knowing.

We should note that a similar trajectory took place at about the same time in the philosophy of science. The Vienna Circle and Russell and Whitehead sought a totally formal, completely abstract model of science and therefore (in their eyes) of all knowledge. A direct and rather concrete understanding of representation and reference were central to the positivists principle of verification in which the only legitimate verification came through direct reference to sense experience, thus idealizing the correspondence theory of truth (that true claims are only those that can be shown to "correspond" to reality). The cognitivist model of reference mirrored the correspondence theory of truth and the Vienna Circle's ideal of knowledge that they modeled directly on their understanding of science, which was (for them) the only source of knowledge. Cognition was modeled as the manipulation or computation, in rule-governed processes, of bounded, completely abstract internal representations of sense experience. Once this process was completely formalized, it would be "multiply-realizable," that is, enactable not only in brains but in any number of different kinds of computational machines.

The positivist, cognitivist goal of a completely formalized and validated system shipwrecked in several ways: Goedel demonstrated that a completely formalized system could not be proven to be consistent and would still contain true propositions that could not be demonstrated to be true within that system. Studies of the actual conduct of science (like those of Hanson, Kuhn, Toulmin) found it to be much messier than could be easily formalized. The crucial distinction between data and theory collapsed as scholars realized that the data are never "raw" or "neutral" but are always approached in the context of some theory. Thus the "correspondence theory of truth" was found not to correspond to any truth. All this directly cut the ground out from under any simple positivism and verificationism and indirectly cut the ground out from under the dismissal of religious knowledge that positivism engendered. This positivistic model of knowledge was replaced either by a more open and flexible model of science as in Imre Lakatos, or a radically pluralistic one as in Paul Feyerabend, or a purely pragmatic model as in Stephen Toulmin. This story has been told in several places (Brown, 1979; Urmson, 1969; and by me in Jones, 1981) and recently summarized by the philosopher William Abraham in a way relevant to the topic of this book when he wrote in 2013 about what he calls evidentialism which is similar to what I am calling verificationism,

> In Britain this was undermined (in a story that has never been properly told) by the work of Basil Mitchel. . . . Mitchel attacked the hidden assumptions about the nature of evidence and cracked open the whole evidentialist enterprise from within. In North America, as we know, Alvin Plantinga and others dismantled the whole evidentialist enterprise more radically by challenging the need for the kind of evidence that [evidentialism] championed. We now know the whole field of epistemology is up for grabs; the range of *desiderata* has multiplied; so the space for robust forms of theism is enormous. . . . More generally, the wider changes in epistemology over the last generation have completely altered the landscape where the prospects for theology are concerned. (3)

My suggestion is that neuropsychological research on embodiment both contributes to this dismantling of positivism (by weakening over-reliance on abstract models of representation) and also expands the framework for epistemological discussion and thus can be doubly helpful to theology.

However, if you demote or complexify the idea of human understanding as the manipulation of internal representations and direct reference, what do you put in its place? What is knowledge if not simply representation of and reference to something known? Research on the role of embodiment offers at least two alternatives.

One alternative beyond strict representationalism is that rather than only the formal computing of disembodied, amodal representations (ones that seem completely disengaged from any sensory modes), human understanding almost always engages multi-modal sensory, bodily episodes. Remembering or thinking about a cup evokes all the physiological processes associated with picking up a cup. Understanding a friend's sadness involves modeling that sadness (through the use of so-called mirror neurons) in ourselves. One way of conceptualizing this entanglement of understanding with embodiment is to view understanding primarily as a process of simulation rather than representation. In this vein, Yeh and Barsalou (2006) write, "People represent a category by simulating experiences of its members. To represent chairs, for example, people simulate the experience of a chair. Besides representing how a chair might look and feel, people might simulate actions taken toward chairs, introspective evaluations about their aesthetics and comfort, and so on. . . . We assume that a multimodal simulator underlies a concept" (351–352). To know something, then, is to simulate it in an embodied way. Reflecting on the possibility of a life beyond death or experiencing a meditative insight into the ultimate origin and constitution of the self or connecting a passage from a sacred text to a life problem can be understand as embodied, multi-modal simulations that may be psychologically or spiritually compelling.

But what would make such simulations compelling? Research suggests that so-called abstract concepts are more complex, that is, their simulations cross and involve more cognitive domains than concrete concepts (see, for example, Barsalou & Weimer-Hastings, 2005) and may therefore involve more modalities. What may make an abstract concept more compelling is the number of different domains it may evoke and connect together. There is an important research implication here. This suggests a simple study in which subjects are asked to list their associations to God, church, and so on (or comparable terms in their tradition) in one minute. Comparisons could be made among devoted believers and less devoted believers, agnostics, and militant atheists. The hypothesis would be that more devout believers would produce more extensive and elaborate associations as exemplified in the studies reported in Barsalou and Weimer-Hastings (2005). Presumably those who found such terms as "God" or "creation" compelling would have more associations to these terms.

A similar study could be conducted along narrative lines. Subjects would be asked to narrate episodes when they thought of God (or Jesus, or the Buddha, or Krishna, for example) and to describe their thoughts, feelings, memories, bodily sensations. Going beyond a list of associations, a narrative might evoke some of the different domains involved in the hypothesized simulation occurring during these thoughts. So the model of cognition as multi-modal simulation presents one empirically testable alternative to the cognitivist claim that religious cognition is primarily abstract representation. Instead, a claim is found to be compelling in part, not simply because it has been demonstrated to represent something external, but rather because it is richly associated with other claims and experiences.

Another alternative to demoted ideas of representation and reference besides conceiving of human understanding as embodied simulation, coming out of an embodied-relational model, is a pragmatic turn. Understanding is here modeled as a way of making one's way through life. One might study the ways in which people are aided in interacting with the world of experience by doing so in a religious way—being guided by a set of moral guidelines (of course non-religious people do that too but for the religious person these moral guides are embedded in a larger, transmoral context of worship, life in community, study of a tradition, etc.), prayerfully seeking the presence of God in everyday events, being grateful to God for positive events and relying on "religious coping" when disasters befall one, reflecting regularly on sacred teachings, practicing meditation and contemplation. If living in this way is found to be helpful and lead to flourishing, then that serves as a support for the religiously lived life (Barrett & Wildman, 2009).

Much post-Kantian theology has been obsessed with the problem of justification. The cognitive dimension of the religious life is virtually reduced to trying to obtain a state of justified belief. This, of course, goes along with a cognitivist concern about representation. The question of justification is in part a question of representation. How can we justify our claim that our beliefs actually represent something real? If we demote or complexify the category of representation and supplement or replace it with a more complex and pragmatically oriented approach, paralleling the more pragmatic turn in the philosophy of science, then the issue of justification shifts from providing warrants for abstract beliefs to providing examples of the gains of living by those beliefs. Here the extensive psychological research on topics such as religious coping, religion and health, post-traumatic growth, the possible pro-social impact of religion (as reviewed in chapter 3) turn out to have epistemological as well as psychological and epidemiological importance.

For example, research finds consistent correlations between religiosity and well-being, happiness, and flourishing, although the correlations can differ depending on how religiosity is measured and the cultural context of the devotees (recent review in Lun & Bond, 2013; see also Myers, 2000). Decades of research on religion and mental health have consistently found that many religious beliefs and practices significantly contribute to mental and physical health (reviews in Jones, 2004; Miller & Kelley, 2005; Oman & Thoresen, 2005). And religion's ability to contribute to psychophysical resilience and help people cope with the vicissitudes of life is widely recognized in the psychological literature (reviews in Gall & Guirguis-Younger, 2013; Koenig, 2013). If the results of our cognitive processes are partly justified in terms of how they help us make our way through the world, then these avenues of empirical work offer justification for commitment to the religiously lived life.

In addition to this empirical research on the positive impact of the religiously lived life, there are other, obvious, practical effects of such a life. One of them, which circles back on the epistemological issues we've been discussing, is the grounding religion gives to ethical values. This is important epistemologically, and not just morally, because of the developing area of what is often called "virtue epistemology." For example, the philosopher Wayne Riggs argues that a broad notion of understanding or wisdom may be a higher epistemic good than acquiring justified true beliefs. He writes, "The focus on propositions, truth, justification, and knowledge that has been the mainstay of epistemology for some time is not appropriate to the subject of epistemic virtue. Our epistemic aspirations go beyond the mere collection of true propositions, even beyond the acquisition of knowledge" (2003: 226). Virtue is as important as propositional knowledge to the rationally well-lived life. Virtue, these philosophers argue, may be essential to our deeper epistemological goals. Along with providing arguments and evidentiary experiences, by providing values and moral guidance, religions can contribute to the search for virtuous knowledge and thereby provide another pragmatic support for the lived religious life.

Embodiment-based research not only allows for a broader range of justifications for religious belief; it radically alters the nature of belief itself. I have been suggesting that post-Kantian epistemology has been too narrowly focused on issues of representation, reference, and finding warrants for beliefs. It has been reinforced in this by certain trends in cognitive science that have depended on a singularly cognitivist model. These are important issues. And brilliant work has been done on them by contemporary philosophers of religion (Alston, Plantinga, and Swinburne). And given that an (outmoded) positivism (which focuses on precisely those issues) seems to dominate the public discussion of theism, atheism, and religion in the West, it remains crucial for theologians to continue to creatively address and resolve those quasi-positivistic issues.

So, an embodied-relational paradigm makes two important contributions to the contemporary discussion in theological epistemology. First, as we have seen, research coming out of an embodied-relational paradigm underscores some of the problems and limitations with approaches that focus only on concerns regarding representation and reference. And this, in turn, should constrain appeals to early twentieth-century positivistic and verificationist criteria in discussions of religious issues.

Second, an embodied-relational paradigm offers theology at least two alternative, empirically grounded, epistemological paths away from that earlier positivism and cognitivism.

One alternative to the positivist epistemology, as we have seen, is a more complex, multi-modal model of cognition as embodied simulation that involves more attention to the connection between cognition and affect and an acknowledgment of the role of somatosensory activity in cognition. Attention to these factors would necessarily enrich our models of representation. More fully understood, religious cognition (like all cognition) is more than simply the manipulation of abstract representations of sense experience. Therefore appropriate means of validating a commitment to a religiously lived life must logically involve more complex processes of validation than merely justifying separate religious claims with reference to discrete sense experiences. Epistemological attacks on religion that only refer to individual beliefs taken out of context miss the target of the fully lived religious life by many miles.

Another alternative to positivism for theology is a pragmatic appreciation of the epistemological importance of the impact of lived religion (as researched by psychologists and others in areas such as coping, resilience, health, meaning-making, pro-sociality, and so on) in the evaluation and validation of religious commitments. Such psychological research generally supports the day-to-day significance of the fully lived religious life.

To summarize this section on epistemological pluralism in theology, as seen from an embodied-relational perspective, belief is no longer simply a cognitive state. Beliefs (in any domain) are much richer and more complex realities than simply ideas or opinions about what is or is not the case. Beliefs are not simply the result of abstract computational processes acting on sense data; rather, they arise from complex, interacting non-linear dynamics involving not just physical sensing and rational thinking but also emotional processing, bodily simulations, and inputs coming in below the level of awareness. Our sense organs are not just input devices to feed computational machines in our heads. Our sense organs and the entire, interconnected neural networks and muscle spindles they are joined with are all constituent parts of the act of believing and claiming to know. Simple beliefs about the sheer existence of physical objects, for example, are also multi-modal; but these less complex beliefs may involve fewer cognitive interconnections and the simulation of fewer sensory modalities. But research suggests that cognitively sophisticated concepts in theology (along with the natural sciences, the humanities, and cognitive neuroscience itself) are complex, multi-modal, embodied activities (Barsalou & Weimer-Hastings, 2005; Yeh & Barsalou, 2006). For purposes of empirical investigation, cognitive neuroscience must necessarily narrow its focus and radically reduce that complexity. But we must never completely lose sight of that complexity when we make claims and evaluate arguments, especially in the case of religion. In brief, an embodied-relational perspective broadens epistemological discourse. And in such a broadened epistemological framework, religion may appear more epistemologically compelling and its claims more solidly justified than it does in narrower, cognitivist, and positivist frameworks.

Perceiving God: Embodied-Relational Knowing and the Argument from Religious Experience

In the West, since at least the Reformation, religion has been increasingly conceived of as a set of beliefs. And since the so-called Age of Reason those beliefs have increasingly been questioned. When religion is thought of as a set of beliefs, two challenging questions immediately occurred: how do such beliefs arise, and how might they be justified? One common answer to both questions has been the existence of religious experience. Some claim that religious experiences are the source of religious beliefs and their occurrence provides the best evidence for the truth of those beliefs.

Conversely, others have proposed naturalistic answers to the first question—the source of religious beliefs—and argued that such naturalistic accounts of the origin of religious experiences and their concomitant religious beliefs eliminates the second question—the truthfulness of religious beliefs—from consideration. One of the first to do this was Sigmund Freud who provided an alternative account of the origin of religious beliefs that he thought rendered them impossible to justify (an analysis of Freud's argument can be found in Jones, 1996). A more current parallel answer to the first question is provided by the proponents of evolutionary, cognitive psychology, many of whom also feel that their answer to the first question eliminates the second (for a critical review, see Jones, 2016). Both Freud and many contemporary cognitive scientists seek to demonstrate (correctly in many cases) that natural, human factors are at work in the production of religious beliefs. But they seem to then assume, without offering any arguments, that the presence of those natural processes within religious belief and practice means that religious claims are false. It is almost universally asserted that such findings prove that religion is a purely natural phenomenon. Clearly these findings do no such thing. All they suggest is that natural, human processes are at work in religion (something virtually no one denies). That does not logically mean that *only* natural processes are present; rather, it simply entails that some of the processes involved in religion are natural. If it should be the case (and I am not arguing that it is the case) that some non-natural processes were also at work in the development of a religious outlook, a purely naturalistic method would never find them (remember that schemas and frames of reference allow us to see some things and blind us to others). As a psychologist of religion I certainly think that religion is a human phenomenon. I am not arguing otherwise here. I am just pointing out that Freud and contemporary cognitive science find common human cognitive processes are at work in religion. That's all.

Obviously I think that the psychology of religion in its many forms adds to our knowledge of religion in important ways. But logically it does not go beyond that to eliminate all other possible factors. Some seem to assume that if natural processes are at work, nothing else can be. But no argument is offered to support that assumption. Why the assumption that there must only be one set of causes or influences at work in the world? That the world is not complex enough to contain a plurality of influences? Can we not count beyond one?

Such findings cannot be used to prove (in a strong sense) that religion is simply a natural phenomenon. Rather, these findings assume that religion is a natural human phenomenon. Such an assumption is basic to any scientific study of religion. Any psychological study of religion must begin from that assumption; otherwise, religion could not be an object of scientific investigation. But having started by assuming that religion is a natural phenomenon, one cannot then turn around and say that the cognitive science of religion proves it. To argue that way is to mistake conclusion for premise.

Justin Barrett has addressed the same concern about whether naturalistic explanations make other accounts necessarily irrational or unconvincing. He argues at length that there is no logical or necessary reason to always prefer naturalistic explanations and that providing naturalistic explanations does not logically or necessarily vitiate religious claims (Barrett, 2007). Clark and Barrett state the obvious when they write, "Showing that natural causes are involved in the production of a belief tells us nothing about the truth or falsity of that belief. . . . Both natural and supernatural explanations may be true" (2011: 655).

From cognitive science we learn that religious ideas and behaviors are human artifacts, utilizing human cognitive systems, and that they are constrained and shaped by these systems. The same is no doubt true of economics, physics, and cognitive science. But we do not usually say that tells us anything about the truth of the claims found in those domains. A person who studies the motivations that propel a person to be an economist and the cognitions employed there would be (to paraphrase a statement I heard from Justin Barrett) flabbergasted if someone said his research answered the question of whether the law of supply and demand holds true in a globalized economy. A person who studies the motivations that propel a person to be a physicist and the cognitions employed there would be flabbergasted if someone said his research answered the question of whether string theory is correct. Freud and some cognitive psychologists say that learning about the motivations that propel a person's religious practices and the cognitions employed there implies that religion false. That is a serious logical error (Clark & Barrett, 2011; Visala, 2014). As the atheistic philosopher J. L. Mackie, having reviewed the history of such arguments, put it, "Even an adequate, unified natural history which incorporated all these factors would not in itself amount to a disproof of theism. . . . [N]o account of the origin of a belief can settle the question of whether that belief is true or not" (1982: 197). As a psychologist of religion, I am certainly convinced that religious experiences involve natural, human neuropsychological processes. But that does not suggest either that naturalistic models alone provide a complete account of such experiences nor that the presence of these natural processes automatically vitiates the religious claims derived from them.

On the other hand, many post-Enlightenment theologians invoked the occurrence of religious experience as both the source of religious beliefs and a justification for them. This was in line with the post-Enlightenment outlook that insisted that knowledge arose directly from experience. In this process our minds were essentially passive blank slates on which sense experience wrote beliefs. Implicit here was a parallel between religious experience and sense experience. As we shall see in chapter 5, this analogy has a long tradition in Christian theology. But in the early days of Christian theology the parallel performed a very different function than it did in post-Enlightenment thought. In the modern period, the epistemological function of religious experience has been primarily to serve as a warrant for religious beliefs in a way analogous to using sense experience to warrant beliefs about external reality: how do I know there is a tree there? I see it with my own eyes. How do I know God exists? I experience "His" presence. But religious experience is far from indubitable. So it turned out that in order to use religious experience to warrant religious beliefs, one first had to provide warrants for the veracity of religious experience. And one might therefore soon find oneself in an infinite regress of warrants for warrants.

One of the most brilliant modern attempts to rescue the use of sense perception as a model for religious experience and to use it to warrant religious beliefs is William Alston's 1991 book *Perceiving God*. The core of Alston's argument is what he calls his "Theory of Appearing." The thrust of this theory is to reject the notion that all experience is mediated or categorized; some is direct and immediate. Alston writes

> I do not agree . . . that all experience of objects involves interpretation, taking an object to be such-and-such. No doubt normal, adult perception, and spiritual perception as well, is heavily conceptualized. . . . Normal perception is shot through with "interpretation." Nevertheless, what makes this a matter of perceiving a house, rather than just thinking about it or remembering it, is the fact of *presentation, givenness*, the fact that something is presented to consciousness, is something of which I am *directly aware*. . . . Thus I cannot agree that to perceive a house *is* to interpret our experience as manifesting a house." (1991: 27–28, italics in original)

Thus "sensory experience essentially involves a *presentation* of objects to consciousness in a way that does not *necessarily* involve the application of general concepts to those objects" (1991: 38, italics in original). That is Alston's "Theory of Appearing."

This, of course, is not really a "Theory" of appearing but is rather a phenomenological description of appearing. The *experience* of sense perception is clearly direct and immediate in the way Alston describes. We do not experience some red, green, and black sense-data and then reflectively interpret that as meaning that we are seeing a brick house with a green lawn and shingled roof. Rather, we just "see a house." Later, of course, in describing the experience we will use concepts like house, bricks, lawns, and so on. And if asked to defend the claim that we really saw a house, we will again describe in detail the features of our experience that go with the objects we call houses—roofs, windows, doors. But Alston rejects the idea that the deployment of such concepts is involved in the direct perception of the house. "From the fact that we use concepts to identify something as of a certain type (How else?!), it does *not* follow that *what* we are identifying 'involves' concepts or judgments"

(1991: 41, italics in original). Concepts and judgments inevitably enter into our descriptions and justifications of our experiences when challenged, but the "raw" experience of something present to my senses is immediate.

From here it is, for Alston, only a short distance to characterize certain types of religious (he uses the word "mystical") experiences as forms of perception. He includes several first-person accounts of people's experiences of God in which they clearly use sensory, perceptual language to describe their experiences ("God was present . . . my consciousness perceived him"; "I saw Christ at my side or, to put it better, I was conscious of Him"; "[the soul] sees Him [God] clearer than one man sees another." Quotes from 1991: 13). Such statements fit easily within Alston's "Theory of Appearing" in which something appears or is presented to the subject (1991: 55); that is, "mystical experience can be construed as *perception* in the same generic sense of the term as sense perception" (1991: 66).

For the religious person there is clear epistemological gain here. In response to the obvious question as to whether mystical experience is really an experience of a divine reality, Alston has a ready answer—"the question of whether mystical experience does count as a genuine perception of God is just a question of whether it is what it seems to its subject to be" (1991: 66). Rather than having to provide a (potentially endless) string of warrants for one's beliefs, a "perceptual construal" means "that a claim to be perceiving God is prima facie acceptable just on its own merits . . . provided that a direct realist understanding of perception is in general possible" (1991: 67, 66).

But Alston stands in the tradition of defending religion as a set of beliefs. So his task remains demonstrating that religious experience, or more precisely, religious/mystical perceptions, can serve as a valid basis for beliefs based on those perceptions. While some perceptual beliefs involve a network of other beliefs (I see a vapor trail in the sky and believe a plane has probably passed overhead even though I don't see it), some, Alston argues "are based on perceptual experience *directly*" (1991: 78, italics in original). I believe there is a man walking down the street because I see a man walking down the street. I may be mistaken that it is my friend John but I cannot be mistaken that I see a man walking down the street. Of course it might be a transsexual but Alston is impatient with counterfactuals like that. A skeptic might reply that one's belief that there is a man there is not direct but rather is based on the belief that you are seeing a man walking down the street. Alston considers it a "decisive refutation" of that position that we do not normally find it necessary to formulate a belief about our experience in order to rely on it. Rather "experiential presentations themselves are quite enough to elicit belief about

the perceived object" (1991: 82). Rejecting his position, he says, confuses what
a belief is based on (in this case, direct perception) and what is required to defend or justify that belief if challenged (presenting assumptions and warrants
about the experience). So while acknowledging that "background beliefs not
infrequently figure in the total basis of perceptual belief," there remains "con-
siderable scope for purely immediately justified perceptual beliefs" (1991: 93).
Among such, Alston argues, are beliefs about God arising from and justified
by mystical perceptions.

But is it really valid to rely on mystical perceptions to justify religious
beliefs? Having argued for the fundamental, phenomenological equality of
mystical perceptions and sense perceptions, Alston turns and makes a stunning
move. He argues that there is no way to demonstrate conclusively that sense
perception is reliable! He goes through an extensive catalogue of arguments
used to demonstrate the reliability of sense perception (that sense perception
has a record of reliability, that we rely on sense perception, and so on and so
on) and shows that each one is clearly circular. They all presuppose what they
seek to demonstrate—the reliability of sense perception. If challenged on my
claim that there is a tree outside my office window, I can enumerate what I am
seeing and point out that these are the characteristics of trees in my part of
the country. But I only know these are characteristics of trees and that the
comparison holds by relying on sense perception. I may experience an illusion in which two lines appear to be different lengths but on measurement
they turn out to be the same. But the only way I know the measurement is
accurate is through sense perception. I can only verify my sense perception in
terms of my sense perception. And I cannot argue for the validity of a perceptual belief that there is a tree outside my window without talking about trees.
So, Alston concludes, "We are unable to give a non-circular demonstration,
or even a strong supporting argument for the reliability of SP [sense percep-
tion]" (1991: 143).

Is his point that we should be radical skeptics and not rely on sense perception? Certainly not! Such a position is impossible to live out in practice.
Rather we should recognize that "epistemic circularity does not prevent justification" (1991: 148). That I must rely on sense experience and categories
directly connected to an experience (using tree language to explain seeing a
tree) in order to justify beliefs based on that experience should not vitiate
that justification. Thus we come back to where we began (and perhaps see it
anew). Alston concludes, therefore "it is eminently *reasonable* for us to form
beliefs in the ways we standardly do" (1991: 159, italics in original), that is by
using what Alston calls "doxastic practices" (practices that form our beliefs).

Standard doxastic practices are warranted through a "practical rationality"; that is, that they are acceptable if they are internally consistent and do not directly contradict other established practices in any fundamental way and have proven to be useful and reliable over time. Of such a practice, it is *"rational to suppose that its doxastic outputs are prima facie justified"* (1991: 183, italicized in original).

Arguments can certainly be brought against the reliability of mystical perception and the justification of beliefs based on it. However, since mystical perception and sense perception are closely allied, any strong arguments against the reliability of mystical perception would also tell against sense perception—for example, that we must use religious language (based on religious beliefs and experiences) to describe and validate such experiences. But we have seen that exactly the same circularity characterizes the description and justification of sense experiences. We must use "tree language" or "house language" to justify our belief that we have seen a tree or a house. If that is no bar to validating ordinary sense experience, it should be no bar to validating mystical experience. And, Alston claims, religious traditions fit the criteria for established doxastic practices and so the beliefs produced by them on the basis of mystical perceptions should also be granted prima facie justification.

It is important to note that Alston has done two things here: (1) he has produced arguments showing that religious perceptions are similar enough to ordinary sense experience that arguments that would undermine the validity of religious perceptions would also undermine the validity of ordinary sense experience; and (2) he has argued that it is rational to claim that beliefs based on religious experience are thereby justified when religious perceptions are located in the context of accepted doxastic practices. The second depends on the first in a way that the first does not depend on the second. I cannot use religious perceptions to justify religious beliefs without first showing that religious perceptions are valid perceptions. But I can claim that religious experience is a valid form of perception without necessarily using that claim to justify a set of beliefs. That is, religious perceptions, if valid in some sense, may perform functions other than justifying a set of beliefs. That is the subject of chapter 5.

From the perspective I've taken here, there is much to approve of in Alston's argument. Especially important is his defense of religious perceptions. He is clearly correct that most (if not all) of the arguments usually deployed against religious experience as a form of perception would also undermine the veridicality of ordinary sense perception. Or, to put it more positively, it is reasonable enough to conceptualize religious experience as a form of perception that can give rise to and validate religious beliefs in the context of religious doxastic practices, and that such practices can be warranted by practical reason, that is, by the kind of pragmatic justifications discussed previously in this chapter.

On the other hand, his "Theory of Appearing" is not as convincing in the context of contemporary psychology. Phenomenologically, perceptional experience clearly has that direct, immediate quality that Alston attributes to it. But how much epistemic weight can that be given? Very little, I think, given that even a perceptual experience that feels unmediated is, neuropsychologically, incredibly complex. For example, color perception is often taken as the epitome of direct perception; it is claimed that one cannot be mistaken that one is "seeing red" if the color "red" appears. But it turns out that different cultures divide the spectrum up very differently, and some have many more color terms than others, so presumably some may not even see what we call red. It is also the case that the same "red" object appears to be a different shade or hue when placed next to differently colored objects or in front of differently colored backgrounds. Gibbs (2005: 44–45) cites studies that demonstrate color vision is not simply retinal impressions and that "color" does not mark out a simple property of objects in the world. In this regard Varela et al. write, "We cannot account for our experience of color as an attribute of things in the world by appealing simply to the intensity and wavelength composition of the light reflected from the area" (1991: 160; see also 157–171 for more research that undercuts "the objectivist [who] assumes that surface reflectances are to be found in some pregiven world that is independent of our perceptual and cognitive capacities," 166). Rather, color vision too is a reciprocal and interactive process in which "color properties are enacted by the perceptual-motor couplings of animals with their environments" (44). So even color vision, often taken as the paradigm of "direct" perception is, rather, contextual and variable.

Then there is the rumor that Eskimos see seven (or is it five?) different kinds of snow. Presumably, they actually have a different perceptual experience from mine when looking at a snow bank. Now one might reply, yes, but you all see something called a "color" or a "cold, white substance." But such a vague "appearance" has little or no epistemic content. It is not clear how much information something so vague can really convey or what sorts of beliefs or claims (beyond "I am seeing *something*") it could really support. Given that even simple perceptions like color or snow are, in fact, so psychologically complex, reducing them only to their quality of "directness" or "immediacy" creates a description that is so vague and abstract ("*something* is presented to me") that virtually no content can be derived from that aspect of the experience alone—certainly not content as complex as "I am in the presence of divine being."

Beyond that, there is much research to suggest that people simply do not see things right in front of their eyes if they have no schema for them or if their schemata lead them to expect something else. The experience of optical illusions makes this clear. It also makes clear that the mind is active, not passive as Alston implies, in perception and other experiences, a point we will get to shortly. Consider figures 4.1 and 4.2. Are the lines in figure 4.1 curved or straight? Test them with a straight edge if you see them curving. In figure 4.2, are the vertical lines the same length? Measure them if you think they are not.

FIGURE 4.1.

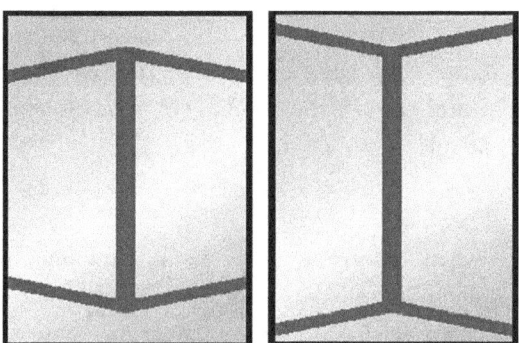

FIGURE 4.2.

In figure 4.3 look at the white dots in the centers of the two images. Are they the same size? Yes.

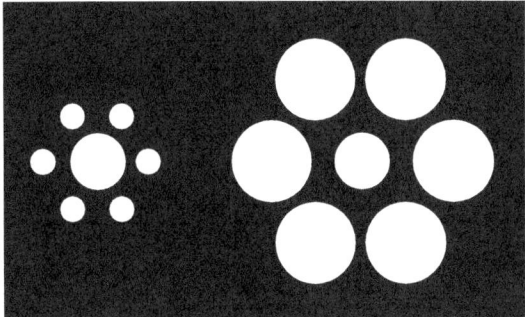

FIGURE 4.3.

And in figure 4.4, do you see a triangle? But there is no triangle there.

FIGURE 4.4.

You cannot help seeing curved lines when there are really only straight lines. Or two white dots of different sizes when there are only two dots of the same size. Or vertical lines of different lengths when there are only lines of exactly the same length. The mind transforms the stimuli so that you do not see what is really there, and in the last one, the mind fills in the lines you see but which are not there. The mind determines what you see. It fills in missing pieces or transforms the stimuli based on its expectations. These are not "interpretations" but rather what you actually perceive. Even if you know intellectually there is no triangle on the page, you will still see one here. The most dramatic case is watching men playing basketball and missing a gorilla (actually a man in a gorilla suit) walking right in the midst of them. Or under hypnosis, people will hallucinate sounds and sights that are experientially and neurologically indistinguishable from actual sounds. Perception is simply never as direct and unmediated as Alston's "Theory of Appearing" implies. And the perceiving mind is never as passive as that theory assumes.

Also, the experiential "sense" that there is simply a vague "appearance" occurring is too slender a reed on which to hang any significant epistemic claims. And such a theory about the veracity of pure appearing is unconvincing, given how easily we can all be mistaken not just about what is in front of our eyes and ears but even about whether anything is there or not—missing gorillas that are there and really seeing a triangle or hearing music that are not there. It is not just that we can be mistaken about the content of an appearance, but we can be mistaken about appearance itself. We may miss experiencing the appearance of something that is presumably impacting on our retinas; and we may have an "appearance experience" that has all the marks of a veridical appearance (including the neurological underpinnings), except that it is a hypnotic illusion. Despite Alston's often brilliant arguments, to a psychologist (this one at least), a "theory" that only deals with "appearing" is too content free to give rise to or warrant claims that have substantial content, like those found in the world's religions. And the cognitive passivity involved in such a theory is simply not supported by any evidence. All the evidence we have points to the activity of the mind (and body) in even the most basic sensory experiences, that, as we said earlier, perception is something we do, not something done to us.

Pointing out the complexity and ambiguity of perceptual experience and the way it is constrained by psychological processes could, in fact, help Alston's cause, however. Presumably atheists' and agnostics' experiences also are constrained by the same processes that constrain the experiences described in Alston's "Theory of Appearing." Thus it is reasonable to argue that the atheist and agnostic may miss the awareness of the divine because they have no schema for it or the categories they do hold do not allow them to perceive the divine. When they claim there is no evidence for the existence of God, what they are really claiming is that there is no evidence that they are aware of. Fair enough. But to what extent is their awareness limited and constrained by their own set of convictions and assumptions? Would they perceive the divine presence even if it was there? Or would they miss it like the spectators concentrating so intently on the game that they miss the gorilla in its midst?

So does all this mean Alston's theory of perceiving God is totally wrong-headed? No! Quite the reverse. It has important things to tell us about the nature of those religious experiences that are seen to be a form of sense experience. Once we reframe his argument along the lines of more current theories of perception, the importance of his analysis becomes clearer. One major theme emphasized in the preceding chapters is that human understanding is usually

an interactive, relational process. Perception and cognition mean active exploration of the world of our experience, not passive reception of it. Another major
theme is that perception is a full-bodied process. Hearing, seeing, tasting, and
touching involve not only ears, eyes, and tongues, but they also involve somatosensory neurons and proprioceptive spindles and muscle memories.

How would our understanding of religious perception change if we
thought of it as a process of embodied interaction with the world around us?
First, religious understanding is embodied understanding. It is not abstract
ratiocination. Posture, breathing, movement, sights, smells, and sounds that
engage the senses, and bodily imagery all enter into our religious knowing.
Proprioception may also figure into religious understanding, not just the "five
senses." Second, embodied understanding is active understanding. In contrast to Alston's position, I have underscored the importance of the schemas,
expectancies, and even unconscious processes that go into our perceptions.
They are not problematic features to disown. They are the foundations on
which to build better theories and practices. There is no perceiving in everyday life, in science, or in religion, without them. Rather than ignoring or
downplaying them, they should be critically and consciously developed so
that any possible "perception" of God is deepened.

In addition, we must not forget that perception is an ongoing, embodied
interaction with the world. That aspect is lost in laboratory experiments, neurological studies, and philosophical discussions that freeze and dissect a single
moment of ecstatic experience, a single moment of perception, a single moment of cognitive activity. Such synchronic, cross-sectional approaches yield
information necessary for understanding the functioning of human perceptual, neurological, and cognitive systems (as well as information crucial for
clinical diagnosis). But they obscure or obliterate the ongoing life of the organism and what led up to and followed after the moment of observation or
intervention.

An embodied perspective insists that (while important) only a very incomplete understanding of religious perceptions can result from a singular
focus on isolated and decontextualized moments of experience, whether that
is an fMRI image of the brain, a psychophysiological report on the effects
of a period of meditation, an experiment that tests religious cognition, or a
philosophical analysis of a momentary religious perception. Such studies and
analyses are important and greatly contribute to the understanding and practice of religion. But those undertaking them and those seeking to learn from
them must not lose sight of the larger context of the religiously lived lives
that are their natural home. Equally important (in terms of understanding

religion) is understanding how these mystical moments, these meditative practices, these cognitive activities fit into and transform and are transformed by an ongoing, lived religious life. That, it seems to me, is where the questions of the reliability and validity of religious perceptions get answered. Their reliability and validity is not demonstrated so much by whether one can brilliantly construct arguments that connect occasional religious experiences directly to specific religious beliefs. Rather, their reliability and validity are demonstrated by whether they enable Jews to "do justice, show mercy and walk humbly with G-D," enable Christians to "love God with all their heart and mind and soul and their neighbors as themselves," enable Buddhists to taste "*shunyata*" and mobilize "*Bodhichitta*," enable Hindus to "pierce the veil of *maya*," and enable Muslims to submit to the peace of Allah.

This is not the kind of justification of beliefs that Alston aims at. But from my standpoint, his rather linear understanding of how beliefs get justified, along with the abstraction and passivity that characterizes his theory of appearing, are the weakest aspects of his argument. His strength is in his defense of the veridicality of religious perceptions and his insistence they be treated along the lines of other perceptions and not subject to additional criteria that would not be demanded of other perceptual claims. His weakness comes in attempting to use such experiences to warrant particular religious beliefs by the deployment of direct, linear arguments. Put another way, my disagreement with Alston is with his approach to religious epistemology as primarily involving justified belief rather than as a whole gestalt of practice/experience/reflection. Living religion is not about belief in propositions taken out of context; it is about a whole life of practice and reflection. Dead religion is about beliefs taken out of context.

Understanding religious perception in this manner goes a long way toward weakening the strongest argument against the analogy between spiritual perception and ordinary perception: that there is a virtually universal consensus about ordinary perception and almost complete disagreement and difference about any alleged spiritual perception. First, it is hardly logical to compare a simple perception of a physical object (a tree) with a complex experience like the awareness of God. A more accurate analogy would be a more complex perceptual experience like seeing a painting by Picasso, tasting a fine wine, parsing the harmonies in a Bach fugue, or reading an elaborate pathology slide. Here there is much greater variance in the accounts of those perceptual experiences, not so different from that found in the religious domain. Note also that in all these cases—the painting, the wine, the fugue, the pathology slide—perception can be trained and improved, a point we will return to in chapter 5 in relation to any possible "spiritual sense."

Also, this objection may well overstate the amount of consensus in even the simplest perception. As we have seen, there can be variations and differences in perceiving colors like red and green or in seeing snow across cultures. More important, these objections again reprise an outmoded positivist epistemology that depended on a "myth of the immaculate perception" in which "sense data" could be experienced directly and clearly differentiated from any "cognitive" overlay. Rather, as we have seen, schemas and categories enter into even the simplest perception and they are deeply intertwined in the complex perceptual processes involved in examining an X-ray, interpreting a bubble chamber photograph, or perceiving nature as reflecting the glory of God. Religious perception is not the "(mis)interpretation" of a "bare" experience any more than seeing a green tree or reading an X-ray is.

There is a deeper and related issue at work here as well. Arguments that use religious experience as a source of justification for belief proceed in a rather linear fashion: religious experience **X** entails (or at least strongly supports) religious belief **Y**. The same is true of arguments (like those of Richard Swinburne) that seek to defend religious beliefs by a Bayesian calculus of probability by summing up all the possible arguments for (say) God's existence to conclude that God's existence is more probable than not. Such approaches, while clearly in the mainstream of philosophical discussion (skeptical and theistic), tend to treat particular religious experiences and specific religious beliefs in isolation. The metaphors of argument I am using here are derived more from non-linear models in cognitive psychology and neuroscience. On this view, religious perceptions are not treated as isolated warrants for belief but rather as one part of the whole fabric of the religious life including other arguments for the existence of God, the transforming effects of religious practice, the impact of living according to a certain moral code, the experience of community, the critical study of and reflection on one's beliefs, and so on. All these elements are not simply additive in a linear calculus of probability. Rather, they mutually work together, interacting in a non-linear way, to produce a "form of life" which is more compelling and self-validating than any element taken on its own or all of them together combined in a strictly linear fashion.

Conclusion

An embodied-relational epistemology and the empirical and clinical evidence supporting it have much to contribute to theology and to the psychology of religion. Psychologically, it suggests additional ways of theorizing religious cognition and additional avenues for study and research. By downplaying the issues of reference and representation, models of embodied action minimize some of the problems those topics have created for theology. And reframing the idea of religious perception in more embodied ways can strengthen the argument from religious experience by tying it more closely to contemporary theories of perception and broadening and deepening its epistemological validity by considering it in a non-linear perspective that emphasizes the way in which the beliefs, practices, reflections, and experiences that constitute the religiously lived life together give rise to a reality much richer and more complex than the sum of all these parts treated in isolation or in a linear fashion.

5

Living Religion

CAN RESEARCH ON embodied knowing help us understand the traditional notion of a "divine sense" or a "sense of the divine"? Perhaps not if the body is understood only in mechanistic, Cartesian terms. We have already raised the question of whether the idea of a "spiritual sense" requires the concept of a "spiritual body" and how that might be understood from an embodied-relational perspective and the twin ideas of the embodied mind and the mind-suffused body.

The idea that humans have a spiritual sense goes back to the earliest days of Western thought. For example, Plato's model of contemplation appears to have involved a direct apprehension of the eternal forms by means of the "eyes of the soul." This was part of Plato's argument for the eternality of the soul: the ideal forms (for example, mathematics) were eternal and unchanging; to be able to perceive them, the soul must be eternal and unchanging too. It is not clear whether he meant that humans literally had two sets of eyes, a physical set and a parallel spiritual set, or whether he was using perceptual language metaphorically to refer to some transcendental experience that was similar to perception but was not literally sensory. This difference (or confusion?) continues through most Christian centuries and the writings of many Christian authors (for examples, see Gavrilyuk & Coakley, 2012): do we literally have two parallel sets of sensory organs (bodily and spiritual) or does spiritual perception occur through our regular, physical sense organs when they are in a transformed or ecstatic condition? Or is there another alternative?

And this is only one of many differences among authors throughout the Christian centuries as well as among parallel writers from other traditions (Cattoi & McDaniel, 2011). Gavrilyuk and Coakley speak, in a bit of an understatement, of the "rich vocabulary of spiritual perception" in the Christian tradition (2012: 3). Karl Rahner calls for a "doctrine of the spiritual senses," but that seems much too formalized for what is really a welter of images, metaphors, and occasionally some more philosophical reflections. I am not equipped to enter into a historical and exegetical discussion that would attempt to sort out some of this confusion. Nor is that necessary for my own argument here. In reference to Plato, Gavrilyuk and Coakley (7) speak of a "direct, perception-like apprehension" of the eternal. That phrase captures what I would mean by a spiritual sense: an experience that is phenomenologically as direct as regular sensation, that can be described in the language of ordinary sensory perception, and that carries an awareness of an external, divine, and transcendental reality. It does not have to be literally sensory, such as actually hearing a voice or seeing a vision, but it cannot be simply a vague hunch with no epistemic content or a moment of daydreaming with no sense of externality.

Nor, on my definition, can it be only awe and wonder at the majesty and complexity of nature that does not directly push through and beyond itself to the apprehension of a transcendental source or ground. Thus religious naturalism, such as Ursula Goodenough's (1998) "sacred depths of nature" or Wesley Wildman's religious naturalism's "engagement with value structures and flows in the depths of nature" (2011: 248), are limiting cases here. Like most religious naturalists, both authors extensively deploy the metaphor of depth, presumably (and explicitly in Wildman's writings) in opposition to a strong notion of divine transcendence. Barrels of theological ink have already been drained dry by the issues of divine transcendence and immanence and I do not intend to spill any more here. I have already referred to Christianity's Logos doctrine and its image of nature as the Body of Christ and to the Mahayana Buddhist teaching about the Dharmakyia all of which point at a divine reality immanent within nature. But the Logos and the Universal Buddha nature are also transcendental in a stronger sense than most religious naturalists would accept; both would exist if/when the natural world ceased to exist, and the natural world depends on them for its existence but they do not so depend on the natural world. More on this discussion would take us far beyond this book's scope. I am therefore sympathetic to the religious naturalists' project and often moved by the beauty of their writings. And I think they would agree with me that there is more to reality than only what can be described by current physical science, so they are not physicalists in the sense used here nor do they fall under the critique of physicalism advanced earlier in the book. On the other hand, I do not find their arguments against a more robust transcendentalism and even "supernaturalism" philosophically necessary or logically convincing or spiritually compelling. So for the purpose of my argument here I retain the phrasing that a spiritual sense is the apprehension of something eternal and transcendental, as well as being a "direct perception-like apprehension."

Embodiment-based research suggests that even the most transcendental experience will be expressed in language that reflects our embodiment: we will be *lifted up* to heaven, we will *ascend* experientially to heaven on Jacob's ladder; we will *see, taste*, or *touch* the presence of God or the reality of *shunyata*; we will be *moved* by the experience. For example, Dionysius writes:

> I also think that each of the parts of the human body can provide us with images which are quite appropriate to the powers of heaven. One could say the powers of sight suggest their ability to gaze upward toward the lights of God and, at the same time, to receive softly, clearly, without resistance but flexibly, purely, openly, yet impassibly, the enlightenment coming from the Deity. The powers to discern smells indicate their capacity to welcome fully those fragrances which elude the understanding and to discern with understanding those opposites which must be utterly avoided. The powers of hearing signify the ability to have a knowing share of divine inspiration. Taste has to do with the fill of conceptual nourishment and their receptiveness to the divine and nourishing streams. Touch is understanding how to distinguish the profitable from the harmful. [*Celestial Hierarchy* xv.3 in Gavrilyuk, 2012: 98]

Dionysius is clearly using the five senses as symbols of the different aspects of the spiritual life. I do not think he is literally saying that discernment comes through the sense of touch or smell brings us the unification of opposites. But from another perspective his reliance on the body as an image or icon of the mystical path is not coincidental. Even at the highest point in which all cognition is (according to Dionysius) transcended and we have gone completely out of ourselves and "being neither oneself nor someone else, one is completely united by a completely unknowing inactivity of all knowledge, and knows beyond the mind by knowing nothing" [*Mystical Theology* 1.3 in Gavrilyuk, 2012: 103], even in this completely transcendental state, we are still in the body (as Paul says) and that embodiment is still, unconsciously, impacting our understanding.

Even at these transcendental heights, Dionysius continues to refer to "seeing" that aspect of God that can be "known," even if the "knowing" is also a form of "unknowing" and that "seeing" is shrouded in "darkness." So while we "see" and "know," we are also "surpassed by the infinity beyond being, intelligences by that oneness which is beyond intelligence. Indeed the inscrutable One is out of the reach of every rational process" (*Divine Names*, I.I, in Gavrilyuk, 2012: 102). My task here is hardly to try to resolve the paradox about a form of "knowing" that transcends knowledge that generations of scholars of "mysticism" have been unable to resolve. Rather, my point is simply that from the perspective of cognitive psychology an experience or awareness that literally was beyond all cognition would be impossible to encode in memory and so recall, impossible to speak of in even the most paradoxical terms, impossible to refer to even in metaphor and symbol. One possible resolution is to claim that in Dionysius our senses are "stretched and extended" or are "simplified, unified, extended and ultimately transcended" (Gavrilyuk & Coakley, 2012: especially 102–103). This implies that the "spiritual sense" is a profound transformation of our ordinary senses, rather than being an additional or parallel set of senses. Put another way, it implies that a spiritual sense is something we develop, not something we automatically possess. An embodied-relational perspective would support the claim that any "spiritual sense" must represent the training, expanding, and transforming of our bodily senses.

The Neurology of Our Expanded Awareness

Several questions about this claim to "see God" even in Dionysius's carefully nuanced way, arise from an embodied perspective. One is how such experiences are to be understood given the insistence that perception is a psychologically active phenomenon, however passive it may appear phenomenologically. As with Alston, this is one of the places where a psychological account and some phenomenological accounts diverge most sharply. It seems clear (to a psychologist) that even the experience of transcending (ordinary) awareness takes place in the context of our awareness. If we are conscious of an experience (as we are by definition) and are able to remember it (i.e., encode it in memory), the psychologist assumes it must be mediated through our neurological and cognitive systems. To say otherwise is not only to claim that there is an aspect of the human person that is non-physical (that is, to affirm dualism in some sense) but that can still be known through our physical brains and bodies (which dualism certainly can affirm). But to go beyond that and claim that there are actual experiences and noetic processes that go on in a way completely detached from our bodies and our neurological/cognitive systems. That goes beyond what even dualism requires and is a claim that it is very hard (I would say impossible) to make coherent unless we greatly enlarge our common conception of what is meant by a "body."

So the claim to transcend our ordinary experience probably cannot mean that we transcend awareness altogether. It certainly can mean that we transcend ordinary, linear rationality. In fact, this framework of embodied knowing sketched here can provide neurological models for such a process of transcending ordinary, linear rationality. This model of embodied knowing emphasizes that all our cognitive processes, including formal rationality, and their underlying neurological substrates are instantiated in a more encompassing, interconnected network that also includes affect and proprioception and the non-linear interaction among different sensory modalities.

Gallagher, for example, emphasizes the importance of these intermodal communications, say, between vision and proprioception (2005: 78–81). The body schema itself, in which cognition is embedded, is an intermodal system that unites proprioception with the sensory and motor systems. Gallagher presents evidence that such intermodal connections are there from birth. So even at the most basic neurological level, formal rationality and its neurological underpinnings are not self-contained and encapsulated (say, in autonomous modules) but are rather encompassed in a broader network comprising many other cognitive and neurological systems. As we saw in the first chapter, Lisa Feldman Barrett and her colleagues present research demonstrating that human cognition and behavior involve deep neural interconnections between diverse central nervous system domains including reason, emotion, and sensation working together. And the "Human Connectome Project" not only maps a different way of dividing up the cortex but, at the same time, uncovers dense interconnections among all these areas. So abstract rationality is embedded rationality; embedded in and embraced by a more complex and extended network of sensing, affect, and other bodily processes. This reciprocal, interacting network—which extends beyond the body through its ongoing, reciprocal interactions with the lived world it both finds and creates (as D. W. Winnicott puts it)—may be one neurological foundation for our capacity to know in ways beyond our abstract, linear rationality.

Another model with similar implications is that of dual, interacting cognitive systems (Watts, 2013). There is growing agreement in cognitive psychology that human cognition involves at least two subsystems: a mostly (but not entirely) unconscious, more intuitive, fast-reacting "implicational" system; and a slower, more conscious, deliberate, and more linguistic "propositional" system in which ratiocination plays a major role. There is also general agreement that the intuitive system provides the assumptions that guide the propositional system's activity. This model implies that "cognition" is more than calculation. And that rational cognition depends upon intuitive, immediate cognition for its governing outlooks and presuppositions. On the other hand, the implicational, intuitive system depends upon the propositional system for the verbal articulation of its insights; although its insights can also be expressed by such non-verbal means as art, music, dance, and liturgy. Watts suggests that the sense of "ineffability" that often (but not always) accompanies spiritual experiences arises in part from the attempt to translate experiences originating in the intuitive system into the modes of expression used by the propositional system. Here is another neurological basis for understanding (and grounding in neuroscience) experiences that transcend our ordinary (in our culture) cognition.

Another neurological foundation for the claim of a larger cognitive context in which abstract, linear rationality is only a part (and not the whole) is the dual-hemispheric nature of the brain. There was a time when this distinction of the left hemisphere organized for language and linear rationality and the right hemisphere organized for more integrative, intuitive, and artistic processes dominated neurological thinking. By the time I got my training, this over-simplification was being critiqued and rejected. I was taught (with good reason) to be skeptical of these over-simplifications. As so often happens historically, this distinction is making a comeback in a more complex and nuanced form. For example, Ian McGilchrist (2009), while insisting that both hemispheres are involved in virtually all cognitive activities, argues that the right hemisphere is more contextual, direct, and intuitive (it sees the forest more than the trees) and that it "is more true to the nature of things" (198). He presents a series of studies that suggest that the right hemisphere is more basic and provides the "grounding" for the left hemisphere's more abstract and de-contextualized rationality. This parallels the findings from cognitive psychology that the intuitive, implicational cognitive subsystem provides the assumptions that govern the ratiocination carried out by the propositional subsystem. For McGilchrist, the more abstract and linear left-hemispheric activity arises from and, in order to be experienced as compelling, must return to the more basic contextual, intuitive knowing of the right hemisphere. Here too linear rationality (the "left hemisphere") can and, according to McGilchrist, should be transcended by being encompassed by experiences arising from the right hemisphere (a similar point is made in Watts, 2014).

However neurologically formulated, implicit in all these models is the claim that humans have many (more than just two actually) different neurologically grounded ways of perceiving the world and processing information; and that is an important point about human nature that we forget at our peril. That is one of the main arguments of McGilchrist's wide-ranging book. And such a claim, based in neurology or not, is an important corrective to philosophies that would insist on only a limited version of sensory input and valorize only one form (the "left brained") of cognitive processing as the only sources of knowledge. In different ways, all these neurological models suggest that cognitive balance, coherence, realism, and wisdom depend on repositioning ordinary rationality in larger, more encompassing (transcendental if you will) experiential and noetic frameworks.

All of this involves complexities *within* an individual person's sensory- and information-processing systems. In addition, an individual person, however internally complex, is not a self-contained, atomic unit but rather is in continual reciprocal interaction with his or her environment. Part of that interaction is that a person continually receives information on many different levels and through many different channels, not just the traditional five senses. Are we aware of all the possible information that is impinging on us at any one moment? There is no reason to think that we are and many reasons to think we are not. And so it is only logical that expanding our sensory capacities through disciplined practices might well provide us additional information, including information relevant to the spiritual life, that goes beyond the information that is ordinarily (that is, within the constraints of our current schemas) processed by our five senses and by our ordinary rationality. To limit information only to what is regularly known through the five senses, especially only to the information that gets through a very narrow set of schemas and is only processed by them (say, those limited by a positivist, physicalist philosophy), and then to assert that this is all the knowledge there is can hardly be called logical. One implication of the model of the spiritual sense as an expansion of our ordinary senses would be that embodied practices (like those described earlier in this book) increase our sensitivity to more of the information that is constantly impinging on us. And religious training provides schemas that enable us to perceive, organize, make sense of, and integrate some of that information into our ongoing lives.

So the phenomenological awareness of transcending ordinary rationality and expanding and stretching our sensory apparatus can certainly be psychophysiologically grounded within an embodied-relational perspective. Such a perspective makes clear that information can come into the central nervous system from many more sources than simply the five senses and can (and should) be processed in more than a strictly amodal, linear way. Most important here may be proprioceptive information. And it is crucial to recognize the ways in which these inputs can interact in a non-linear fashion to generate new cognitive connections that we might well experience as deeper insights and intuitions. From an embodied perspective, there is no reason to limit our sources of information processing simply to the five ordinary senses and to linear ("left-brained") cognition. This perspective, in fact, implies that we have many other possible sources of information and modes of processing information. This makes neurological sense of Dionysius's and others' suggestion that accessing those other sources requires a stretching and expanding of our more ordinary sensory sources and modes of information processing.

This proposal has important implications for living religion. A religion mainly organized around propositional, "left-brained" cognition—that is, one whose homilies are primarily practical or intellectual (concrete suggestions for daily life, doctrinal or exegetical lessons) and whose practices are primarily instrumental ("meditate to lower stress," "sing together to increase the sense of community") will not ultimately be transformative, however much (as McGilchrist might argue) they are congruent with a "left-brained" culture. A religion that evokes no transcendental sensibility is as one-sided neurologically as a religion that is all emotion and employs no reflective cognition. Here again is a more complex model of human nature that is congruent with religious teaching.

Transformative Practice

If a spiritual sense is something we develop through the transformation of our ordinary senses, how might such a transformation of the senses come about? Here the embodied-relational perspective has something important, although not new, to contribute: presumably that training, expanding, and transforming would involve bodily practices—different postures, breathing exercises, movements of various kinds, and perhaps visualizations. All of these disciplines, which can be understood in the context of embodied knowledge, have a long history in the religions of humankind. Religious perception is not abstract ratiocination. Posture, breathing, movement, sights, smells, and sounds that engage the senses, along with bodily metaphors, can all enter into our religious perceptions. Proprioception can also figure into religious perception. Many meditative techniques (as well as certain psychotherapeutic ones) and bodily practices like yoga or martial arts facilitate and deepen proprioception. These disciplines explicitly or implicitly expand and deepen our sensory capacities and our bodily awareness and make us more sensitive to increasingly subtle proprioceptive sensations and other sensory inputs.

For example, research using various brain imagery techniques finds that various meditative and contemplative practices can lessen the activation in the parts of the brain associated with processing painful stimuli, thus making the individual less emotionally reactive and so potentially more open to new information; they can increase connectivity between various brain regions, can produce changes in areas associated with processing self-referential material, can alter brain areas in a way that increases an individual's proprioceptive abilities, and can produce lasting structural changes in other parts of the brain (Kang et al., 2012; Lutz et al., 2004; Taylor et al., 2012). For example, meditation "alters information processing in the brain, increasing the contribution of interoception to perceptual experience" (Farb et al., 2012: 15) and strengthens "present-moment awareness" (Taylor et al., 2012: 4). It may also improve executive functioning (McNamara, 2009). Even when done in a purely secular setting for purely instrumental reasons (in this case, stress management), meditation can increase a person's spiritual outlook (Shapiro, Schwartz, & Bonner, 1998). Research also finds that meditation can increase empathic behavior (Condon et al., 2013) and transform the neurological structures that appear to support such behavior (Lee et al., 2012).

That an intentionally undertaken spiritual practice can transform the way in which a person processes information and perceives the world and themselves within it, as well as altering relevant neuro-anatomical structures, has far-reaching epistemological consequences. Spiritual disciplines can make available to their practitioners sources of information and means of processing it (in consensually validated ways) that are not available to others. Religious knowing is trained and disciplined knowing in ways analogous to learning to differentiate fine wine or pick up the subtle diagnostic features of an X-ray or brain scan. Thus some of the information that serves to validate and justify religious perceptions, beliefs, and the religiously committed life in toto may be available *only* to those willing to engage the relevant disciplines and may become more accessible as the individual continues in those practices. This may be the most controversial and unhappy implication of this discussion of embodiment and religious knowing (a conversation with Tom Simpson was very helpful in clarifying this point).

An Embodied Spiritual Sense

While Plato saw the body as the prison-house of the soul and Descartes sup-posedly saw the body and soul as totally incompatible realities (as do some yogic texts), many religious traditions affirm an intimate interconnection between the soul or spirit and the body: the soul is the form of the body, Aristotle and Aquinas famously claimed; the body is an expression of the soul suggests Neo-Platonism, as when Plotinus claims that the body is in the soul rather than the soul being in the body; and the body is the temple of the Holy Spirit says Saint Paul. These more intimate portrayals from Western religious traditions imply that the human soul or spirit makes its presence known through the body. And in the East, martial arts traditions derived from Buddhism speak of the "chi" or "ki" as a spiritual life force that enlivens the body; Tantric texts in Hinduism and Buddhism talk of subtle, spiritual forces or powers that circulate through the body. All of these make it clear that a radical, oppositional dualism of soul or spirit and body is not the posi-tion most commonly associated with world religions. And if perception and cognition are embodied activities (as they surely are), then they may well also have a spiritual potential or dimension.

An embodied-relational framework provides additional perspectives on these traditional models of bodily spiritual perception: it supports the idea that a spiritual sense is a transformation of our ordinary senses; it provides insights into the neurological underpinnings of the phenomenon of transcending our ordinary sensory experience and cognition by pointing to the ways in which the neurological foundations of ordinary cognition are situated in a neurologically more encompassing interacting psychophysio-logical network of neurons and receptors; and it stresses the crucial role of embodied practice in that transformation. But along with pervading a new perspective on this traditional idea, can it also provide further models of what might comprise a spiritual sense? Two possibilities.

First, we have insisted that our bodies connect us to the world around us (Clark, 2008; Clark & Chalmers, 1988; Noe, 2009). Embodied-relational knowledge is both situated and extended (to use some of the language from the embodied cognition literature in a rather different way). This was prob-ably one of the most radical claims of the embodied cognition model, even though it is not a new claim. Quite the reverse, it as an ancient religious and philosophical vision—that we are intimately connected to the world around us. But it is a vision that goes against the grain of the modern project's sin-gular valorization of the isolated and autonomous individual, a valorization that drives the contemporary world's economic and political systems as well as much of its ethical, philosophical, and even religious discourses. In contrast, Gibbs writes that "the agent and the world are not really separate, because they are "'mutually specifying'" (2005: 17). Some contexts are so intense that "the person and the environment are so tightly coupled that it is better to conceive of the two as constituting a single conceptual system rather than two independent systems" (154). Accounts of piloting a plane or a race car, engaging in martial arts combat, or experiencing ecstatic moments of connection with nature all illustrate this. Such moments of intensity reveal the deeper ontological truth that we exist only as interconnected beings. This more porous and less bounded view of the self may be the most radical implication of embodied-relational research.

But such truths are revealed not only in moments of intensity and ecstasy. There are practices that also deepen our ongoing sense of connection, our "oneness," with the world around us. Walking meditations when all our concentration is on the sensations of our feet touching the ground or the floor. Or martial arts stances that "ground" us, rooting us in the earth. These and many other disciplines intensify our sensation of relatedness to the physical earth. And through the earth to the cosmos, to the universe which, according to Ephesians and Colossians, is the Body of Christ.

Embodied-relational knowing with its discussion of the reciprocally interacting mind also reminds us of these connections and relations. This is a claim about human nature that a psychology of embodiment shares with other psychological paradigms such as contemporary relational psychoanalytic and attachment theories. We are inherently relational creatures. On the other hand, mainstream cognitivism is a radically individualistic paradigm. Its object of study is the individual isolated in the laboratory, performing tests while staring at a computer screen, or sitting alone at a desk filling out questionnaires. Extreme forms of cognitivism even more radically decontextualize the person by speaking of a brain kept alive in a vat. From such theoretically based laboratory research when applied to religious cognition we learn important things about how the mind processes religious information, especially under stressful circumstances: which religious concepts are more implicit than explicit; what religious ideas come quickest to mind; what roles do emotions play in religious cognition; are we more inclined to use more abstract apersonal or more anthropomorphic, personal images when thinking about God. These are important things to know. But if these more individualistic models and research designs completely define human nature for us, then the relationally interconnected dimension of human life will be obscured.

That relational dimension can have important theological ramifications. Theologically (as we said earlier) we can ask, How far does that reciprocal, relational knowing extend? Beyond the brain to the whole body? Beyond the body to the interpersonal and social worlds? Beyond the interpersonal and social worlds to the physical cosmos? And the religious person refuses to stop there. His or her extended, relational understanding extends still further to relate to and engage with a more encompassing, sacred reality. In addition, as I argued decades ago in conjunction with the move from Freudian (and Jungian) to relational models within psychoanalytic psychology, relational models in any discipline can easily generate theological connections. Models of human nature that idealize the autonomous individual and decry any hint of dependency almost always have secularizing results. They hide our dependencies, even from ourselves, and obscure the networks of interconnection on which we inevitably depend: with the natural world that supplies us with air to breathe and food to eat; with societies that build our roads, staff our schools, lay down our infrastructures of travel and communication; with other persons who provide the crucial lifelines of attachment and affiliation necessary for human flourishing. They also enable us to maintain the illusion of the "self-made man," an illusion so fundamental to our current economic and political climate. Spiritually too, in such a context of forgetting our fundamental interconnectedness, claims of dependency upon a more encompassing or transcendental source are anathema. More relational models, if we allow them to generalize to the furthest possible extent, enable us to recognize and affirm our dependency on the ultimate source of our existence (Jones, 1991a).

Because of these interconnections that come to us through our body, our body functions as the unconscious center of perception, providing the sense of spatial orientation, distance, and perspective from which everything seen is configured. Merleau-Ponty says that through my body "things of intersensory significance become possible for us.... To have a body is to possess a universal setting, a schema of all types of perceptual unfolding" (1962: 326). He speaks of a logic that the body and the world have in common: "There is a logic of the world to which my body in its entirety conforms" (326). The world of our experience is organized around our bodies; we are at the center of a world of experience radiating out from us. Our perceiving and knowing is thus shaped by our embodied history. Every body has a history. Understanding what a person knows means more than examining that individual's thought processes. It means attending to the history of that person and his or her situatedness in nature, in history, and in culture. Bodies connect us to each other, to nature, and to culture and history that have shaped our experience of being embodied as well as shaping our bodies themselves (as experience shapes our brains and exercise shapes our bodies). Bodies also connect us to the cosmos, the universe, that cosmic Body of Christ.

So one form of spiritual sensing, taking off from our embodied and situated knowings, involves the expansion of our senses out to their farthest limits. Thereby we recognize that we are indeed situated creatures, embraced by and interconnected with a more encompassing and transcendental reality. Such a sense of our cosmic and transcendental situatedness is in continuity with our more mundane deployments of our embodied knowing. Through such an awareness, embodied perception becomes spiritual perception through the extension and expansion of our sensory capacity, both in imagery exercises and in actual and direct perception, so that we come to experience our deep interconnection with the world around us, especially the natural world. That sense of "union" with the cosmos is one commonly reported element in many accounts of spiritual experience from many different traditions.

A Direct Sense of the Divine

The purpose of this section is to connect the argument of this chapter about embodiment itself as a spiritual sense with the Christian theological tradition. A medieval and a modern Christian theologian, the anonymous author of Cloud of Unknowing *and Friedrich Schleiermacher are discussed in relation to that position. Those readers not inclined toward a rather technical, theological discussion can easily skip this section and go directly to the next section on spiritual senses as spiritual practices.*

So far we have focused on our experiences coming through our primary bodily senses such as sight, touch, smell, and sound. But do we also have embodied experience that is not sensory in that sense? The answer is yes. The awareness we have of our own body does not come through vision or touch: sensations of pain, or awareness of the positions of our limbs, or our location in space. The body itself is a sensory system. It is not just that the body has five (or more) senses; these five senses are embedded in a larger sensory system called the body. As we have said, a person is not a self-contained, atomic unit but is rather in continual reciprocal interaction with his or her environment. Part of that interaction is that the person is continually receiving information on many different levels and through many different bodily channels, not just the traditional five senses. Taking proprioception as an analogue, we can train ourselves to sense more of what impinges on us.

One task of spiritual discipline is to train our sensing capacities by enlarging our capacity for awareness of more of what is there. Part of what is there is the presence or action of God in sustaining us in existence. Every living theistic tradition insists that (in contrast to eighteenth-century Deism) God did not simply create the world and retire. The divine Spirit is continually active in sustaining the universe in existence. Even theologians who disclaim the notion that God intervenes in history are inclined to affirm that in some way God sustains the created order in being.

Consider two anonymous classic late medieval English Christian texts by the same author—*The Cloud of Unknowing* and *The Little Book of Private Counsel*. In the latter book, the author writes, "God is your being" (anonymous: 136). God is the cause of everything that exists but God is also the "being," that is, the essence, nature, or the basic reality ("being" can mean all those things in this context) of each of us and of everything that exists. "He is thy being and in him thou art that thou art, not only by cause and by being, but also he is in thee both by cause and by being. . . . All things be in him by cause and by being and he be in all things their cause and their being" (137). For this author "being" is not just a state or synonym for "existing." Rather, "being" is a reality in itself, like life or living. Hence some say, "God is my life." Not just that God is the *cause* of my life but that God *is* my life. Likewise for this author, God *is* my being, the reality "in whom I live and move and have my being." God is a more fundamental reality than a cause; God is the very being of the things on which causes work.

Since God is the central reality or basic nature of our existence (and not just the cause of it), the most basic spiritual practice is simply to deepen our awareness of our existence through which one learns that "the most fundamental starting point and goal of contemplation is a direct perception and clear awareness of one's own existence, the direct feeling on your own being" (141). This is a spiritual practice that is open to everyone; even the simplest and most ignorant people know that they exist. That is the most basic starting point of the spiritual journey, the simple awareness of our own existence. Since God is our nature and our existence, the author is suggesting that by deepening and expanding our awareness of our nature and our existence, we will encounter the reality of God. Eventually, of course, even that awareness of our own existence must be transcended if we are to experience "the gracious feeling of God's [own] self" (155–156). Exploring those most transcendental experiences are far beyond the scope of this book. The medieval author's proposal is that an awareness of our existence can be the "doorway" (his metaphor) into our awareness of God. We must keep in mind that his is a treatise of practical spirituality, not an essay on abstract theology. When the author says, "God is your being," he is not ontologizing the divine in the manner of theologians like Paul Tillich, who says "God is the ground of being," or John Mcquarrie, who says "God is holy being," or even Thomas Aquinas, although the author might accept such a claim. Rather, the medieval author is here making an epistemological point, that we can come to know God through a disciplined, contemplative exploration of our experience of our own existence in which our existence becomes "transparent" (my metaphor) to the divine existence.

Of course, this epistemological point presupposes a very radical ontology. It only makes sense to claim that we can know God through a contemplation of our own existence, essence, or nature if our existence, essence, or nature is somehow linked or joined with the divine essence. The author is careful to distinguish God's mode of existence from ours since God exists in God's-self and we exist only in dependence on God; God is our "being" but we are not in any way God's "being" (136). Still, the author comes very close to suggesting that our essence ("being") is also God's essence ("being"), that is, that we share in the divine essence common to God and to us. "All that thou art, that thou art completely unto him that is as he is . . . [which] is the blissful being both of himself and of thee" (144). A striking claim indeed, that our nature, at its deepest core, is the "blissful" nature of God.

So, our awareness that we exist, that we "are," leads this author directly to God since "God is your being." Thus, we can relate to God directly through a sense of our own existence. It is not that we realize that we exist and then logically reason to a cause of our existence (as Descartes proposes). The reality of God is not a deduction from our existence but rather our existence becomes transparent to the reality at its heart. What might that mean? From an embodied knowing perspective, that would clearly involve our embodiment. We know we exist through our bodies (this would be another element of anti-Cartesianism in this embodied-relational model). Our physicality is our main mode of existence (at least in this life and, if you believe in the resurrection of the body, in the life to come). Part of our embodied spiritual practices, on this model of our spiritual senses, would be practices that deepen our proprioception. Becoming more deeply aware of the heart of our existence, of our "being," means, among other things, becoming more deeply aware of our embodiment. In this way, proprioception would be at the core of our spiritual sense.

Proprioception is clearly more direct and immediate than awareness coming through the five ordinary senses. Thus, this practice would contain that sense of immediacy that the classical authors almost always attribute to the spiritual senses but which, we have argued, is a misleading claim in relation to our ordinary five senses, at least in the context of contemporary psychology.

An approach to theology that sounds similar to the unknown, late medieval author but is really quite different is that of the nineteenth-century German theologian Friedrich Schleiermacher. Schleiermacher grounds theology in the domain of "feeling" [Gefuhl] or "immediate self-awareness" [unmitelbares Selbsbewusstsein—which, in the 1920s Mackintosh and Stewart translated as "immediate self-consciousness"; since then, self-consciousness has acquired other connotations so I am preferring "self-awareness"] (Mackintosh & Stewart, 1968: 5). For Schleiermacher, "feeling" and "immediate self-awareness" refer to the same thing—the way the self is present to itself—feeling is not just a mood or a passing emotion. Rather, it is the awareness of the self's unified existence that is behind the individual's thoughts and actions. The particular feeling that is crucial here Schleiermacher calls "the feeling of absolute dependence" [schlechthin abhangig] which he says "is the same thing as being in relation with God" (12; the German could also be translated as "being in a conscious [bewusst] relationship [Beziehung] with God," thus emphasizing the element of awareness that is so crucial for Schleiermacher). Thus, for Schleiermacher, "the direct inward expression of the feeling of absolute dependence is the consciousness of God [Gottesbewusstsein]" (25). Our awareness of absolute dependence is our awareness that we did not create ourselves, that we are dependent on an unknown "whence" for our existence, and that "the *Whence* of our receptive and active existence, as implied in this self-consciousness, is to be designated by the word 'God'" (Mackintosh & Stewart, 1968: 16).

He contrasts the direct, inward [unmittelbare innere] self-awareness with a "sensory" [sinnlich—which the translators denote as "sensible" but again, times have changed and I think is now better translated "sensory" and it can also mean sensual, even erotic] self-awareness. Schleiermacher clearly thinks that feeling and self-awareness are unmediated (the literal meaning of "unmittelbare") and in that way distinct from sensory knowledge that comes to us through our regular channels of perception and serves as the object of our thoughts and intentions. Whether he is correct or not in that claim of "immediacy" is not so crucial here. He clearly wants to contrast this awareness of God with sensory awareness and so certainly does not consider this an awareness that comes through the senses. The medieval author claims we have a direct awareness that we exist (and I have argued that is an embodied, proprioceptive awareness) that leads directly to an awareness of God "who is our being." Schleiermacher claims we have a direct awareness of our dependency on an unknown "whence" that is identical to an awareness of being in relationship to God. But for Schleiermacher that awareness has nothing to do with any bodily or proprioceptive awareness. Embodiment does not seem to figure all that much in Schleiermacher's account. Nor is there any suggestion that this awareness comes through a transformation of the senses. Quite the reverse. For Schleiermacher it is completely inward and potentially continuously present. But Schleiermacher, like the classical authors (and like Alston), is at pains to insist that the awareness of God is direct and immediate. He also insists that our immediate awareness of God is intimately bound up with our immediate awareness of our existence. In this sense, his position is similar to that of the author of the *Little Book of Private Counsel*. For both, a direct *awareness* of existence is the means to a direct *awareness* of God.

Spiritual Senses as Spiritual Practices

The *Cloud* and Schleiermacher point to a deep connection between, maybe even an equating of, our awareness of our existence and our awareness of God. This presents another avenue into the discussion of embodiment and the possibility of a spiritual sense: through an awareness of our own existence, that is, through proprioception. There are meditative practices in many different traditions for improving proprioception. The simplest is just a "body scan," in which the person gets into a meditative posture or position, relaxes (usually through breathing concentration), and begins to direct his or her attention to different parts of the body, usually starting with the feet and ending with the face and head. Obviously engaging in bodily practices such as yoga, walking meditation, tai chi, martial arts, dance, or vocal training can also increase proprioception. The same is often true with athletics. And sometimes when people are being treated for a disorder that requires regular monitoring (sugar/insulin levels for diabetes or blood pressure for cardiac conditions), and especially when they are learning self-regulation through biofeedback, they develop increased proprioception related to their disorder. Often this is trial and error learning so that people learn to perceive these proprioceptive conditions but they cannot tell you how they do it. So there is little question that proprioception is a skill that can be improved.

Deepening one's proprioceptive abilities in this way can lead to a deepening awareness of one's existence as an embodied person. And following the author of the *Cloud of Unknowing*, I am suggesting that being consciously aware of the state of one's existence (and not just having the ratiocination that "I exist" à la Descartes) can be another source of spiritual perception.

This awareness involves, among other things, an increased awareness of one's embodiment as intimately connected with existing. That is, an increased awareness of location (the sense of your body on a chair or a bed or a meditation cushion, or your orientation of sitting or lying) or your movement through space (the feel of feet on the ground, of motion over distance, of muscular action and breathing). Over time, this deepening awareness of embodied existence can produce a shift in consciousness. In my experience, practitioners often refer to this shift in consciousness with embodied metaphors of sinking or dropping—dropping into a deeper state of consciousness characterized by calm, peace, relaxation; and more awareness of their bodies, breathing, heartbeat, points of stress and tension; and an awareness of subtler environment impacts like the movement of air, fainter sounds, and changes in temperature and light. Here the boundaries around the self soften. One of the results is a more profound sense of connection with the surrounding world and a stronger sense of groundedness, which can open up into an awareness of being grounded in a transcendental source. But such sensations and perceptions are very subtle. Context is important to give them more content.

Another important implication of this model is that embodied cognition is active cognition. In contrast to Alston's position, embodied cognition underscores the importance of the schemas, expectancies, and even unconscious processes that go into our perceptions. They are not problematic features to deny. There is no perceiving in everyday life, in science, or in religion without them. And when we get to complex perceptions like those involved in scientific experimentation, medical diagnosis, or religious perceiving, those schematic processes are inevitably and necessarily the result of training. I might walk into a biology lab and a student might call me over to look through a microscope and say to me, "Look Dr. Jones, you'll see mitochondria." Nice try. But not a chance. I have no idea what mitochondria look like or how to differentiate them from similarly appearing cellular structures. I would probably be receiving the same retinal impressions as my student. Although as we've seen even that is in doubt given the way some research suggests that perception may be a two-way interaction, not just retinas sending information to brains but brains also sending information to retinas that may influence what information impacts them (Noe, 2009; Teske, 2013). But even if, at some concrete level, I was receiving the same retinal impressions, I still would not "see" mitochondria. However, if I really studied cell biology, did the required laboratory experiments, and had my work critiqued by an expert, then I would eventually be able to "see" mitochondria. I would have developed the categories, laid down the neuronal connections, and learned the necessary skills. Using a microscope in biological research is a skill that can be learned, trained, and improved on as judged by previously trained experts. The same is true of medical diagnosis. You cannot learn diagnosis from simply reading a textbook. God help you if you go to a doctor whose only diagnostic training involved memorizing a pathology textbook. The only way you can learn it is by going on rounds in the clinic, observing patients, practicing and being critiqued by previously trained experts. Diagnosis is a skill that can be learned, trained, and improved on as judged by previously trained experts. The same is often true with interpreting the results that come back from the pathology lab or that appear on a picture produced by a neurological scan. Similarly, skills develop with wine tasting or musical training. It's not just that Alston is, from a psychological perspective, incorrect in his theory of direct appearing. Such a theory of direct perception is unnecessary.

To be spiritually fruitful, the practice of deepening one's proprioceptive abilities needs to be done in the context of the spiritual life, just as learning to use a microscope properly has to be done in the context of studying biology or learning diagnosis has to be done in the context of clinical training. One doesn't learn to use a microscope for biological investigation by just walking into a lab and occasionally staring into one. Nor does one learn diagnosis by just wondering around the wards of hospitals and making random observations. One is sure to miss subtle but crucial cues in that way. Likewise, a practice intended to deepen one's spiritual perception must be done in a spiritual context. That's how spiritual disciplines were traditionally done in Christianity and that is how they are done today in traditional Buddhist cultures. These contexts provide the tools with which to observe, whether it is cellular processes or symptoms of a disorder or the divine presence one is seeking to see. And these contexts provide the categories and frameworks into which one's observations fit in order that they make sense, fall into a coherent pattern, and are fruitful for further investigation and reflection.

There are two consequences of what I am saying here: that the spiritual perception that arises out of a disciplined practice is not totally direct or completely unmediated and that it is contextualized. Neither of these need be a problem. As regards the first, the "myth of the immaculate perception" is a myth and sets an epistemological ideal that no human experience can reach. As regards the second, following Alston's arguments, there is no logical difference here between religious perceptions and learning microscopy, medical diagnosis, or wine tasting. There is no logical or necessary reason that would justify including those as valid practices and excluding a disciplined, communal religious practice.

Of course, Alston would resist both of those ideas because he was using religious perception primarily as means to justify and validate religious beliefs. I am not doing that. Rather, I am saying that religious perceptions can play a crucial role in the larger context of a lived religious life in which beliefs play an important part but so do processes of personal and moral transformation, times of worship and devotion, and acts of service. It is not at all clear to me that justified belief is any more important than any of those. This whole integrated and interactive complex of phenomena makes up the lived religious life and is, in a non-linear way, greater than the sum of its parts taken in isolation. And it is this whole integrated complex that should be the subject of any process of verification rather than a few isolated beliefs abstracted out of their lived context and studied in isolation. Perceptual religious experiences can and should serve to strengthen one's religious commitments but not simply by providing stronger warrants for one's beliefs (although they may well do that) but rather by intensifying one's awareness of the presence of God in one's life and in the world around one. That, I am suggesting, is the main purpose of these experiences—to strengthen one's awareness of the presence of God.

If we are talking about a spiritual *perception*, we are talking about embodiment since perception is clearly an embodied activity. So all religious perceptions or religious experiences can, and should, be understood as embodied events, including those more narrowly called "mystical" and reported in the standard books on mysticism as well as in the opening chapters of Alston's *Perceiving God*. They all involve neuronal activations, tacit somatic simulations, expressions derived from bodily metaphors. And they are all affected by posture, breathing, movement, and concentration. No matter how transcendental is the state of consciousness they evoke, such mystical moments are still profoundly and inescapably embodied.

Spiritual Sensing as Embodied-Relational Activity

We have proposed that an embodied-relational paradigm suggests that the spiritual sense can easily be understood in at least two ways: (1) as the sense of interconnection and relationship with the cosmos that is rooted in our interconnections through our bodies with the world around us that can expand into a sense of relationship with a more encompassing and transcendental reality; and (2) as the proprioceptive sense of our own existence becoming more transparent to a divine source. In addition, the connection between embodiment and religious cognition is seen in the ways in which active, embodied religious practices impact cognition and understanding. Two kinds of practices have been reviewed here. First, practices that stretch, expand, and transform our sensory awareness in ways that make us more aware of the spiritual dimension of life and perhaps more able to "perceive God." Such practices are supported by studies of the ways in which meditative and contemplative practices impact our perceptual processes. And second, practices that deepen our capacity for proprioception, which might sensitize us to deeper aspects of our existence or "being" (in the words of the author of *The Cloud*). This embodied spiritual sense comes through a more subtle deepening of our "being," which would clearly be an embodied perception. Both of these awarenesses would fit my definition of spiritual sensing as the "direct, perception-like apprehension of a transcendental reality." And both can be cultivated through embodied practices. The details of such disciplines and the instructions for engaging them are far beyond the scope of this text. This is not a manual of spiritual practice. Rather, it is an extended empirical and theological argument to support engaging in such embodied practices by pointing to research that suggests such embodied practices can transform our perceptual and information generating processes and by supplying reasons to think that the effects of such practices, when located in a doxastic context, epistemically support the religiously lived life. This is one of the most radical and uncomfortable conclusions of this book: that some of the information that justifies and validates religious claims and the whole religious life in which they are embedded only becomes available gradually as one lives within and practices that life.

Conclusion

EMBODYING RELIGION

THE TWO PRIMARY intellectual pillars supporting many of the current arguments against theological claims, supposedly drawn from cognitive neuroscience (and science in general), are a physicalist metaphysics and a positivist epistemology. Both have been analyzed here and found wanting. The theoretical and scientific problems with physicalism have only been summarized in this book since they are extensively developed in other places that are alluded to in the text and notes. But even these brief summaries should be sufficient to show that physicalism is hardly the uncontested and self-evident viewpoint that it is often made out to be in the popular media. And while embodied-relational paradigms that are the subject of this essay can certainly be used (and have been used) in support of a reductive physicalism, I have suggested ways in which some versions at least of embodied knowing might also support other perspectives on the nature of the physical world (particularly that part of the physical world known as our body) and more complex models of human nature and even certain types of dualism. So even research on embodiment is not a direct and unambiguous support for physicalist metaphysics.

On epistemological concerns, the paradigms of embodied knowing have a more direct bearing. But they come late to the game here. The post–World War II period saw increasingly trenchant attacks on logical positivism and its verificationalism. In different ways, Goedel, Wittgenstein and followers, Kuhn, Lakatos, and many others all cut the ground out from under a positivist epistemology. However, a form of it survived in the artificial intelligence world and from there it easily migrated into cognitive science. Early artificial intelligence and cognitive science research programs kept alive the focus on reference and representation long after they had been substantially critiqued, compromised, or rejected within much philosophy of science. Some research on embodiment and cognition raises significant questions about constructs like reference and representation even from within cognitive science. Nuancing and constraining any reliance on models of reference and representation also weaken any positivistic deployment of neuroscience, especially in regard to religion.

The weakening of these two pillars supporting the attacks on religion in the name of science is an important but primarily negative result. It removes objections to but does not provide any positive support for a religiously lived life. This book has argued that models of embodied knowing have something positive to contribute here. First, they often emphasize the way in which each person (including that individual's ways of perceiving, thinking, and feeling) is embedded in a cultural context and a historical lineage. In that sense, all cognition is embodied and all embodied cognition is contextualized. An embodied approach demands of us that we recognize the ways in the experiences we undergo, the data we pay attention to, the schemas we deploy, the forms of cognition we rely on, the arguments we find compelling are all shaped by those contexts. Recognizing that suggests (1) a certain humility about the limits of the claims we make and the reasons for them, whether in neuroscience or theology; and (2) different domains of understanding require different methods of justification. This book has argued that the appropriate object of justification for theological claims is the religiously lived life, not isolated propositions. I also understand there is a certain degree of inevitable relativism in that recognition. We will return to that issue in a moment.

The epistemological position taken here, that some of the justifications for the religiously lived life become more available as one lives that life, parallels the argument of Paul Moser in *The Elusive God* (2008). And I thank Tom Simpson for pointing this out. Moser and I agree that some process of personal transformation is required to fully engage with the epistemological concerns associated with religion. His model of that process of transformation appears rather different from mine but his discussion of skepticism is very valuable. Such a claim about the epistemic priority of personal transformation is explicit in the training of Tibetan Buddhist thinkers and implicit in the works of the early Christian theologians who were mainly monks or others with disciplined spiritual practices; but it goes against the grain of the post-Enlightenment insistence that all claims be based on publicly accessible grounds. But we have long since left that Enlightenment wish behind. The grounds for deciding between differing forms of string theory or different cosmological models are hardly publicly accessible and the grounds for deciding among various treatments for prostate cancer only slightly more so.

Several readers vigorously raised the problem of religious pluralism as a reason to reject my argument out of hand, since its heavy reliance on contextualism and pragmatism offers no way to resolve the differing claims among the various religions. Wildman raises a similar issue in relation to Alston's position, but Wildman does not see it as undermining Alston's argument, only the use Alston makes of it. And I agree. The issue of religious pluralism is implicit in Alston's "theory of appearing" since not only the Protestant Jesus to whom Alston is devoted but also Krishna, the Bodhisattva of compassion Avalokitesvara, and the Blessed Virgin Mary are, even now, the subject of appearances.

The issue of religious pluralism is a very deep issue here for sure and I certainly cannot resolve it in this brief space. But I will make some observations. The first is a matter of social location or the sociology of knowledge, an issue (in my experience) that many philosophers and theologians want to avoid. Several of those who raised this question about my position taught theology or philosophy of religion in implicitly or explicitly denominational contexts, or contexts in which they were not faced with the variety of religions on a regular basis. So the complexities of the issue of religious pluralism may not directly confront them daily and they may be able to avoid them most of the time. On the other hand, I taught for almost fifty years in deeply pluralistic environments: every class of mine contained representatives of virtually all the world's religions as well as many who were militantly anti-religious. And so I felt ethically required to include readings from more than one tradition in my courses and to openly confront the issue of religious pluralism directly in the face of students from a variety of very different religious perspectives. And I taught in a department and a university made up of colleagues and friends from all the major religious traditions and those vigorously opposed to any religious commitments. And over the years I have participated in many so-called interreligious dialogues and groups. All that has made me exquisitely sensitive to the complexity of many of the concerns connected to the topic of religious pluralism and forced me to wrestle with them. Even with my own Christian commitments, I automatically reflect on religious issues in a pluralistic framework. That is clear even here where I make reference to texts or constructs from many religions. In addition, when people speak of resolving the issue of religious pluralism, it is rarely clear to me what they are really asking for. Until what would count as a resolution of the issue is more obvious, it is hard to know how to address it.

On the other hand, the position I have outlined here does have some implications for understanding the issue of pluralism. My contextualist position holds that truth claims can only be made within particular contexts that are shaped by consensual assumptions and practices. Claims within a context will be understood and adjudicated by those who share those assumptions and practices. Those who do not share them will find the claims made there hard to understand and maybe even nonsensical. There is clearly a degree of relativism in such a position. I do not think it need be a vicious relativism but I think it is inevitable given the nature of human understanding.

For example, I am convinced that human beings possess choice and intentionality and can engage in self-regulatory activities where their conscious choices can cause changes in their physiological processes. Such a conviction is the basis of my work in behavioral medicine; I think it can be demonstrated in the laboratory with biofeedback and hypnosis; I think there are models within physics that make such processes comprehensible within natural science. But I have many colleagues who are complete determinists, who think that conscious experience and intentionality are epiphenomenal, and that any such experimental results are misconceptions. Within a reductionistic, physicalist framework, their claims make perfect sense and are in fact the inevitable entailments of that framework. But I am working in a different context, with different assumptions and practices. Each of our claims only makes sense in the contexts in which we do our work. I do not think that is a vicious kind of relativism but rather a statement about the way human understanding is constituted. Rather, I name this a "critical relativism" that calls on all human knowers to be conscious of the limits and relativities built into all their claims and that I hope yields a virtue I have called "epistemic humility." All this is spelled out in more detail in my book *The Texture of Knowledge* (1981). To some extent claims can be adjudicated across contexts by their agreement with other relevant and widely accepted claims as long as the limitations of even widely accepted claims are openly acknowledged—and more important, adjudicated by their pragmatic usefulness in solving pertinent problems and answering important questions.

So all religions and their secular critics voice their claims in the context of specific assumptions, convictions, and practices. This does not resolve the problem of religious pluralism. As I have said, I have no idea what that would really look like. But it does help us understand some of aspects of that problem. Given this contextualism, it is not necessarily illogical for particular religions to make particularistic and parochial claims. But such claims will make sense only within the context of that particular religion. Thus, it is illogical to insist that those outside a particular religion should share those claims. They won't. Those claims are only compelling in the context of those particular religious assumptions and practices.

There is no context-free claim from nowhere. Anyone who addresses the issue of pluralism does so from within some context. Someone may stand outside all particular religious contexts and then insist that those who belong to particular religions should give up their particular claims. But that makes sense only in an outside-of-all-religions context. Those inside religious traditions will probably not go for it. That, from my perspective, is what makes the problem of religious pluralism so epistemologically deep and intractable.

In addition, the embodied-relational approach also contributes to our understanding of what it means to say, especially in the case of religion, that claims are "properly supported." Arguments that either attack or defend isolated religious claims taken out of context miss the mark. Given the insistence that embodied cognitive activity is embedded in a context, properly supporting religion means supporting the religiously lived life in which its doxastic practices, perceptions, epistemic values, and cognitive activities, including affirmations of belief, are embedded. Put another way, what is fundamentally at issue in justifying religious beliefs is justifying the lived religious life that gives rise to those beliefs. And that life is the non-linear result of many, many interrelated and reciprocally interacting domains—leading an ethically informed life, engaging in spiritual disciplines; times of study, worship, devotion, and service; and critical study and reflection; and affirmation of statements of belief.

One element in that gestalt that has been of particular concern in this text are those experiences that we might legitimately call perceptions of the divine that result from the development of a spiritual sense or a capacity for spiritual perception. We have detailed two possible forms of such a spiritual sense that can be neurologically grounded in the embodiment of our cognitive and perceptual processes. Given that our bodies connect us to the world around us and even to the cosmos at large, we can conceptualize a spiritual sense as a sense of our cosmic embodiment and interconnection with all that exists. Another model of a spiritual sense derived from an embodied perspective is to conceptualize a spiritual sense as a sense of our own existence that has become transparent to its ultimate source. Both represent direct, perception-like apprehensions of something divine or transcendental. Insisting that such spiritual senses can be trained through embodied practices means that any perceptions generated in this way become noetic or doxastic by their embeddedness in practices or contexts that generate the categories in which they make sense and can be integrated into life. Any information we become aware of in these ways will be expressed in body-based language. Such embodied spiritual senses provide powerful epistemic support for the religiously lived life not primarily as sources of evidence to warrant propositional truths but as crucial elements in the larger gestalt of the lived religious life in which belief is one, but only one, important part. Once the debris left behind by the collapse of physicalism and positivism have been cleared away, an embodied understanding of the spiritual senses and the personal impact of a religiously lived life can be a powerful part of any reconstruction or reappropriation of that life. But, of course, the only way you can fully know that is true is to engage in the attempt to live such a life yourself.

Notes

INTRODUCTION

I hold that religion, in this case Christianity, is fundamentally a set of practices, an argument I make and illustrate historically in my 2003 book, *The Mirror of God: Christian Faith as Spiritual Practice*, New York: Palgrave. The point is not that belief is unimportant or should be ignored but rather that beliefs only make sense in and can be warranted by a context shaped by practices.

CHAPTER 1

Again I must begin by thanking Fraser Watts for inviting me to Cambridge to be a part of his Psychology of Religion Research Group, especially its ongoing project on embodied cognition and religion, as well as again thanking the other members of that group for welcoming me to join them in their work, which introduced me to some of this research on embodiment.

The material reviewed in this chapter is taken from the books listed in the bibliography and referenced in the text. For more detailed discussion of the role of embodiment in human understanding and some of the research investigating it, these books should be consulted. When I arrived in Cambridge to work with the project on embodied cognition going on there, I was given a draft of a paper by Mark Williams and colleagues from Oxford entitled "Embodied Cognition and Emotional Disorders," which was the basis of much of the group's discussions. It too contained an excellent review of this material that was very helpful to me. In addition, in 2012 I attended a conference on embodied cognition in Loccum, Germany, at which John Teske gave a fine paper also reviewing this research. He kindly sent me a copy of the paper almost immediately, which was exceedingly useful. A shorter version of that paper has been published in 2013 in *Zygon* and that is how it is cited in the text and bibliography.

CHAPTER 2

The first part of this chapter reprises arguments and commentaries I have been making for over twenty years, starting with Jones (1992a). A fuller version of my refutation of the physicalist position can be found in Jones (2016), *Can Science Explain Religion?* New York: Oxford University Press; and, especially in relation to the mind-body dilemma and the related problem of "top down causation," in Jones (2005), "Mind, Brain, and Spirit—A Clinician's Perspective; or, Why I Am Not Afraid of Dualism," in *Soul, Psyche, Brain*, edited by Kelly Bulkeley, New York: Palgrave Press. There the arguments alluded to here are developed in more depth and from there much of this section is derived. Other extensive arguments that undermine physicalism can be found in the works by Crane, Nagel, and Plantinga in the bibliography.

Again, I am using the term "physicalism" in a restricted sense as the position that claims that all of reality is (or will be) amenable to a complete, natural scientific description and explanation. This can be contrasted here with "naturalism" of which there are a variety of forms that lay claim to realities beyond a reductive, natural scientific account.

Paul Bloom suggests that our immediate experience of minds as different from bodies results from a miscarriage of our evolved cognitive systems that make us, in his words "intuitive dualists" subject to being misled by our "folk psychology." I am quite critical of this argument in Jones, *Can Science Explain Religion?*

In working through the implications of the embodied-relational paradigm for the mind-body dilemma and developing the position I call here "embodied dualism," I was helped exceedingly by the introduction to the book *Persons* by my Rutgers' colleague Dean Zimmerman (Inwagen & Zimmerman, 2007) and by his paper and the other papers in the *Soul Hypothesis* book. Citing his wonderful phrase "the mind-suffused body" gives me another chance to thank my Cambridge colleague Leon Turner for our many very helpful discussions of these and other topics and for his willingness to read many very rough versions of this text.

While in Cambridge I had the privilege of several discussions with George F. R. Ellis, professor of applied mathematics at the University of Cape Town, about the possible role of quantum effects in the ordinary world and the implications of quantum theory for our understanding of the physical world. He kindly gave me copies of two, as-of-then unpublished, papers on this subject, which are listed in the bibliography. See also George Ellis (2016), *How Can Physics Underlie the Mind*, Berlin: Springer.

CHAPTER 3

In March 2014 I was invited to give a series of lectures on embodied knowing at Uppsala University in Sweden. The meaning-making approach is very influential there and my colleagues' encouragement to write something about embodiment and meaning-making was the impetus for this chapter. I am especially grateful to professors Valerie DeMarinis and Maria Lillas for their encouragement.

The story of the rise and fall of existentialism within modern, North American theology is most ably told by Gary Dorrien, *The Making of American Liberal Theology*, vol. 2 (2003), *Idealism, Realism, and Modernity—1900–1950*; and vol. 3 (2006), *Crisis Irony, and Postmodernity—1950–2005*, Louisville: John Knox Press. Accounts of this history by two who helped shape it can be found in Paul Tillich (1967), *Perspectives on 19th & 20th Century Theology*, New York: Harper & Row, and John Macquarrie (1981), *Twentieth Century Religious Thought*, New York: Charles Scribners.

A readable and still useful account, including primary texts, of the philosophical background of existential psychology and its concern with meaninglessness can be found in Walter Kaufman (1960), *Existentialism from Dostoevsky to Sartre*, New York: Meridian Books; see also Heine et al. (2006).

CHAPTER 4

I had just drafted the section of this chapter on possible research projects growing out of an embodied approach, especially how movement and posture might impact the effects of spiritual practices, when Kevin Ladd from Indiana University showed up in Cambridge and described conducting exactly the types of research I was suggesting, especially on whether posture and movement shape the effects of religious practices. I am grateful to Kevin for sharing his ingenious research designs and preliminary results with me. I am looking forward to additional interesting findings coming out of his work. A moving first-person account of experiencing some of these embodied practices can be found in Barbara Brown Taylor (2009), *An Altar in the World*, New York: HarperCollins, especially chapter 4.

Wesley Wildman (2011) offers a similar critique and response to Alston's theory of appearing but in the service of a rather different project: that is, in defense of a religious naturalism while I am obviously indirectly defending a form of classical Christian theism. Reading his clear and cogent presentation forced me to return to my text and more clearly differentiate my embodied theistic position from religious naturalism.

My book *Can Science Explain Religion?* critiques those evolutionary psychologists who think (like Freud) that proposing theories of the origin of religion based on our evolved psychological systems can do away with the claims of religion. For more on Freud, see Jones (1991a).

CHAPTER 5

In the discussion of the late medieval English treatise, *The Little Book of Private Counseling*, I used the text from (1944) *The Cloud of Unknowing and The Book of Privy Counselling* (ed.) P. Hodgson, New York: Oxford University Press. The page numbers are from that edition; the translations and transliterations are my own.

In the discussion of Schleiermacher, I relied on the translation by H. R. Mackintosh and J. S. Stewart (1968). *The Christian Faith by Friedrich Schleiermacher*,

Edinburgh: T & T Clark. And the German text F. Schleiermacher (1960), *Der Christliche Glaube*, vol. 1, Berlin: deGruyter. I also used *F. Schleiermacher On the Glaubenslehre*, (1981), trans. J. Duke & F. Fiorenza, Atlanta: Scholars Press—AAR Texts and Translations #3. My translation of the central terms in Schleiermacher's text are as follows: Feeling—Gefuhl; Self-consciousness—Selbstbewusstsein; Absolute—schlechthin; Dependence—abhangig. I am grateful to Analena Schriever for her suggestions on German usage.

Bibliography

Abraham, W. (2013). "Turning Philosophical Water into Theological Wine." *Journal of Analytic Theology*, 1/1: 1–16.

Abraham, W. (2012). "Analytic Philosophers of Religion." In P. Gavrilyuk. & S. Coakley (eds.), *The Spiritual Senses*, 275–290. Cambridge: Cambridge University Press.

Adams, F., & K. Aizawa. (2009). "Why the Mind Is Still in the Head." In P. Robins & M. Aydede (eds.), *The Cambridge Handbook of Situated Cognition*, 78–95. Cambridge: Cambridge University Press.

Adams, F., & K. Aizawa. (2001). "The Bounds of Cognition." *Philosophical Psychology*, 14/1: 43–64.

Aizawa, K. (2007). "Understanding the Embodiment of Perception." *Journal of Philosophy*, 104/1: 5–25.

Alibali, M. W., D. C. Heath, & H. J. Meyers. (2001). "Effects of Visibility between Speaker and Listener on Gesture Production." *Journal of Memory and Language*, 44: 169–188.

Alston, W. (1991). *Perceiving God*. Ithaca, NY: Cornell University Press.

Anderson, Michael L. (2010). "Neural Re-Use as a Fundamental Organizational Principle of the Brain." *Behavioral and Brain Sciences*, 33: 245–313.

Anderson, Michael L. (2008). "Circuit Sharing and the Implementation of Intelligent Systems." *Connection Science*, 20: 239–251.

Anderson, Michael L. (2007). "Evolution of Cognitive Function via Redeployment of Brain Areas." *Neuroscientist*, 13: 13–21.

Anderson, Michael L., Michael J. Richardson, & Anthony Chemero. (2012). "Eroding the Boundaries of Cognition: Implications of Embodiment." *Topics in Cognitive Sciences*, 4: 1–14.

Andres, M., X. Seron, & E. Oliver. (2007). "Contribution of Hand Motor Circuits to Counting." *Journal of Cognitive Neuroscience*, 19: 563–573.

Anonymous. (1944). *The Cloud of Unknowing and The Book of Privy Counselling*, ed. P. Hodgson. New York: Oxford University Press.

Antonovsky, A. (1987). *Unraveling the Mystery of Health*. San Francisco: Jossey-Bass.

Arbib, M., & M. Hesse. (1986). *The Construction of Reality.* Cambridge: Cambridge University Press.

Atran, S. (2002). *In Gods We Trust.* New York: Oxford University Press.

Baker, M., & S. Goetz (eds.). (2011). *The Soul Hypothesis.* New York: Continuum.

Barrett, L. F. (2014). "The Conceptual Act Theory." *Emotion Review,* 6/2: 292–297.

Barrett, L. F. (2009a). "The Future of Psychology: Connecting Mind to Brain." *Perspectives on Psychological Science,* 4/4: 326–339.

Barrett, L. F. (2009b). "Understanding the Mind by Measuring the Brain: Lessons from Measuring Behavior" (Commentary on Vul et al., 2009). *Perspectives on Psychological Science,* 4/3: 314–318.

Barrett, J. L. (2007). "Is the Spell Really Broken? Bio-psychological Explanations of Religion and Theistic Belief." *Theology & Science,* 5/1: 57–72.

Barrett, J. L. (2004). *Why Would Anyone Believe in God?* Walnut Creek, CA: Altamira Press.

Barrett, L. F. (2006). "Are Emotions Natural Kinds?" *Perspectives on Psychological Science,* 1/1: 28–58.

Barrett, L. F., & J. A. Russell. (1999). "The Structure of Current Affect Controversies and Emerging Consensus." *Current Directions in Psychological Science,* 8/1: 10–14.

Barrett, L. F., & A. B. Satpute. (2013). "Large-scale Brain Networks in Affective and Social Neuroscience: Towards an Integrative Functional Architecture of the Brain." *Current Opinion in Neurobiology,* 23/3: 361–372.

Barrett, N., & W. Wildman. (2009). "Seeing Is Believing." *International Journal for Philosophy of Religion,* 66/2: 71–86.

Barsalou, Lawrence W. (2008). "Grounded Cognition." *Annual Review of Psychology,* 59: 617–645.

Barsalou, Lawrence W. (1999). "Perceptual Symbol Systems." *Behavioral and Brain Sciences,* 22: 577–660.

Barsalou, Lawrence W. (1993). "Flexibility, Structure, and Linguistic Vagary in Concepts: Manifestations of a Compositional System of Perceptual Symbols." In A. C. Collins, S. E. Gathercole, & M. A. Conway (eds.), *Theories of Memory,* 29–101. Hillsdale, NJ: Erlbaum.

Barsalou, L.W., W. K. Simmons, A. K. Barbey, & C. D. Wilson. (2003). "Grounding Conceptual Knowledge in Modality-specific Systems." *Trends in Cognitive Sciences,* 7: 84–91.

Barsalou, Lawrence, & K. Weimer-Hastings. (2005). "Situating Abstract Concepts." In D. Pecher & R. Zwaan (eds.), *Grounding Cognition,* 129–163. New York: Cambridge University Press.

Baumeister, R. (1991). *Meanings in Life.* New York: Guilford Press.

Bechara, A., A. R. Damasio, H. Damasio, & S. W. Anderson. (1994). "Insensitivity to Future Consequences Following Damage to Human Prefrontal Cortex." *Cognition,* 50: 7–15.

Beckes, Lane, & James A. Coan. (2015). "Relationship Neuroscience." In Mario Mikulincer, Phillip R. Shaver, Jeffry A. Simpson, & John F. Dovidio (eds.), *APA Handbook of Personality and Social Psychology*, Vol. 3: *Interpersonal Relations*, 119–149. Washington, DC: American Psychological Association.

Berneiri, Frank. (1988). "Coordinated Movement and Rapport in Teacher-Student Interactions." *Journal of Nonverbal Behavior* 12: 120–138.

Bernstein, R. (1983). *Beyond Objectivism and Relativism*. Philadelphia: University of Pennsylvania Press.

Berti, A., G. Bottini, M. Gandola, L. Pia, N. Smania, A. Stracciari, I. Castiglioni, G. Vallar, & E. Paulesu. (2005). "Shared Cortical Anatomy for Motor Awareness and Motor Control." *Science*, 309: 488–491.

Bohm, D. (1975). "Quantum Theory as an Indication of a New Order in Physics." *Foundations of Physics*, 5: 93–109.

Borghi, A., & F. Cimatti. (2010). "Embodied Cognition and Beyond." *Neuropsychologia*, 48: 763–773.

Boroditsky, L. (2000). "Metaphoric Structuring: Understanding Time through Spatial Metaphors." *Cognition*, 75: 1–28.

Boyer, P. (2001). *Religion Explained*. New York: Basic Books.

Bray, P. (2013). "Bereavement and Transformation." *Journal of Religion and Health*, 52/3: 890–903.

Brown, H. (1979). *Perception, Theory, and Commitment: The New Philosophy of Science*. Chicago: University of Chicago Press.

Bryant, D., & G. Wright. (1999). "How Body Asymmetries Determine Accessibility in Spatial Function." *Quarterly Journal of Experimental Psychology*, 52: 487–508.

Buber, M. (1970). *I and Thou*, trans. W. Kaufman. New York: Scribner.

Burge, Tyler. (1986). "Individualism and Psychology." *Philosophical Review*, 95: 3–45.

Bush, L. K., C. L. Barr, G. J. McHugo, & J. T. Lanzetta. (1989). "The Effects of Facial Control and Facial Mimicry on Subjective Reactions to Comedy Routines." *Motivation and Emotion*, 13: 31–52.

Cacioppo, J. T., J. R. Priester, & G. G. Bernston. (1993). "Rudimentary Determination of Attitudes: II. Arm Flexion and Extension Have Differential Effects on Attitudes." *Journal of Personality and Social Psychology*, 65: 5–17.

Cardinali, L., F. Frassinetti, C. Brozzoli, C. Urquizar, A. Roy, & A. Farne. (2008). "Tool Use Induces Morphological Updating of the Body Schema." *Current Biology*, 19: 478–479.

Catttoi, T., & J. McDaniel (eds.). (2011). *Perceiving the Divine through the Human Body*. New York: Palgrave.

Chalmers, D. (1995). "Facing Up to the Problem of Consciousness." *Journal of Consciousness Studies*, 2/3: 200–219.

Chandler, J., & N. Schwartz. (2009). "How Extending Your Middle Finger Affects Your Perception of Others." *Journal of Experimental Social Psychology*, 45: 123–128.

Chao, L. L., & A. Martin. (2000). "Representation of Manipulable Man-Made Objects in the Dorsal Stream." *NeuroImage*, 12: 478–484.

Chemero, Antony. (2009). *Radical Embodied Cognitive Science*. Cambridge, MA: MIT Press.

Chu, C. J., N. Tanaka, J. Diaz, B. L. Edlow, O. Wu, M. Hämäläinen, S. Stufflebeam, S. Cash, & M. A. Kramer. (2015). "EEG Functional Connectivity Is Partially Predicted by Underlying White Matter Connectivity. *NeuroImage*, 108: 23–33.

Clark, A. (2010a). "Memento's Revenge: The Extended Mind, Extended." In R. Manary (ed.), *The Extended Mind*, 43–66. Cambridge, MA: MIT Press.

Clark, A. (2010b). "Coupling, Constitution, and the Cognitive Kind." In R. Menary (ed.), *The Extended Mind*, 81–99. Cambridge, MA: MIT Press.

Clark, A. (2008). *Supersizing the Mind: Embodiment, Action, and Cognitive Extension*. New York: Oxford University Press.

Clark, A., & David Chalmers. (1998). "The Extended Mind." *Analysis*, 58: 10–23.

Clark, K. J., & J. Barrett. (2011). "Reidian Religious Epistemology and the Cognitive Science of Religion." *Journal of the American Academy of Religion*, 78/3: 639–675.

Clayton, P., & P. Davies. (2006). *The Re-emergence of Emergence*. New York: Oxford University Press.

Coakley, S. (2009). "Dark Contemplation and Epistemic Transformation." In O. Crisp & M. Rea (eds.), *Analytic Theology*, 280–312. Oxford: Oxford University Press.

Coakley, S. (2002). *Powers and Submissions*. Oxford: Blackwell.

Coakley, S. (ed.). (1997). *Religion and the Body*. Cambridge: Cambridge University Press.

Cole, M., L. Hood, & R. McDermott. (1997). "Concepts of Ecological Validity: Their Differing Implications for Comparative Cognition." In M. Cole & Y. Engestroem (eds.), *Mind, Culture, and Activity*, 48–58. New York: Cambridge University Press.

Condon, P., G. Desbordes, W. Miller, & D. DeSteno. (2013). "Meditation Increases Compassionate Responses to Suffering." *Psychological Science*, 24/10: 2125–2127.

Condon, W. S., & L. W. Sander. (1974). "Neonate Movement Is Synchronized with Adult Speech." *Science*, 183: 99–101.

Corwin, A. (2012). "Changing God, Changing Bodies: The Impact of New Prayer Practices on Elderly Nun's Embodied Experience." *Ethos*, 40/1: 394–410.

Crane, T. (1995). "The Mental Causation Debate." Proceedings of the Aristotelian Society, Supplementary Volume.

Crane, T., & D. H. Mellor. (1990). "There Is No Question of Physicalism." *Mind*, 99: 185–206.

Damasio, A., & H. Damasio. (1994). "Cortical Systems for the Retrieval of Concrete Information." In C. Koch & J. Davis (eds.), *Large Scale Neuronal Theories of the Brain*, 61–74. Cambridge, MA: MIT Press.

Damasio, A. R., T. J. Grabowski, D. Tranel, R. D. Hichwa, & A. R. Damasio. (1996). "A Neural Basis for Lexical Retrieval." *Nature*, 380: 499–505.

Damoiseaux J., & M. Greicius. (2009). "Greater than the Sum of Its Parts: A Review of Studies Combining Structural Connectivity and Resting-state Functional Connectivity." *Brain Structure and Function*, 213: 525–533.

De Jaegher, Hanne, Ezequiel Di Paoulo, & Shaun Gallagher. (2010). "Can Social Interaction Constitute Social Cognition?" *Trends in Cognitive Sciences*, 14: 441–447.

Dijksterhuis, A., & J. A. Bargh. (2001). "The Perception-Behavior Expressway: Automatic Effects of Social Perception on Social Behavior." In M. P. Zanna (ed.), *Advances in Experimental Social Psychology*, 23: 10–40. San Diego, CA: Academic Press.

Dijkstra, K., M. P. Kaschak, & R. A. Zwaan. (2007). "Body Posture Facilitates Retrieval of Autobiographical Memories." *Cognition*, 102: 139–149.

Dimberg, U. (1982). "Facial Reactions to Facial Expressions." *Psychophysiology*, 19: 643–647.

Duguid, M., & J. Goncalo. (2012). "Living Large: The Powerful Overestimate Their Own Height." *Psychological Science*, 23/1: 36–40.

Duncan, S., & Barrett, L. F. (2007). "Affect Is a Form of Cognition: A Neurobiological Analysis." *Cognition and Emotion*, 21/6: 1184–1211.

Ehrsson, H., Geyer, S., & Naito, E. (2003). "Imagery of Voluntary Movement…Activates Corresponding Body-part-specific Motor Representations." *Journal of Neurophysiology*, 90/5: 3304–3316.

Ellis, G. F. R. (2013). "The Functioning of Complex Systems: How Can Physics Underlie the Human Mind?" Unpublished Text.

Ellis, G. F. R. (2012). "On the Limits of Quantum Theory: Contextuality and the Quantum-Classical Cut." Unpublished Text.

Farb, N., Z. Segal, & A. Anderson. (2012). "Mindfulness Meditation Alters Cortical Representations of Interoceptive Attention." *Social Cognitive and Affective Neuroscience*, 8/1: 15–26.

Farrer, C., N. Franck, N. Georgieff, C. D. Frith, J. Decety, & M. Jeannerod. (2003). "Modulating the Experience of Agency: A Positron Emission Tomography Study." *NeuroImage*, 18: 324–333.

Farrer, C., & C. D. Frith. (2002) "Experiencing Oneself vs. Another Person as Being the Cause of an Action: The Neural Correlates of the Experience of Agency." *NeuroImage*, 15: 596–603.

Federman, A. (2011). "What Buddhism Taught Cognitive Science about Self, Mind and Brain." *Enrahoner*, 47/1: 39–62.

Feyerabend, P. (1993). *Against Method*. New York: Verso.

Fodor, Jerry. (2000). *The Mind Doesn't Work That Way*. Cambridge, MA: MIT Press.

Forest, A. L., D. R. Kille, J. V. Wood, & L. R. Stehouwer. (2015). "Turbulent Times, Rocky Relationships." *Psychological Science*, 26/8: 1261–1271.

Freeman, Walter J. (2001). *How Brains Make Up Their Minds*. New York: Columbia University Press.

Freeman, W. (1991). "The Physiology of Perception." *Scientific American*, 264/2: 78–85

Bibliography

Freyd, J. J. (1987). "Dynamic Mental Representations." *Psychological Review*, 94: 427–438.

Fuller, R. C., & D. E. Montgomery. (2015). "Body Posture and Religious Attitudes." *Archive for the Psychology of Religion [Archiv Fur Religionspsychologie]*, 37/3: 227–239.

Gall, Y., & M. Guirguis-Younger. (2013). "Religious and Spiritual Coping." In K. Paragment, J. Exline, & J. Jones (eds.), *APA Handbook of Psychology, Religion and Spirituality*, Vol. 1, 349–363. Washington, DC: American Psychological Association.

Gallagher, S. (2005). *How the Body Shapes the Mind*. Oxford: Oxford University Press.

Gallagher, S., & D. Zahavi. (2008). *The Phenomenological Mind*. New York: Routledge.

Gallese, V., & A. Goldman. (1998). "Mirror Neurons and the Simulation Theory of Mind-Reading." *Trends in Cognitive Science*, 12: 493–501.

Gavrilyuk, P. (2012). "Psuedo-Dionysius the Areopagite." In P. Gavrilyuk & S. Coakley (eds.), *The Spiritual Senses*, 86–103. Cambridge: Cambridge University Press.

Gavrilyuk, P. & S. Coakley (eds.). (2012). *The Spiritual Senses*. Cambridge: Cambridge University Press.

Gibbs, R. (2005). *Embodiment and Cognitive Science*. Cambridge: Cambridge University Press.

Gibson, J. J. (1979). *The Ecological Approach to Visual Perception*. Boston: Houghton-Mifflin.

Glasser, Matthew F., Timothy S. Coalson, Emma C. Robinson, Carl D. Hacker, John Harwell, Essa Yacoub, Kamil Ugurbil, Jesper Andersson, Christian F. Beckmann, Mark Jenkinson, Stephen M. Smith, & David C. Van Essen. (2016). "A Multi-Modal Parcellation of Human Cerebral Cortex." *Nature*, 536/7615: 171–178.

Glenberg, A. M. (1997). "What Memory Is For." *Behavioral and Brain Science*, 20: 1–55.

Glenberg, A. M., & M. P. Kaschak. (2003). "The Body's Contribution to Language." In B. Ross (ed.), *The Psychology of Learning and Motivation*, Vol. 43, 93–126. New York: Academic Press.

Glenberg, A. M., J. L. Schroeder, & D. A. Robertson. (1998). "Averting the Gaze Disengages the Environment and Facilitates Memory." *Memory and Cognition*, 26: 651–658.

Goldin-Meadow, S. (2003). *Hearing Gesture: How Our Hands Help Us Think*. Cambridge, MA: Harvard University Press.

Goldman, A. (2006). *Simulating Minds: The Philosophy, Psychology, and Neuroscience of Mindreading*. New York: Oxford University Press.

Goodenough, Ursula. (1998). *The Sacred Depths of Nature*. New York: Oxford University Press.

Goodman, N. (1984). *Of Mind and Other Matters*. Cambridge, MA: Harvard University Press.

Greicius, M. D., Kaustubh Supekar, Vinod Menon, & Robert F. Dougherty. (2009). "Resting-State Functional Connectivity Reflects Structural Connectivity in the Default Mode Network." *Cerebral Cortex*, 19/1: 72–78.

Haggard, Paul. (2005). "Conscious Intention and Motor Cognition." *Trends in Cognitive Science*, 9: 290–295.

Haimovici, A., E. Tagliazucchi, P. Balenzuela, & D. R. Chialvo. (2013). "Brain Organization into Resting State Networks Emerges at Criticality on a Model of the Human Connectome." *Physical Review Letters*, 110/17: 178101–178104.

Happold, F. C. (1970). *Mysticism*. London: Penguin Books.

Hauk, O., I. Johnsrude, & F. Pulvermüller. (2004). "Somatotopic Representation of Action Words in Human Motor and Premotor Cortex." *Neuron*, 41/2: 301–307.

Hegarty, M. (2004). "Mechanical Reasoning as Mental Simulation." *Trends in Cognitive Science*, 8: 280–285.

Heine, S., T. Proulix, & K. Vohs. (2006). "The Meaning Maintenance Model." *Personality and Social Science Review*, 10/2: 88–110.

Heintzelman, S., & L. King. (2014). "Life Is Pretty Meaningful." *American Psychologist*, 69/6: 561–574.

Holden, J., G. van Orden, & M. T. Turvey. (2009). "Dispersion of Response Times Reveals Cognitive Dynamics." *Psychological Review*, 116: 318–324.

Honey, C. J., O. Sporns, L. Cammoun, X. Gigandet, J. P. Thiran, R. Meuli, & P. Hagmann. (2009). "Predicting Human Resting-state Functional Connectivity from Structural Connectivity." *Proceedings of the National Academy of Sciences*, 106/6: 2035–2040.

Horn, A., D. Ostwald, M. Reisert, & F. Blankenburg. (2014). "The Structural-functional Connectome and the Default Mode Network of the Human Brain." *NeuroImage*, 102: 142–151.

Hung, I. W., & A. A. Labroo. (2011). "Firm Muscles to Firm Will Power." *Journal of Consumer Research*, 37/6: 1046–1064.

Hurley, S. (1998). *Consciousness in Action*. Cambridge, MA: Harvard University Press.

Inagaki, T., & N. Eisenberger. (2013). "Shared Neural Mechanisms Underlying Social Warmth and Physical Warmth." *Psychological Science*, 24/11: 2272–2280.

Intraub, H., & J. F. Hoffman. (1992). "Reading and Visual Memory: Remembering Scenes that Were Never There." *American Journal of Psychology*, 105: 101–114.

Inwagen, P. van, & D. Zimmerman (eds.). (2007). *Persons*. Oxford: Oxford University Press.

Isenhower, Robert W., Michael J. Richardson, Claudia Carello, Reuben M. Baron, & Kerry L. Marsh. (2010). "Affording Cooperation: Embodied Constraints, Dynamics, and Action-Scale Invariance in Joint Lifting." *Psychonomic Bulletin & Review*, 17: 342–347.

Janoff-Bulman, R. (1992). *Shattered Assumptions*. New York: Free Press.

Janoff-Bulman, R., & C. Frantz. (1997). "The Impact of Trauma on Meaning: From Meaningless World to Meaningful Life." In M. Power & C. Brewin (eds.), *The Transformation of Meaning*, 91–106. Hoboken, NJ: Wiley.

Jones, J. (2016). *Can Science Explain Religion? The Cognitive Science Debate*. New York: Oxford University Press.

Jones, J. (2006). *Waking from Newton's Sleep: Dialogues on Spirituality in an Age of Science*. Eugene, OR: Wipf and Stock.

Jones, J. (2005). "Mind, Brain, and Spirit—A Clinician's Perspective; or, Why I Am Not Afraid of Dualism." In Kelly Bulkeley (ed.), *Soul, Psyche, Brain*. New York: Palgrave Press.

Jones, J. (2004). "Religion, Health, and the Psychology of Religion: How the Research on Religion and Health Helps Us Understand Religion." *Journal of Religion and Health*, 43/4: 317–328.

Jones, J. (2003). *The Mirror of God: Christian Faith as Spiritual Practice*. New York: Palgrave, 2003.

Jones, J. (1997). "The Real Is the Relational: Relational Psychoanalysis as a Model of Human Understanding." In J. A. Belzen (ed.), *Hermeneutical Approaches in Psychology of Religion*. Amsterdam: Rodopi.

Jones, J. (1996). *Religion and Psychology in Transition*. New Haven: Yale.

Jones, J. (1992a). "Can Neuroscience Provide a Complete Account of Human Nature?" *Zygon*, 27/2: 187–202.

Jones, J. (1992b). "Knowledge in Transition: Towards a Winnicottian Epistemology." *Psychoanalytic Review*, 79/2: 223–237.

Jones, J. (1991a). *Contemporary Psychoanalysis and Religion: Transference and Transcendence*. New Haven, CT: Yale University Press.

Jones, J. (1991b). "The Relational Self: Contemporary Psychoanalysis Reconsiders Religion." *Journal of American Academy of Religion*, 59: 119–135.

Jones, J. (1989). "Personality and Epistemology: Cognitive Social Learning Theory as a Philosophy of Science." *Zygon*, 24/1: 23–38.

Jones, J. (1984). *The Redemption of Matter: Towards the Rapprochement of Science and Religion*. Lanham, MD: University Press of America.

Jones, J. (1982). "The Delicate Dialectic: Religion and Psychology in the Modern World." *Cross Currents*, 32: 143–153.

Jones, J. (1981). *The Texture of Knowledge: An Essay on Religion and Science*. Lanham, MD: University Press of America.

Jones, J. (1972). "Reflections on the Problem of Religious Experience." *Journal of the American Academy of Religion*, 40: 445–453.

Kang, D-H., H. Jo, W. Jung, S. Kim, Y. Jung, C. Choi, U. Lee, S. An, J. Jang, & J. Kwon. (2012). "The Effect of Meditation on Brain Structure: Cortical Thickness Mapping and Diffusion Tensor Imaging." *Social Cognitive and Affective Neuroscience*, 8/1: 27–33.

Kelso, J. A. S. (2009). "Synergies: Atoms of Brain and Behavior." In D. Sternad (ed.), *Progress in Motor Control*, 83–91. New York: Springer.

Kihlstrom, J. F. (2002). "The Seductions of Materialism and the Pleasures of Dualism." *Journal of Conscious Studies*, 9/11: 3–29.

Kille, D., A. Forest, & J. Wood. (2012). "Tall, Dark, and Stable: Embodiment Motivates Mate Selection Processes." *Psychological Science*, 24/1: 112–114.

Kober, H., L. F. Barrett, J. Joseph, E. Bliss-Moreau, K. Lindquist, & T. D. Wager. (2008). "Functional Grouping and Cortical–subcortical Interactions in Emotion: A Meta-analysis of Neuroimaging Studies." *Neuroimage*, 42/: 998–1031.

Koenig. H. (2013). "Religion and Spirituality in Coping with Acute and Chronic Illness." In K. Pargament, A. Mahoney, & E. Schafranski (eds.), *APA Handbook of Psychology, Religion, and Spirituality*, Vol. 2, 275–295. Washington, DC: American Psychological Association.

Koenig, H., D. King, & V. Carson. (2012). *Handbook of Religion and Health*. New York: Oxford University Press.

Koltko-Rivera, M. (2004). "The Psychology of Worldviews." *Review of General Psychology*, 8/1: 3–58.

Kosslyn, Stephen M. (1994). *Image and Brain*. Cambridge, MA: MIT Press.

Kosslyn, Stephen M., W. L. Thompson, & G. Ganis. (2006). *The Case for Mental Imagery*. New York: Oxford University Press.

Krauss, R. M. (1998). "Why Do We Gesture When We Speak?" *Current Directions in Psychological Science*, 7: 54–59.

Kuhn, T. (1972). *The Structure of Scientific Revolutions*. Chicago: University of Chicago Press.

Ladd, K. L., M. L. Ladd, J. Harner, T. Swanson, T. Metz, K. S. Pierre, & D. Trnka. (2007). "Inward, Outward, Upward Prayer and Big Five Personality Traits." *Archive for the Psychology of Religion*, 29/1: 151–175.

Lakens, D., I. Schneider, N. Jostmann, & T. Schubert. (2011). "Telling Things Apart." *Psychological Science*, 22/7: 887–890.

Lakoff, G., & M. Johnson. (1980). *Metaphors We Live By*. Chicago: University of Chicago Press.

Lee, Tatia, M. C., Mei-Kei Leung, Wai-Kai Hou, Joey C. Y. Tang, Jing Yin, Kwok-Fai So, Chack-Fan Lee, & Chetwyn C. H. Chan. (2012). "Distinct Neural Activity Associated with Focused-Attention Meditation and Loving-Kindness Meditation." *PLoS ONE*, 7/8: Article e40054.

Levin, D. T., & D. J. Simons. (1997). "Failure to Detect Changes to Attended Objects in Motion Pictures." *Psychonomic Bulletin and Review*, 4: 501–506.

Lindquist, K., & L. F. Barrett. (2006). "Constructing Emotion." *Psychological Science*, 19/9: 898–903.

Lindquist, K. A., T. D. Wager, H. Kober, E. Bliss-Moreau, & L. F. Barrett. (2012). "The Brain Basis of Emotion: A Meta-analytic Review." *Behavioral and Brain Sciences*, 35/3: 121–143.

Longo, M. R., & S. F. Laurenco. (2007). "Space Perception and Body Morphology: Extent of Near Space Scales with Arm Length." *Experimental Brain Research*, 177: 285–290.

Lotze, M., P. Montoya, M. Erb, E. Hulsmann, H. Flor, U. Klose, N. Birbaumer. & W. Grodd. (1999). "Activation of Cortical and Cerebellar Motor Areas during Executed and Imagined Hand Movements: An fMRI Study." *Journal of Cognitive Neuroscience*, 11/5: 491–501.

Lun, V., & M. Bond. (2013). "Examining the Relation of Religion and Spirituality to Subjective Well-Being across National Cultures." *Psychology of Religion and Spirituality*, 5/4: 304–315.

Lutz, A., L. Ggreischar, N. Rawlings, M. Ricard, & R. Davidson. (2004). "Long Term Meditators Induce High Amplitude Gama Synchrony during Mental Practice." *Proceedings of the National Academy of Science*, 101: 16369–16373.

Machery, E. (2007). "Concept Empiricism: A Methodological Critique." *Cognition*, 104: 19–46.

MacIver, M. A. (2009). "Neuroethology: From Morphological Computation to Planning." In P. Robbins & M. Aydede (eds.), *The Cambridge Handbook of Situated Cognition*, 480–504. New York: Cambridge University Press.

Mack, A., & I. Rock. (1998). *Inattentional Blindness*. Cambridge, MA: MIT Press.

Mackie, J. (1982). *The Miracle of Theism*. New York: Oxford University Press.

Mackintosh, H. R., & J. S. Stewart. (1968). *The Christian Faith by Friedrich Schleiermacher*. Edinburgh: T & T Clark.

Mahon, B. (2015). "The Burden of Embodied Cognition." *Canadian Journal of Experimental Psychology*, 69/2: 172–178.

Mahon, Bradford, & Alfonso Caramazza. (2008). "A Critical Look at the Embodied Cognition Hypothesis and a New Proposal for Grounding Conceptual Content." *Journal of Physiology*, 102: 59–70.

Martin, A., L. G., & T. Matlock. (2004). "Fictive Motion as Cognitive Simulation." *Memory & Cognition*, 32: 1389–1400.

McGilchrist, I. (2009). *The Master and His Emissary*. New Haven, CT: Yale University Press.

McNamara, P. (2009). *The Neuroscience of Religious Experience*. Cambridge: Cambridge University Press.

McNeill, David. (2005). *Gesture and Thought*. Chicago: University of Chicago Press.Medin, Doug L., & Edward Shoben. (1988). "Context and Structure in Conceptual Combination." *Cognitive Psychology*, 20: 158–190.

Meier, B. P., & M. D. Robinson. (2004). "Why the Sunny Side Is Up: Associations between Affect and Vertical Position." *Psychological Science*, 15: 243–247.

Meissner, W. W. (1984) *Psychoanalysis and Religious Experience*. New Haven, CT: Yale University Press.

Merleau-Ponty, M. (1962). *Phenomenology of Perception*, trans. C. Smith. London: Routledge & Kegan Paul.

Michael, C., & M. Cooper. (2013). "Post-Traumatic Growth Following Bereavement." *Counseling Psychology*, 28/4: 18–33.

Michaelson, P., J. Vetter, & J. Zacks. (2006). "Lateral Somatotopic Organization during Imagined and Prepared Movements." *Journal of Neurophysiology*, 95/2: 811–822.

Miller, L., & B. Kelley. (2005). "Relationships of Religiosity and Spirituality with Mental Health and Psychopathology." In R. Paloutzian & C. Park (eds.), *Handbook of the Psychology of Religion and Spirituality*, 460–478. New York: Guilford Press.

Moser, P. (2008). *The Elusive God*. Cambridge: Cambridge University Press.

Mottonen, R., & K. Watkins. (2009). "Motor Representations of Articulators Contribute to Categorical Perception of Speech Sounds." *Journal of Neuroscience*, 29/31: 9819–9825.

Murphy, N. (1999). "Supervenience and the Downward Efficacy of the Mental: A Nonreductive Physicalist Account of Human Action." In R. J. Russell, N. Murphy, T. C. Meyering, & M. M. Arbib (eds.), *Neuroscience and the Person: Scientific Perspectives on Divine Action*, 147–164. Notre Dame, IN: University of Notre Dame Press.

Myers, D. (2000). "The Funds, Friends, and Faith of Happy People." *American Psychologist*, 55/1: 56–67.

Nagel, T. (2012). *Mind and Cosmos*. Oxford: Oxford University Press.

Nagel, T. (1965). "Physicalism." *Philosophical Review*, 74/3: 339–356.

Nair, S., M. Sagur, J. Sollers, N. Consedine, & E. Broadbent. (2015). "Do Slumped and Upright Postures Affect Stress Responses?" *Health Psychology*, 34/6: 632–641.

Niedenthal, P. (2007). "Embodying Emotion." *Science*, 316: 1002–1005.

Niedenthal, P., M., Lawrence, W. Barsalou, P. Winkielman, S. Krauth-Gruber, & F. Rice. (2005). "Embodiment in Attitudes, Social Perception, and Emotion." *Personality and Social Psychology Review*, 9: 184–211.

Noë, A. (2009). *Out of Our Heads*. New York: Hill and Wang.

Noë, A. (2004). *Action in Perception*. Cambridge, MA: MIT Press.

Nöe, A., & E. Thompson. (2004), "Are There Neural Correlates of Consciousness?" *Journal of Consciousness Studies*, 11: 2–28.

Ogden, P., K., Mintu, & C. Pain. (2006). *Trauma and the Body: A Sensorimotor Approach to Psychotherapy*. New York: W.W. Norton.

Oman, D., & C. Thoresen. (2005). "Do Religion and Spirituality Influence Health?" In R. Paloutzian & C. Park (eds.), *Handbook of the Psychology of Religion and Spirituality*, 460–478. New York: Guilford Press.

Oosterwijk, S., K. Lindquist, E. Anderson, R. Dautoff, Y. Moriguchi, & L. F. Barrett. (2012). "States of Mind: Emotions, Body, Feelings, and Thoughts Share Distributed Neural Networks." *NeuroImage*, 62: 2010–2028.

Oudejams, R., C. Michaels, F. Bakker, & M. Dolne. (1996). "The Relevance of Action in Perceiving Affordances: Perception and the Catchableness of Fly Balls." *Journal of Experimental Psychology: Human Perception and Performance*, 22: 879–891.

Paloutzian, R., & C. Park. (2005). *Handbook of Psychology of Religion and Spirituality*. New York: Guilford Press.

Pargament, K. (2007). *Spiritually Integrated Psychotherapy*. New York: Guilford Press.

Pargament, K. (1997). *The Psychology of Religion and Coping*. New York: Guilford Press.

Park, C. (2010). "Making Sense of the Meaning Literature." *Psychological Bulletin*, 136/2: 257–301.

Park, C., D. Edmondson, & T. Blank. (2009). "Religious and Non-religious Pathways to Stress-Related Growth in Cancer Survivors." *Applied Psychology: Health and Well-Being*, 1: 321–335.

Park, C., D. Edmondson, & A. Hale-Smith. (2013). "Why Religion? Meaning as Motivation." *APA Handbook of Psychology of Religion and Spirituality*, Vol. 1, 157–171. Washington DC: American Psychological Association.

Park, C., & S. Folkman. (1997). "Meaning in the Context of Stress and Coping." *Review of General Psychology*, 2: 115–144.

Parsons, L. M. (1987). "Imagined Spatial Transformations of One's Body." *Journal of Experimental Psychology: General*, 116: 172–191.

Petersen, S. E., & O. Sporns. (2015). "Brain Networks and Cognitive Architectures." *Neuron*, 88/1: 207–219.

Plantinga, A. (2006). "Against Materialism." *Faith and Philosophy*, 23/1: 3–32.

Polyn, S. M., V. S. Natu, J. D. Cohen, & K. A. Norman. (2005). "Category-Specific Cortical Activity Precedes Retrieval Memory Search." *Science*, 310: 1963–1966.

Potter, M. C., J. F. Kroll, B. Yachzel, E. Carpenter, & J. Sherman. (1986). "Pictures in Sentences: Understanding without Words." *Journal of Experimental Psychology: General*, 115: 281–294.

Powel, T., R. Gibson, & C. Collin. (2012). "TBI 13 Years On: Factors Associated with Post-Traumatic Growth." *Disability and Rehabilitation*, 34/17: 1461–1467.

Presson, C. C., & D. R. Montello. (1994). "Updating after Rotational and Translational Body Movements: Coordinate Structure of Perspective Space." *Perception*, 23: 1447–1455.

Proffitt, D. R. (2006). "Embodied Perception and the Economy of Action." *Perspectives in Psychological Science*, 1: 110–122.

Pulvermüller, F. (2005). "Brain Mechanisms Linking Language and Action." *Nature Reviews Neuroscience*, 6: 576–582.

Putnam, H. (1992). *Renewing Philosophy*. Cambridge. MA: Harvard University Press.

Putnam, H. (1987). *The Many Faces of Realism*. LeSalle, IL: Open Court.

Richardson, Michael L., B. R. Fajan, K. Shockley, M. A. Riley, & M. T. Turvey. (2008). "Ecological Psychology: Six Principles for an Embodied-Embedded Approach to Behavior." In Paco Calvo & Toni Gomila (eds.), *Handbook of Cognitive Science: An Embodied Approach*, 161–197. New York: Elsevier.

Richter, W., R. Somorjai, R. Summers, M. Jarmasz, R. S. Menon, et al. (2000). "Motor Area Activation during Mental Rotation Studied by Time-Resolved Single-Trial fMRI." *Journal of Cognitive Neuroscience*, 12: 310–320.

Riggs, W. (2003). "Understanding Virtue and the Virtue of Understanding." In M. De Paul & L. Zagzebski (eds.), *Intellectual Virtue*, 203–226. Oxford: Clarendon Press.

Riskind, J., & C. Gotay. (1982). "Physical Posture Could Have Regulatory or Feedback Effects on Motivation and Emotion." *Motivation and Emotion*, 6/3: 273–298.

Rizzolatti, G., & L. Craighero. (2004). "The Mirror-Neuron System." *Annual Review of Neuroscience*, 27: 169–192.

Robinson, H. M. (1976). "The Mind-Body Problem in Contemporary Philosophy." *Zygon*, 11: 346–360.

Rowlands, Mark. (2003). *Externalism: Putting Mind and World Back Together Again*. Montreal: McGill-Queen's University Press.

Sagioglou, C., & T. Greitemeyer. (2014). "Bitter Taste Causes Hostility." *Personality and Social Psychology Bulletin*, 40/12: 1589–1597.

Schleiermacher, F. (1960). *Der Christliche Glaube*, Vol. 1. Berlin: deGruyter.

Schnall, S., J. Bentos, & S. Harvey. (2008b). "With a Clean Conscience. Cleanliness Reduces the Severity of Moral Judgments." *Psychological Science*, 19: 1219–1222.

Schnall, S., J. Haidt, G. L. Clore, & A. H. Jordan. (2008a). "Disgust as Embodied Moral Judgment." *Personality and Social Psychology Bulletin*, 34: 1096–1109.

Scholz, J., M. C. Klein, T. Behrens, & H. Johansen-Berg. (2009). "Training Induces Changes in the White-matter Architecture." *Nature Neuroscience*, 12: 1370–1371.

Schwartz, D. L. (1999). "Physical Imagery: Kinematic vs. Dynamic Models." *Cognitive Psychology*, 38: 433–464.

Schwartz, D. L., & J. B. Black. (1996). "Analog Imagery in Mental Model Reasoning: Depictive Models." *Cognitive Psychology*, 30: 154–219.

Shapiro, S., G. Schwartz, & G. Bonner. (1998). "Effects of Mindfulness-Based Stress Reduction on Medical and Pre-medical Students." *Journal of Behavioral Medicine*, 21/6: 581–599.

Shaw, A., S. Joseph, & P. Lindley. (2005). "Religion, Spirituality, and Posttraumatic Growth." *Mental Health, Religion and Culture*, 8: 1–11.

Simons, D., & C. Chabris. (1999). "Gorillas and Our Midst: Sustained Inattentional Blindness for Dynamic Events." *Perception*, 28: 1059–1074.

Sinigaglia, C., & G. Rizzolatti. (2011). "Through the Looking Glass: Self & Others." *Consciousness and Cognition*, 20/1: 64–74.

Solomon, K. O., & L. W. Barsalou. (2001). "Representing Properties Locally." *Cognitive Psychology*, 43: 129–169.

Sotiropoulos, S., S. Jbabdi, S. N. Sotiropoulos, T. E. Behrens, S. N. Haber, & D. C. Van Essen. (2015). "Measuring Macroscopic Brain Connections in Vivo." *Nature Neuroscience*, 18/11: 1546–1555.

Sporns, O. (2013). "The Human Connectome: Origins and Challenges." *NeuroImage*, 80: 53–61

Sporns, O. (2011). "The Human Connectome: A Complex Network." *Annals of the New York Academy of Sciences*, 1224/1: 109–125.

Stepper, S., & F. Strack. (1993). "Proprioceptive Determinants of Emotional and Non-Emotional Feelings." *Journal of Personality and Social Psychology*, 64: 211–220.

Strack, F., L. L. Martin, & S. Stepper. (1988). "Inhibiting and Facilitating Conditions of the Human Smile: A Nonobtrusive Test of the Facial Feedback Hypothesis." *Journal of Personality and Social Psychology*, 54: 768–777.

Sugovic, M., & J. Witt. (2011). "Perception in Obesity." *Visual Cognition*, 19/10: 1323–1326.

Sweetser, E. (1998). "Regular Metaphoricity in Gesture: Bodily-Based Models of Speech Interaction." *Acts of 16th International Congress of Linguistics*. Paris: Elsevier.

Sweetser, E. (1990). *From Etymology to Pragmatics*. Cambridge: Cambridge University Press.

Taylor. S. E. (1983). "Adjustment to Threatening Events." *American Psychologist*, 38: 1161–1171.

Taylor, V., V. Dancault, J. Grant, G. Cavone, E. Breton, S. Roffe-Vidal, J. Cortemanche, A. Lavarenne, G. Marrelec, H. Benali, & M. Beauregard. (2012). "Impact of Meditation Training on the Default Mode Network during a Restful State." *Social Cognitive and Affective Neuroscience*, 8/1: 4–14.

Teske, J. (2013). "From Embodied to Extended Cognition." *Zygon*, 48/3: 759–781.

Teske, J. (2011). "Externalism, Relational Selves, and Redemptive Relationships." *Zygon*, 46: 183–203.

Teske, J. (2006). "Neuromythology: Brains and Stories." *Zygon*, 41: 169–196.

Teske, J., & R. Pea. (1981). "Metatheoretical Issues in Cognitive Science." *Journal of Mind and Behavior*, 2: 123–178.

Thelen, E., & L. Smith. (1994). *A Dynamic Systems Approach to the Development of Cognition and Action*. Cambridge, MA: MIT Press.

Thompson, E. (2005). "Empathy and Human Experience." In James D. Proctor (ed.), *Science, Religion, and the Human Experience*, 261–285. New York: Oxford University Press.

Tillich, P. (1967) *Perspectives on 19th & 20th Century Theology*. New York: Harper & Row.

Tillich, P. (1957). *Systematic Theology*, Vol. 2. Chicago: University of Chicago Press.

Tillich, P. (1952). *The Courage to Be*. New Haven, CT: Yale University Press.

Tillich, P. (1951). *Systematic Theology*, Vol. 1. Chicago: University of Chicago Press.

Tipper, S. (2010). "From Observation to Action Simulation." *Quarterly Journal of Experimental Psychology*, 63/11: 2081–2105.

Tipper, S. (2004). "Attention and Action." In M. S. Gazzaniga (ed.), *Cognitive Neurosciences III*, 3rd ed., 619–629. Cambridge, MA: MIT Press.

Tomkins, Silvan. (1979). "Script Theory: Differential Magnification of Affects." In H. E. Howe & R. A. Dienstbier (eds.), *Nebraska Symposium on Motivation*, Vol. 26, 21–36. Lincoln: University of Nebraska Press.

Tsakiris, M., M. D. Hesse, C. Boy, P. Haggard, & G. R. Fink. (2007). "Neural Signatures of Body Ownership: A Sensory Network for Bodily Self-Consciousness." *Cerebral Cortex*, 17: 2235–2244.

Tucker, M., & R. Ellis. (2004). "Action Priming by Briefly Presented Objects." *Acta Psychologica*, 116: 185–203.

Tucker M., & R. Ellis. (2001). "The Potentiation of Grasp Types during Visual Object Categorization." *Visual Cognition*, 8/6: 769–800.

Tucker, M., & R. Ellis. (1998). "On the Relation between Seen Objects and Components of Potential Actions." *Journal of Experimental Psychology: Human Perception and Performance*, 24: 830–846.

Turner, L. (2013). "Individuality in Theological Anthropology and Theories of Embodied Cognition." *Zygon*, 48/3: 808–831.

Ungerleider, M. A., & J. V. Haxby. (2000). "Category-Specificity and the Brain: The Sensory-Motor Model of Semantic Representations of Objects." In M. S. Gazzaniga (ed.), *Category Specificity and the Brain: The Sensory-Motor Model of Semantic Representations of Objects*, 1023–1036. Cambridge, MA: MIT Press.

Urmson, J. (1969). *Philosophical Analysis*. Oxford: Oxford University Press.

Van der Kolk, Bessel A., A. C. MacFarlane, & L. Weisaeth (eds.). (1996). *Traumatic Stress: The Effects of Overwhelming Experience on Mind, Body, and Society*, New York: Guilford Press.

van Orden, G., J. Holden, & M. T. Turvey. (2003). "Self-Organization of Cognitive Performance." *Journal of Experimental Psychology: General*, 132: 331–351.

Vardey, L. (1995). *God in All the Worlds*, New York: Random House.

Varela, F., E. Thompson, & E. Rosch. (1993). *The Embodied Mind*. Cambridge, MA: MIT Press.

Velmans, M. (2000). *Understanding Consciousness*. London: Routledge.

Visala, A. (2014). "The Evolution of Divine and Human Minds." In F. Watts & L. Turner (eds.), *Evolution, Religion, and Cognitive Science*, 56–73. Oxford: Oxford University Press.

Wallace, A. (2007). *Contemplative Science*. New York: Columbia University Press.

Waller, D., Y. Lippa, & A. Richardson. (2008). "Isolating Observer-Based Reference Directions in Human Spatial Memory: Head, Body, and the Self-to-Array Axis." *Cognition*, 106: 157–183.

Waller, D., D. R. Montello, A. E. Richardson, & M. Hegarty. (2002). "Orientation Specificity and Spatial Updating of Memories for Layouts." *Journal of Experimental Psychology: Learning, Memory, and Cognition*, 28: 1051–1063.

Watkins, J. (1982). "A Basic Difficulty with the Mind-Brain Identity Hypothesis." In J. Eccles (ed.), *Mind and Brain: The Many Faceted Problems*, 221–232. New York: Paragon.

Watts, F. (2014). "Religion and the Emergence of Differentiated Cognition." In F. Watts & L. Turner (eds.), *Evolution, Religion, and Cognitive Science*, 109–131. Oxford: Oxford University Press.

Watts, F. (2013). "Embodied Cognition and Religion." *Zygon*, 48/3: 745–757.

Watts, F., & L. Turner (eds.). (2014). *Evolution, Religion, and Cognitive Science*. Oxford: Oxford University Press, 109–131.

Wells, G. L., & R. F. Petty. (1980). "The Effects of Overt Head Movements on Persuasion: Compatibility and Incompatibility of Responses." *Basic and Applied Social Psychology*, 1: 219–230.

Wheatley, T., & J. Haidt. (2005). "Hypnotically Induced Disgust Makes Moral Judgments More Severe." *Psychological Science*, 16: 780–784.

Wildman, W. (2011). *Religious and Spiritual Experiences*. Cambridge: Cambridge University Press.

Willems, R., & P. Hagoot. (2007). "Neural Evidence for the Interplay between Language, Gesture, and Action: A Review." *Brain and Language*, 101/3: 276–289.

Willems, R., L. Labruna, M. D'Esposito, R. Ivry, & D. Cassanto. (2011). "A Functional Role for the Motor System in Language Understanding." *Psychological Science*, 22/7: 849–854.

Williams, J. M., G. Bergljot, & L. Darko. (no date). "Embodied Cognition and Emotional Disorders." Unpublished Paper.

Williams, P. (1997). "Some Mahayana Buddhist Perspectives on the Body." In S. Coakley (ed.), *Religion and the Body*, 205–230. Cambridge: Cambridge University Press.

Wilson, Margaret. (2002). "Six Views of Embodied Cognition." *Psychonomic Bulletin and Review*, 9: 625–636.

Wilson, Robert A. (2004). *Boundaries of the Mind: The Individual in the Fragile Sciences*. New York: Cambridge University Press.

Wilson-Mendenhall, C., L. F. Barrett, & L. Barsalou. (2013). "Neural Evidence That Human Emotions Share Core Affective Properties." *Psychological Science*, 24/6: 947–956.

Wilson-Mendenhall, C., L. F. Barrett, W. K. Simmons, & L. Barsalou. (2011). "Grounding Emotion in Situated Conceptualizations." *Neuropsychologia*, 49: 1105–1127.

Winnicott, D. W. (1971). *Playing and Reality*. New York: Routledge.

Winnicott, D. W. (1965). *The Maturational Process and the Facilitating Environment*. London: Hogarth.

Yalom, I. (1998). *The Yalom Reader*. New York: Basic Books.

Yeh, W., & L. Barsalou. (2006). "The Situated Nature of Concepts." *American Journal of Psychology*, 119/3: 349–384.

Yuaso, Y. (1993). *The Body, Self-Cultivation and Ki-Energy*, trans. S. Nagatomo & M. Hull. Albany: State University of New York Press.

Zago, L., M. Pesenti, E. Mellett, F. Crivello, B. Mazoyer, & N. Tzourio-Mazoyer. (2001). "Neural Correlates of Simple and Complex Mental Calculation." *NeuroImage*, 13: 314–327.

Zimmerman, D. (2011). "From Experience to Experiencer." In M. Baker & S. Goetz (eds.), *The Soul Hypothesis*, 168–201. New York: Continuum.

Index